the prisoner

Robert

The official companion to the classic TV series

RESIGNED

Patrick McGoohan in KAR 120C

the Prisoner

Acknowledgements

All together now – many thanks to the following people for their help, encouragement, knowledge and support:

Patrick McGoohan, Roger Parkes, Lewis and Nan Greifer, Vincent Tilsley, Gerald Kelsey, Moris Farhi, Peter Graham Scott, Tony Sloman, Eric Mival, Angela Marshall, Kenneth Griffith, Annette Andre, Mark Eden, Frank Maher, Frank Rycroft, Robin Llewlyn, Robert S. Baker at Tribune Productions, Mansun, Simon Farnhell and Norma Martin, Dave Barrie, Chris Bentley, Simon Coward at Kaleidoscope, David and Joanne Healey, Ed Ball, Max Hora, Dave and Julie Jones, Chris Perry, Adrain Petford, David Watkins, Colin Bayley, Vaughan Brunt, Janet Davis, Peter Dunn, Simon Ellis, Brian Green, Bob Gunton, Pete Hackney, Graham Bleathman,Steve McKay, John and Helen Moran, Paul Jones, Cult TV, Henry Holland, Robert Ross and Alan Coles (for services above and beyond the call of alcoholism), Slow Dazzle Worldwide, John Reed, Johnny Rogan, Sayer Galib, Howard Heather, Roland Hall, Bernard Hrusa-Marlowe, George Williams, David Buckley, Mark Thomas, Andy Partridge, the staff of the BFI and NFT, Chapter Arts and, last but definitely not least, my dear mum and dad, Bob and Audrey.

The Portmeirion crew: Brian Axworthy, Helweun Vaughan Hatcher, Catherine and Doug Williams, Merfyn and Leri Roberts, Marjorie Beer, Will Parry, Paula McLaughlin, Nel Roberts, Megan Jones and Gabrielle and Richard Eastwood.

At Carlton: Lorna Russell, Adam Wright, Penny Simpson, Sian Facer, Caroline Raudnitz, Sacha Iwanick, Piers Murray Hill, Sylvia Thompson and Garry 'old bab' Lewis.

Special thanks to Jaz Wiseman, whose help with all things ITC was invaluable – this book wouldn't have happened without him – and to Martin Wiggins and Mike Kenwood for being the scourge of the subordinate clause and convincing me that less is, indeed, more.

Dedication

To my wife Rachel, who was there for the arrival and the fall out, and to my inspirational English teacher, Mr Colin Boor: it may have taken nearly 20 years, but I've finally got there.This book is also respectfully dedicated to everyone at Everyman Films involved in bringing *The Prisoner* to the screen, in particular Patrick McGoohan, David Tomblin and the much missed George Markstein.

Six of One is the official appreciation society for *The Prisoner*. They can be contacted at: www.theprisonerappreciationsociety.com

A publication of ibooks, inc.

ibooks, inc.
24 West 25th Street
New York, NY 10010

ISBN 0-7434-5256-9

First ibooks, inc. printing October 2002

Project Editor: Lorna Russell
Picture research: Robert Fairclough, Jaz Wiseman and Marissa Keating
Art Editor: Adam Wright
Design: Robert Fairclough@popco website: www.pop-co.com
Picture research: Robert Fairclough, Jaz Wiseman and Marissa Keating
Production: Janette Burgin

The ibooks World Wide Webb address is: www.ibooks.net
Distributed by
Simon & Schuster, Inc.
1230 Avenue of the Americas
New York, NY10020

Contents

Foreword

Patrick McGoohan is an outstanding actor, and therefore we must not expect an ordinary bloke. I am told that he now lives in the United States of America; in the sun, I hope.

Long ago he appeared on our television screens and startled us all, culminating with a defining series; *The Prisoner.* His colleague was George Markstein, who must have carried in him the dark vision of Jews and Nazis. I have always been convinced, since the day I first saw *The Prisoner*, that this where "I am *not* a number!" was born.

Patrick knew exactly what he was dealing with and he dealt with it.

Unfortunately everything in Britain is degenerating – very fast; law and order, health care, public transport, the postal service, television, everything! So why not the British Theatre? Yes; that too has virtually gone. And McGoohan can crackle on stage too; I have seen and heard him.

Occassionally he has appeared in an American film with a 'Hollywood Film Star'; with McGoohan by his side, you tend not to notice the H.F.S. But there is nowhere – in these miserable days – at least in the English speaking world, to nurture a "flash of lightning"... So, Patrick: enjoy the sun and your family.

Kenneth Griffith
November 2001

Doctor Schnipps (Kenneth Griffith) and his "right lot
of Charlies" in 'The Girl Who was Death'

Left: With Patrick McGoohan as the Prisoner

Introduction: Why?

A series telling the story of an anonymous man held captive in a picturesque, equally anonymous village whose residents all had numbers instead of names has become one of television's most celebrated enigmas. It ran for a mere 17 episodes over 1967 and 1968 and was considered an expensive, commercial failure at the time of its original transmission. Yet *The Prisoner* is now a TV evergreen, constantly repeated around the world and periodically reissued on video and DVD.

Its uniqueness was a result of a collision of interests between star and executive producer Patrick McGoohan and script editor George Markstein, and the way one man's ideas influenced and compromised the other's. As a result, *The Prisoner* was in a constant state of evolution, changing from a spy story with a satirical edge to a self-aware experiment in film making, finally becoming McGoohan's own psychedelic primal scream. As well as exploring conspiracies and promoting the rights of the individual, *The Prisoner* also represented fine acting, great writing, the extension of artistic boundaries to their limits and a concerted attempt to bring feature film production values to television.

The deliberate ambiguity of its format allowed the series to become a cultural melting pot of an era, incorporating almost anything popular or uppermost in the contemporary 1960s zeitgeist. Fringe theatricality, super spy clichés, comedy, spaghetti westerns, surrealism, melodrama, modern art, pop music, fashion and politics can all be found in its stories. The series also borrowed heavily from the arts and classical literature, with sources as rich as George Orwell, Shakespeare, Jean Cocteau and Stanley Kubrick. A volatile mixture, its legacy can be seen in films and TV series such as *Edge of Darkness, The One Game, Twin Peaks, Welcome to Blood City, The Matrix, The Truman Show* and *Cube. The Prisoner* accurately predicted credit cards, cordless phones and twenty-four hour surveillance; for such an earnest programme, it was also full of in-jokes.

If the series is remembered for anything, it should be for its challenge of complacent viewing expectations and its ability to provoke a response in its audience. Interviewed for the documentary *Six into One: The Prisoner File* in 1984, Patrick McGoohan spoke about the extreme reaction which followed the broadcast of the final episode 'Fall Out' in 1968. "No, of course I wasn't angry, not in the least. I was delighted. It's marvellous when people feel enough to be angry. I'd have been very angry and disappointed if they hadn't jammed the switchboards at ATV, and if I can do that again I'll do it again. Watch it, *millions* of 'em, and be outraged! As long as people feel something, that's the great thing. It's when they're walking around not thinking and not feeling, that's where all the dangerous stuff is."

Thirty-five years on from its first broadcast, *The Prisoner* is still TV at its innovative, controversial and subversive best. This book explains why.

Robert Fairclough
November 2001

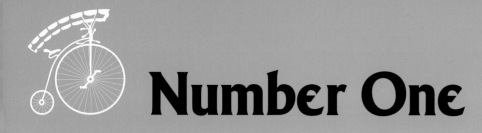

Number One

"It was Christmas Day, and it suddenly occurred to George [Markstein] that Patrick hadn't said if he could have the day off or not. So, he actually took a cab to the studio! There was no one about, but on one of the sound stages, there was a scene lit and there was McGoohan, all on his own, sitting on a stool. 'Hello, George,' he said, surprised. 'What are you doing here?' 'Well,' said George, 'I couldn't remember if you said I could have the day off.' 'George,' Pat said, completely straight-faced, 'on my birthday, *everyone* has a day off!'"

Vincent Tilsley, *The Prisoner* script-writer, 2001

VINCENT TILSLEY'S ANECDOTE NEAtly sums up Patrick McGoohan's character during the making of *The Prisoner* in the mid-sixties: the respect bordering on fear that he inspired in his colleagues, the single-minded drive to achieve perfection no matter what the circumstances and the dry sense of humour. By 1966, McGoohan's singular personality had put him in control of a project he was able to invest with his own personal beliefs and attitudes, an unparalleled position for any actor to be in. " I seek this individuality in everything I do," he said at the time. " In my work and in my private life. It's not easy. I am an actor first, although I'm now going into directing, production and writing, too. I find all these challenges, this total involvement, the most exciting way to live."

When Patrick McGoohan was born on 19 March 1928, his parents were Irish immigrants living in New York. Three months later they returned to Ireland and the young Patrick spent the first seven years of his life on his parents' farm. A strict Catholic upbringing had a profound effect on him: a strong sense of morality subsequently influenced much of his later acting work and career choices.

The McGoohans moved again in 1935, to Sheffield. Already in Patrick's formative life experiences there was a sense of being something of an outsider, particularly as he was an Irish boy in an English city. This may have contributed to the restless period that followed after he left school in 1944, at the age of 16. At his mother's urging, he began training as a Catholic priest, but he didn't complete his studies. He then worked in a steel mill, in a bank and on a chicken farm, before a tentative interest in amateur acting led him to enrol with the Sheffield Repertory Company when he was 19.

His experiences at Sheffield were to redefine his life both professionally and personally. Initially signing on as an assistant stage manager, his career stepped up a gear by accident. "An actor fell ill with appendicitis and I was the only one who knew the play because I'd been prompting it, so I had to go on. The next season I was a fully fledged actor." He also met and married the actress Joan Drummond. He remembers their first rehearsal together vividly: "I was shaking for two days afterwards." Still only in his mid-20s, McGoohan became a devoted family man with the birth of the couple's first child Catherine in 1951 (followed by Anne in 1959 and Frances in 1961). Joan gave up acting to look after Catherine while Patrick developed his career, touring with the Midland Theatre Company based in Coventry before doing two seasons with the Bristol Old Vic.

By now an ambitious young actor, McGoohan moved south from Bristol in search of better roles and a better salary. He alternated between plays at Windsor and Kew before securing his first leading part in a West End production, *Serious Charge,* at the Garrick Theatre in 1955. McGoohan played a vicar accused of homosexuality, highly controversial material for the time. His acting was well received by the critics. Ronald Barker in *Plays and Players* noted that "Patrick McGoohan makes a most refreshing vicar, with a performance remarkable for the amount of light and shade

Left: a 1964 publicity portrait of Patrick McGoohan as John Drake – *Danger Man*

McGoohan with in the Garrick Theatre production of *Serious Charge* in 1955

Above: The cover of the programme for the Lyric Opera House's production of Henrik Ibsen's *Brand*

Right: McGoohan's publicity photograph while at the Lyric

Far right: McGoohan with Dilys Hamlett as Brand's wife Agnes

Below: In the TV play *The Greatest Man in the World* (1958)

it introduces." He then went on to play Starbuck opposite Orson Welles' Ahab in the maverick director's production of *Moby Dick* at the Duke of York's Theatre in 1955.

The then thriving British film industry soon came calling. He became a contract player for the Rank Organisation and by the time of his fourth film, *High Tide at Noon*, McGoohan's name had moved up the cast list to sit comfortably under the banner "also star-ring...". The critics, too, were beginning to notice him; Philip Oakes in the *Evening Standard* commented that "Patrick McGoohan as the villain gives a splendid impersonation of Richard Widmark." A back-handed compliment, perhaps, but it showed the class of actors he was being compared with. The ability to portray vil-lainous roles convincingly led to his first really positive film reviews with *Hell Drivers* in 1957. "What a vil-lain!" exclaimed an anonymous writer in the *Daily Sketch*. "Up until now Mr [Stanley] Baker has been regarded as our toughest screen character. Move over, Mr Baker. McGoohan has just knocked your tough-guy crown for a loop. And he's big enough, rough enough to wear it himself."

Despite an enthusiastic reaction to his film work, it was clear that McGoohan saw himself as a serious actor; he was drawn to parts that had a moral integrity or something to say about the human condition. His last major stage role of the fifties, in Henrik Ibsen's *Brand* in 1959, was to take his career to another level, as McGoohan was able to draw on his own religious back-ground in his portrayal of the central character. Brand

was an uncompromising, tormented priest who put faith in God before everything, even the welfare of his wife and son. His performance was remarkable and embodied the characteristics that were to define both *Danger Man*'s John Drake and the Prisoner: an intense, driven man totally committed to his personal beliefs, distanced from the world around him. Peter Roberts in *Plays and Players* summed up the appeal of the per-formance: "Patrick McGoohan endows the cleric with a fierce, burning power, and tremendous and varying stature." The production was so successful that the BBC remounted it as part of its *World Theatre* series in August 1959. Appearances in other major TV plays followed in the same year, and he was eventually awarded for his small screen prowess with the Guild of TV Producers and Actors award for Best TV Actor of the Year.

McGoohan's successes brought him to the attention of Lew Grade, Managing Director of the Incorporated Television Company Limited (ITC), and he was cast in the lead role of the company's new series *Danger Man*, which initiated the sixties craze for secret agents. Grade summed up McGoohan's appeal succinctly: "It was the way he moved. He moved like a panther – firm and decisive." As a result, he finally found himself as the leading man in a production he was able to influence. Whether his association with Orson Welles inspired him to the same level of involvement in the productions he later worked on is debatable, but there is no doubt that McGoohan was able to exert greater artistic control the more his stature as an actor grew.

For a classically trained actor to appear in what was basically a pulp action series appears to be a questionable career move, but McGoohan's motivation wasn't just financial. If money has been a motive for work, he would have accepted the role of James Bond when film producers Albert R. Broccoli and Harry Saltzman reportedly offered him the part in 1961. That character's amorality, womanising and casual gun-play offended the puritanical, strongly moral side of McGoohan's character. He was far more comfortable with John Drake. Television had stricter controls on what was acceptable for the audience and this policy was in line with his personal concern for presenting acceptable family entertainment. In essence, this meant no romantic involvement for Drake or indulgence in gratuitous violence.

The relaunch of *Danger Man* in an hour-long format in 1964 consolidated McGoohan's stature as an international name (the half-hour series had been less suc-

cessful in syndication in America) and reputedly made him the highest paid actor on television. Bond-style gadgetry aside, McGoohan's tight-lipped performance, now minus an American accent, continued to hold the audience's attention, as Stanley Reynolds observed in *The Guardian*: "It is Drake's complex character that is the biggest draw. Each week he seems to show a different facet; sometimes crassly hard-boiled, sometimes

All Night Long (1961) was a jazz version Of *Othello*, with McGoohan in the Iago role. The soundtrack featured such luminaries as Dave Brubeck, Charlie Mingus and Tubby Hayes

Left: McGoohan received rave critical notices for his part as the psychopathic Red in *Hell Drivers* (1957)

The publicity photo sent out during *The Prisoner*'s initial run on television in the UK

sentimental about old chums who've come down with a deadly case of the double agent, sometimes stricken by pangs of conscience."

By 1966, though, McGoohan had tired of Drake and his restless, perfectionist streak made him keen to embrace new challenges. Lew Grade wanted another series as McGoohan had brought the company considerable commercial success, but a desire to move into film-making had been in his mind since 1960, when he formed Everyman Films with *Danger Man*'s assistant director David Tomblin. McGoohan's popularity presented him with the chance not only to become television's first actor-turned-film-maker, but also to get across in a public forum his own feelings and concerns about mid-sixties society. In effect, *The Prisoner* was the culmination of his career up until that point. As Lewis Greifer, writer of the episode 'The General' and a friend of McGoohan's noted, "Pat was going through a very complex phase at that time of his career, and was very interested in social observation".

McGoohan's complete, almost fanatical commitment to *The Prisoner* impressed those around him. Anthony Davis of the *TV Times* remembers talking to Jimmy Miller, McGoohan's personal assistant of 15 years, and "hearing an amazing eulogy of his boss - of Pat's generosity, sensibility and professionalism."

McGoohan met future *Danger Man* and *The Prisoner* director Don Chaffey while working on *The Three Lives of Thomasina* for Disney in 1962

McGoohan with Don Chaffey during the first location shoot for *The Prisoner* in Portmeirion, September 1966

Alexis Kanner, who worked on three of the episodes clearly found working with McGoohan an inspiring experience. "The absolute driving, rebellious, persuasive, trail-blazing force of McGoohan enabled us to do things that were many years ahead of their time on television," he remembers, "and maybe still are." Producer David Tomblin also praised his friend's dedication: "When you're making a television series, you reckon to get through from 15 to 20 set-ups a day. Pat has often averaged 33 a day, and in one two-day spell achieved 104."

The pressure of being the man in charge of *The Prisoner*, and its demanding production schedule, meant that McGoohan was keen to keep his personal life private. Kenneth Griffith, a friend and colleague, was aware throughout their relationship that he was being kept at a distance: "I was never invited home, not once. I never met his family, although he'd talk a lot about what his wife thought about things... I knew him for a long time, but never got close to him." Frank Maher, McGoo-han's stunt double on both *Danger Man* and *The Prisoner* and also a long-time friend, concurs: "He had this loner bit in his head. Always. Even when he was in a crowd he was alone." Paradox-ically for such a private man, McGoohan was also something of a hell-raiser. "It's no secret that I used to drink a lot" he admits now, and Lewis Griefer confirms that his friendship with the actor revolved mainly around alcohol: "I went out drinking a lot with McGoohan. He was a boozing mate, really." McGoohan ensured that his private and professional life remained separate on the Portmeirion shoot. Catherine Williams, the assistant wardrobe mistress, pointedly recalls: "He wasn't the sort of chap who'd go and sit in the bar with the boys."

During *The Prisoner*'s production, McGoohan was also enthusiastic about the future of Everyman Films: "I own several 'properties' and when I bought them, they could only be done as feature films. Now I can slot them into television – where a cheque for £350,000 is no longer exorbitant." He clearly saw the series as the first stage in a long career in film-making. However, following the generally negative reaction to Everyman Films' first production, and despite Lew Grade's financial commitment to the company's other productions, by 1968 he had decided not to pursue any more projects with his own company.

McGoohan left England for Switzerland, making light of his decision to emigrate: "I never had a penny in a Swiss bank. I just felt like a change and that I had done all I could in England." The truth is rather more complex. At the time of its premiere, *The Prisoner* was a commercial and critical failure, which must have come as a considerable blow to his confidence after the runaway success of *Danger Man*. He had presented himself as (and in the end became) the series' driving force. He said once, "If things go wrong, I am the only one to shoulder the blame." These words returned to haunt him following the adverse reaction to the series. After a charmed rise to fame, he may have felt that the show's perceived failure damaged his credibility as an artist in England.

A seemingly mundane incident may have been another factor in his decision to leave England, but it symbolises many of the injustices *The Prisoner* and, by implication, McGoohan himself, railed against. Frank Maher was present when the incident took place.

"We had arranged to play tennis on Saturday morning and were at his house in Mill Hill. There was a ring on the bell, Pat opened the door and there was a bloke there from the local council. Now, Pat had built a wall round the swimming pool - not a big wall - and the council man, determined to make us sick to death of him, said, 'You can't put a wall there'. Now, you do not

Trusted colleagues: McGoohan with *The Prisoner* producer David Tomblin (above) on the set of 'Living in Harmony' and (left) with stunt double and *Prisoner* stunt arranger Frank Maher during the complex filming of 'The Schizoid Man'

talk to McGoohan and tell him he can't do something. So Pat said, 'What do you suggest I do about it?' 'Pull it down.' 'No.' And this guy was stroppy - you know how they are, a jumped up, officious type with a cheap suit on - and this bloke went on and on and on but in the end we got rid of him... And that's the reason McGoohan sold up and left. He said, 'I'm leaving that wall where it is and I'm going.' Not another word. Off."

Following the small-minded reaction to *The Prisoner*, which had satirised the suffocating petty rules and regulations that his local council was now imposing on him, for McGoohan this encounter must have been the final straw. For a while, though, it looked

With Lee Van Cleef in *The Hard Way* (1979)

as if the actor's future would lie on the big screen as a major Hollywood star. The critical reaction to McGoohan's performance in 1968's *Ice Station Zebra* (the thriller he had made during production of *The Prisoner*), was overwhelmingly positive. *Variety*, the influential Hollywood journal, was highly complimentary: "The film's biggest acting asset is McGoohan, who gives his scenes that elusive 'star' magnetism, a portent of a brilliant career ahead in international film-making... [He] is a most accomplished actor with a presence all his own." The story was picked up in England, with the *Daily Express* reporting that "Patrick McGoohan is wowing the critics in his first Hollywood picture... one critic declared 'He steals the show from everyone but the submarine.'" Press reaction in the UK was equally positive. "McGoohan steals the acting honours and when he finally gives a long explanation of the real meaning of the exercise his exposition is masterly," enthused Ian Christie in the *Daily Express*. Seemingly poised to take on Hollywood, McGoohan decided to settle his family in California.

The Moonshine War (1970) and *Mary, Queen of Scots* (1971) followed, but they were critical successes rather than major box office attractions. McGoohan was again going his own way, working on projects that interested him, rather than cultivating mainstream success.

Once in Hollywood, he was attracted to feature film directing. In 1973, he oversaw *Catch My Soul*, a rock version of *Othello* by Jack Good, which had been inspired by the success of the musicals *Godspell* and *Jesus Christ, Superstar.* It reflected McGoohan's favourite interests of Shakespeare, youth culture and religion – Iago was reinterpreted as the Devil, intent on catching souls. Unfortunately, the film was poorly received, with the direction in particular being singled out for criticism. "Patrick McGoohan's debut as a film director is a sorry mélange of the artie and the smartie," complained Derek Malcolm in *The Guardian*, "with the camera restlessly proving its originality and the *mise-en-scène* tiresomely enslaved by lumpen attempts to move from reality near to the surreal." Sadly, McGoohan has not directed for the cinema since.

By the mid-seventies, commercial success no longer interested him. Financially secure since the sixties, he was free to work as he wished, helping out his old friend Alexis Kanner by appearing in *Kings and Desperate Men* and doing more family entertainment service for Disney in *Baby – Secret of the Lost legend* (1985). Following this film there was a 10-year hiatus in his movie career while he nursed one of his daughters through an apparently incurable illness. Following an operation in 1992, he went into a coma, but by 1995 he was back acting on the big screen, reunited with David Tomblin in Mel Gibson's Scottish epic *Braveheart*. McGoohan played a memorably unhinged Edward I, 'Longshanks', the villainous English king. Even though the part was virtually a cameo and he had few lines of dialogue, he was able to project menace by sheer presence alone. As Kenneth Griffith remarks, "whenever Patrick turns up in a film now, you know it's going to get pretty lively."

In 2001, the man who has lived in four countries seems finally settled. Now a grandfather to five, he is disarmingly frank about his career. Admitting that "I've done an

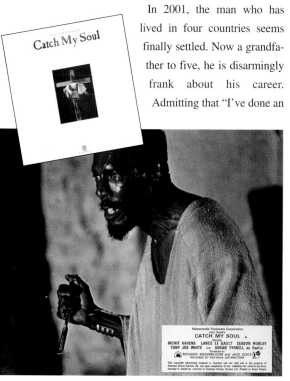

McGoohan's fascination with *Othello* continued when he directed the feature film version of the musical *Catch My Soul* starring Richie Havens in 1973

McGoohan as Dr *Rafferty* (1977), to date his last starring role in a TV series

awful lot of crap," McGoohan has no regrets about never "having done a feature film I really felt good about." His enthusiasm for the series for which he will always be remembered has also been refreshed in recent years, with work on a *Prisoner* movie script and talk of being executive producer on the proposed big screen version. A little out of character, he sent up his most famous role as the ultimate individual, when he was the guest voice of an animated Number 6 in an edition of *The Simpsons* in 2000. He favours his *Braveheart* co-star for the 21st century Prisoner: "the person that I would personally like to play the part of the new Prisoner would be Mel Gibson... We have to wait and see but he would be my number one choice to play it."

McGoohan's career has been an idiosyncratic one: from classical actor, through screen tough guy, to experimental film-maker and now scene-stealing character actor. Often it seems that when the entertainment industry tried to manoeuvre him in one direction, he deliberately reacted against what was expected of him. While he has undoubtedly lived his life and conducted his career on his own terms, Kenneth Griffith, for one, laments his decision to step back early from the limelight: "McGoohan had a tremendous talent and it should have been encouraged and developed. I'd put him in the same league as someone like Jimmy Cagney, definitely. You just don't see their like anymore. The sad thing was, Patrick kept his mouth shut about his own great talent."

TELEVISION AWARDS

1974 Emmy: Outstanding Single Performance by a Supporting Actor in the *Columbo* episode 'By Dawn's Early Light'
1990 Emmy: Outstanding Guest Actor in the *Columbo* episode 'Agenda for Murder'

With Alexis Kanner in *Kings and Desperate Men* (1977)

SELECTED FILM CREDITS

The Dam Busters (1954: director, Michael Anderson); *Passage Home* (1955: director, Roy Baker); *High Tide at Noon* (1956: director, Philip Leacock); *Hell Drivers* (1957: director, C. Raker Endfield); *The Gypsy and the Gentleman* (1957: director, Joseph Losey); *All Night Long* (1961: director, Basil Dearden); *The Quare Fellow* (1962: director, Arthur Dreifuss); *The Three Lives of Thomasina* (1962: director, Don Chaffey); *Dr Syn, Alias The Scarecrow* (1963: director, James Nielson); *Ice Station Zebra* (1968: director, John Sturges); *The Moonshine War* (1970: director, Richard Quine); *Mary, Queen of Scots* (1971: D: Charles Jarrott); *Catch My Soul* (1973: directed); *Kings and Desperate Men* (1977: D.Alexis Kanner); *Escape from Alcatraz* (1979: director, Don Siegel); *Scanners* (1980: director, David Cronenberg); *Baby - Secret of the Lost Legend* (1985: director, Bill L Norton); *Braveheart* (1995: director, Mel Gibson) *A Time To Kill* (1996: director, Joel Schumacher); *Hysteria* (1996: director, René Daalder)

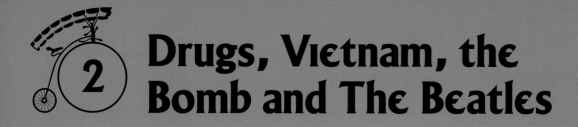

2 Drugs, Vietnam, the Bomb and The Beatles

"1966-7, the summer of love, acid, the Beatles, the whole fashion changing in the Kings Road. Patrick McGoohan... knew there was going to be a change. He wanted very much to be a part of that. He wanted to make this stand that would last forever but would be rooted in that 1966-7 time.... Those of us who were young enough and responding to what was happening well understood what Patrick McGoohan was all about"

Tony Sloman, *The Prisoner* film librarian, 1993

THE PRISONER'S TITLE SEQUENCE IS the perfect shorthand for the series as a definitive piece of mid-sixties popular culture. The opening sequence shows central London and the Houses of Parliament, incorporating both the coolest capital city in the world at the time and easily identifiable symbols of authority. Claps of thunder indicate a storm about to break, as the title character kicks against the status quo by resigning his post, alluding to the fashionable rejection of establishment values. The world the Prisoner lives in has state-of-the-art technology, including the latest in computerised filing systems. The trappings of the man's lifestyle - the sharp suit, the sports car, the swish London apartment and the photos of exotic foreign locations - show him to be a beneficiary of the decade's affluent consumerism. He clearly works for some secret government department, a cold warrior in the secret battle between East and West, which signifies him as a character from the most popular genre of the time, spy fiction. The appearance of enigmatic undertakers suggests death close at hand - an occupational hazard of the man's dangerous employment. It is no surprise that his incarceration in the Village confronts him with all these elements from the first two minutes of the title sequence, through the distorting lens of paranoid fantasy. This section looks at how various social, political and cultural influences came to determine both The Prisoner's structure, and its direction.

"My name's Drake - John Drake"

John Drake, the character played by Patrick McGoohan in Danger Man, was the first of the new breed of Cold War heroes to make it on to celluloid. He was ahead of the first James Bond film by two years, reaching the screen on 11 September 1960. Like his big-screen cousin, Drake reflected an era. His adventures involved unlimited foreign travel and a jet-setting lifestyle, two of the benefits afforded to an independent, upwardly mobile young man in the affluent consumer culture of late fifties and early sixties Britain. Drake and Bond became popular because of the key role of the espionage agent in the Cold War between the opposing power blocs of East and West. If the war couldn't be overt, it was covert – hence the appeal of the spy. Public awareness of the shady profession was heightened by real-life cases such as the defections of Guy Burgess and Donald Maclean in 1951 and Kim Philby in 1963, the Profumo Scandal in the same year, and the frequent expulsion of Soviet diplomats that followed. Drake was also ahead of the game in his application of secret gadgets on his missions. Labour leader Harold Wilson had promoted the "white heat of technology" at the 1963 Labour conference; when the party came to power in 1964, they went on to spend 2.3 per cent of the country's gross national product on scientific development. By the mid-sixties, however, technology was proving to be ambivalent. For every new discovery in science or medicine, there was an increasing stockpile of atomic weapons. Fears about nuclear war, and the fact that a more technologically sophisticated world wasn't necessarily any safer, were articulated in Stanley Kubrick's nervous movie satire *Dr Strangelove* in 1964.

Top: The press conference given by Kim Philby in 1955, where he proclaimed his innocence of spying charges. Above: The hi-tech world of James Bond

Left: Alexis Kanner as Number 48, the embodiment of sixties youth, in the last episode of *The Prisoner*, 'Fall Out'

Alexis Kanner as Number 48 in a break in filming 'Fall Out' and (above) with Richard Poore as Fortinbras in Peter Brook's experimental production of *Hamlet* in 1965

Annette Andre, the 'Watchmaker's Daughter' in the episode 'It's Your Funeral', appeared in the book *Birds of Britain* (1967) as a photographic model with her friend, actress Sue Lloyd. The intention behind the book was to promote women who were the contemporary faces of England, from actresses such as Andre to business women such as Mary Quant. Andre and Lloyd went on a promotional tour of America and succeeded in stopping all the traffic in Lincoln Square in Washington, when they gave the USA its first introduction to the delights of the mini-skirt.

Pop goes politics

It's not surprising that the politically changing climate of the sixties would produce serious satire on television. *The Prisoner* went against the grain of popular spy fiction by inverting the secret agent's command of science and technology. From being its master as Drake and Bond were, it was turned on the agent figure, neutering him – reflecting contemporary fears about the implications of unchecked technological advance.

The programme was very definitely 'pop', too. The artist Peter Blake (later to design the definitive Beatles album cover for *Sergeant Pepper's Lonely Hearts Club Band*) in 1957 defined pop art as "popular (designed for a mass audience); expendable (easily forgotten); low cost, mass produced; young (aimed at youth); witty, gimmicky, glamorous and big business." The synthetic, colourful costumes and smoothly stylised look of *The Prisoner*, together with the programme's generic classification as an action adventure series for a wide audience, and the 'gimmick' of the Rover balloon, numbers and pennyfarthings, meant that the series was as pop as it was possible to get. An abandoned version of the end titles, with the camera zooming into an animated graphic of the Earth as the word 'POP' fills the screen, made the connection with the culture of the time explicit.

The Prisoner was both pop and political. Script editor George Markstein revealed that the Village evolved from his jaundiced view of Harold Wilson's Labour Government. Markstein confessed to a "a deep suspicion of the welfare state. Everything is provided for in the Village. Piped music, games to play, free transport, and the Prisoner's crime is that he wants to escape from the ultimate welfare state." The bright, artificial consumerism of the place was nothing but a diverting exterior. Behind the fiction of the consumer having freedom of choice lurked the reality of the consumer in thrall to the options on offer, as Anthony Burgess astutely observed in *The Listener*. "It is Orwellianism transferred to the world of the advert, in which machines work beautifully, everybody is on a kind of holiday and wears a blazer with a redcoat number... and the interrogators are as jolly as the commercial priests of the washing machine or wrapped cheddar." The classification of the Village inmates as people with numbers instead of names was its most obvious political statement, backed up by the lead character's iconoclastic statement of intent: "I am not a number, I am a free man!"

This combination of the popular with the political made *The Prisoner* symptomatic of a time when barriers were falling throughout the arts. Previously, the use of fantasy and surrealism to make dramatic points on television had been the preserve of one-off plays such as David Perry's *The Trouble with our Ivy* (1961) and Anthony Skene's *File on Harry Jordan* (1965). Now, artistic subversion was employed in popular genre series. While ABC's *The Avengers*, another show hybridised from a gritty thriller, was content to play with fantasy and surrealism in the context of comedy, comic strips and science fiction to spoof espionage, *The Prisoner* applied the same techniques to make social observations in the context of the spy thriller.

Don't mention it, Dad

The Prisoner premiered when Patrick McGoohan was 39. In addition to using the programme to express his own concerns about sixties society, and his individualistic leanings in general, he was also able to bring a mature perspective on contemporary youth, a key factor in the social and political upheaval of the time. "I am extremely interested in modern youth," he said in 1967. "I think people today are concerned at an earlier age about their fellow human beings and the state of the world than at any time in history. Much of their current extremism in clothes and general behaviour is a rebellion against the disastrous state of the world around them." McGoohan clearly saw himself as a rebel. The pseudonyms on his three *Prisoner* scripts show he explicitly identified with the underdog in society: 'Fitz' is a slang term for an illegitimate child; 'Schwarz' an insulting description of blacks; and 'Serf' a medieval term for a slave, (although 'Joseph Serf' was also a fictional character invented by the writer Herman Hesse).

While he sympathised with modern youth, young people are absent for most of *The Prisoner*, apart from attractive young actresses – or 'Prisoner Birds' as the magazine *TV World* predictably called them – the obligatory ingredient of films and film series at the time. Like McGoohan's previous show *Danger Man*, *The Prisoner* went against the prevailing free-love sexual politics of the time, with the actor successfully avoiding several attempts by scriptwriters to get the character involved romantically. This made the Prisoner a character of contradictions. Despite being in tune with the revolutionary feeling of the period, he was very much an establishment rebel, at home in the drawing rooms and corridors of power with the movers and shakers of sixties society, a secret agent so chaste and traditional he has a fiancée who is his boss's daughter.

The identification of *The Prisoner* with sixties youth culture was left until the final episode, 'Fall Out', with the casting of Alexis Kanner as Number 48. At 27, Kanner typified both youthful rebellion and its cutting edge of creativity. Not fitting in with the staid constraints of the BBC's police show *Softly, Softly*, his character Constable Stone had been dropped mid-way through the show's first series in 1966. Before that, Kanner had been a prominent member of Peter Brook's Theatre of Cruelty, a theatrical group set up by the Royal Shakespeare Company and subsidised so that it had a licence to experiment. Its 1964 production of Jean Genet's *The Screens* was censored by the Lord Chamberlain. *Plays and Players* described it as "a kaleidoscope of shifting scenes... a series of shattering images," showing "a world in flux", a description that could be equally applied to *The Prisoner*. Kanner's theatrical pedigree fitted with McGoohan artistic ambitions for the series; the leading man himself was, after all, a trained classical actor. Kanner's edge on the contemporary stage – one critic described him as an "E-type Hamlet" – was ideal for the portrayal of "unco-ordinated youth, which rebels against nothing it can define." Kanner's good looks and public pop star persona also saw him mobbed by young girls at Covent Garden station when PC Stone became popular, and Andrew Loog Oldham, the Rolling Stones' manager, reportedly courted the actor to record a vocal version of the *Softly, Softly* theme tune.

The magical mystery revolution

The other facet of 'Fall Out' that locates *The Prisoner* squarely as part of the sixties was the use of the Beatles' summer of love anthem 'All You Need Is Love'. McGoohan was initially doubtful about its use, as sound editor Eric Mival recalls: "Pat was very concerned that the series would have longevity and he did actually ask if I felt that The Beatles would date it or not. I said I didn't think it would because even then it was terrific stuff they were turning out and it seemed as though it would last as long as the series itself." McGoohan had great foresight in choosing the music of a group, which, like *The Prisoner*

itself, would transcend its initial context. Their career in the sixties in many ways resembled his; both were international, mainstream success stories, and used their commercial clout to push through pioneering, experimental work. *The Prisoner*'s production manager, Bernard Williams, remembers that in the wake of 'Fall Out', McGoohan was their favourite choice as film director: "They thought he was the best thing since sliced bread. They just thought he was really with it, and crazy enough to be right for their material." Certainly, the group's own self-directed, produced and written *Magical Mystery Tour*, screened a few weeks before the final episode of *The Prisoner* over Christmas 1967, was anarchic and shambolic enough to bear comparison with 'Fall Out.' One P. J. Nunn, writing to the *TV Times* after the last instalment, drily commented, "...I have come to the conclusion that it was part two of the *Magical Mystery Tour*." For his part, McGoohan was pleased that the decade's most influential group were on his wavelength. "They knew what I was on about," he said. "Right on the button."

That *The Prisoner* ended in confusion and apocalypse was also consistent with sixties popular culture. Certain films of the time, as a cultural response owing to the uncertainties of life under the bomb, end in a shocking, fatalistic fashion, mostly with the death of the rebellious protagonists at the hands of an oppressive or reactionary opposition. *The Trial* (1962), *Seconds* (1966), *Bonnie and Clyde* (1967) and *The Wild Bunch* (1969) all fit this pattern. The climax of Lindsay Anderson's *If...* (1968) has remarkable similarities with 'Fall Out'; in both, principal characters turn machine guns on the anonymous establishment they have fought against. Questioned about the abstruse finalé, McGoohan confessed, "I can't explain it anymore than the pictures from Vietnam which appear in the paper every day." There was no concise, explanatory conclusion to *The Prisoner* because that last, anarchic instalment was symptomatic of the unresolved contradictions in the culture that produced and defined the series. The show was perfectly timed, built on the fault lines that underscored the decade, before the 'swinging' sixties became cynical.

Meet the new boss
Same as the old boss
'Won't Get Fooled Again', The Who, 1970

Top: Malcolm McDowell and Christine Noonan bring armed revolution to an unamed English public school in *If...* in 1968. The Prisoner did the same for the Village in February of the same year (above)

Left: The Beatles dominated sixties popular culture, from records to toys

The hippy generation unites at Woodstock, 1969

3 Cinema for the Small Screen

"Lew Grade, basically, is a romantic. He believes in so-called wild decisions, crazy ideas, going out on a limb, and that's wonderful. On the spur of the moment he has a hunch, and he plays the hunch."

Patrick McGoohan, 1984

"Lew Grade was amazing. One of the greats. I had a very smart Hillman Minx convertible in those days. I used to park it at the studios in the space marked 'Director - *Danger Man*' and Lew used to park his Rolls Royce beside it. One day he comes steaming on to the set and says, 'Ere, someone's parked a rotten old banger in your parking space!' I said, 'I'm awfully sorry, Lew, that's my wife's. I've just borrowed it for the day'. He said, 'You can't bring that 'orrible old thing in 'ere. You'll have a Rolls Royce tomorrow!' Of course, it never arrived, but the thought was there. That's what he was like."

Peter Graham Scott, Director of *The Prisoner* episode 'The General', 2001

The publicity book and ITC catalogue card for the first series of *Danger Man* and (below) the brochure for the second, internationally successful version of the show

ENTREPRENEUR LEW GRADE RELISHED show business and had a larger than life, colourful personality. "I love the entertainment industry," he once declared. In his time, the Russian immigrant (born Louis Winogradsky in the village of Tokmak near Odessa on Christmas Day 1906) had been a professional Charleston dancer and a successful talent agent. Joining the Birmingham-based Associated TeleVision company in 1955, his far-sighted attitude of making programmes for export abroad was to transform British television and profit many of the creative individuals who worked under Grade's aegis, not least Patrick McGoohan. The high esteem in which Grade held the actor was both to make the production of *The Prisoner* possible and, perhaps, be its undoing.

Entertaining the world

Independent television broke the British Broadcasting Corporation's monopoly in 1955. The BBC's predominantly paternal, semi-educational and middle-class tone was countered by a broadcasting service inspired by the American commercial television networks and their part-

funding through advertising. A more demotic, populist attitude was reflected in game and variety shows – *Beat the Clock, Sunday Night at the London Palladium* – and, in particular, fast-moving action adventure shows. ATV was the first UK broadcasting organisation to commission such series, following the lead of smaller companies such as Towers of London, which had made *The Adventures of the Scarlet Pimpernel* for export to the States in 1954. *The Adventures of Robin Hood*, made by Sapphire Films, was ATV's first international success, running for three years on the American CBS network. In order to expand further into this lucrative market, in 1960 ATV formed the Incorporated Television Company Limited – ITC – to distribute its programmes overseas, with more action/adventure product high on its agenda.

The form of the ITC adventure series was dictated primarily by commercial considerations. A film series made in batches of usually 39 instalments was ideal for syndication; the American networks could repeat the best episodes of the first 26 instalments while another 13 were made, meaning that the given series could run for a whole year. The show could also be screened in any order

Left: Lew Grade, with some of the shows that made him famous

ITC's first American success, *The Adventures of Robin Hood*, starred Richard Greene in the title role

McGoohan began directing on *Danger Man*, with the episode 'Vacation' (1960)

as the episodes were usually self-contained stories. This production specification also allowed for the series being rested due to schedule changes or the audience missing the occasional instalment. The look and content of the ITC shows was also exciting, vibrant and fast moving. Shot on 35mm film – the same film stock was used in the cinema – the stimulating ingredients of historical and modern heroes, beautiful women, fights and chases, pacy incidental music, distinctive title sequences and memorable theme tunes defined a new television vocabulary. Even if the majority of foreign settings the shows favoured were shot in the UK home counties or on the back lot of MGM, Pinewood or Elstree studios, they were definitely mini-movies for television. Patrick McGoohan himself was keen to develop this new form: "I was able to bring on to *Danger Man* film directors who'd held aloof from television as it was considered second-rate at the time; eventually I was able to persuade them." He recruited Charles Crichton, who had directed *The Lavender Hill* Mob for Ealing Studios, Don Chaffey, the director behind *Jason and the Argonauts* and *One Million Years B.C.*, Peter Graham Scott and, for *The Prisoner*, Pat Jackson.

The first series of *Danger Man*, transmitted in England over 1960 and 1961 was the first of the new breed of action shows to be syndicated in the States and Canada. However, it was not successful there until its relaunch as an hour-long series with the overseas moniker of *Secret Agent*. "There was a period where no one wanted to know British TV programmes," Lew remembered. "It was really *Danger Man* that broke the bad run. We sold it to America in 1964 and never looked back." By 1967, the series had made 8 and a quarter million dollars for ITC, and in that year the company received the Queen's Award to Industry, the first time it had been given to a company in the entertainment sector. Lew Grade's foresight had brought in 100 million dollars for the company and the UK economy in ITC's first 12 years of operation.

The persuaders

"*Danger Man* and *The Saint* are shown in virtually every country that has a television," Grade stated proudly in 1966, and the two series had made international stars of their respective leading men, McGoohan and Roger Moore. While other ITC series such as *The Baron* (1966) and *Man In A Suitcase* (1967) relied on an imported American star to secure overseas distribution deals and guarantee an American audience, the popularity of *Danger Man* and *The Saint* was built on home-grown

stars; they were also the only shows of their type to make it beyond one series. Coincidentally, McGoohan and Moore both harboured ambitions of going into film production for themselves – both directed episodes of their own shows – and Grade was persuaded to back them as he was keen to retain the services of his two most popular and profitable leading men. Moore and *The Saint* producer Bob Baker's company, Bamore, was careful to build on the star's established success as a light leading man, never too far from a gun or a girl, with colour seasons of *The Saint* between 1966 and 1968. Bamore restructured as Tribune and tentatively moved into cinema production with *Crossplot* in 1969.

Danger man at work

Everyman Films (retitled from Keystone Films to avoid any possible comparisons with accident-prone comedy policemen), the company McGoohan formed with *Danger Man*'s assistant director David Tomblin in 1960, had ambitions far from *The Saint*'s entertaining fripperies or *Crossplot*'s caper movie vibe. Following his decision to leave *Danger Man*, McGoohan favoured a film adaptation of the role that had made him famous, Ibsen's polemical *Brand*, but Grade persuaded him to build on his status as one of ITC's biggest exports, with a new action-orientated series.

Right from the start, Everyman's proposed new show, *The Prisoner*, was in conflict with established ITC practice. McGoohan feared that the concept couldn't be sustained longer than a mini-series, but he was convinced by Grade to accede to a 26-episode run split into two production blocks of 13 episodes to form a first and second series. Grade clearly wanted a return on his investment for what was a very expensive show. At £75,000 per 52-minute episode, *The Prisoner* was £35,000 more expensive than its nearest ITC rival, and reputedly the most expensive television series made up to 1966, incorporating scratch-built sets, stylised clothing and a six-week location shoot in Wales. Prolonged location filming was unheard of for a TV series during the sixties, but in 1970 Tribune's *The Persauders!* went one better and shot for four weeks on the continent.

The format of the series also went against the grain of established ITC practice: *The Saint, The Baron* and *Man In A Suitcase* all had a weekly change of scene with a small regular cast to give continuity. *The Prisoner* was the opposite. The confinement of the hero to one location that didn't change from week to week demanded a

Cinema for the small screen

"CROSSPLOT"

starring ROGER MOORE · MARTHA HYER · ALEXIS KANNER and CLAUDIE LANGE

A TRIBUNE Production
COLOR by DeLuxe®
United Artists
Entertainment from
Transamerica Corporation

Above and right: Following Roger Moore's role in *The Saint*, his and Bob Baker's company Tribune went into cinema production with *Crossplot* (1969) which co-starred Alexis Kanner

Cool Spies and Private Eyes

Out of This World – Sci-Fi Heaven

Although *Danger Man* is still marketed with the rest of the ITC action canon, *The Prisoner* is now bracketed with science fiction titles

development of both the character's reaction to his environment and his experience of it. It had the elements of a serial rather than a series, with a set of objectives – the escape of Number 6, his search for Number 1, the discovery of who ran the Village – that the audience expected to see resolved. However, *The Prisoner* was a one-off, a hybrid. 'Arrival', the opening episode, and the two-part conclusion, 'Once Upon A Time' and 'Fall Out', fulfil the requirements of the serial. Apart from these stories, *The Prisoner* tries to behave like any other ITC film series where the stories stand alone and can be shown in any order. The distinction between 'series' and 'serial' was lost on the programme's production team with the result that, with a jumbled screening order, there was confused continuity between episodes made first and those made later in the show's run. Having said that, *The Prisoner* is still the only ITC action series to have a concluding episode, even if that denouement does break all the conventions of its genre.

It could be argued that the series' perception by the viewing public was prejudiced by the dominant production practices of ITC. The confusing broadcast order aside, the popular ITC staples of action, a frenetic theme tune, and incidental music that would be at home in any other show on ITC's action/adventure roster, prescribed a certain response in the audience. These factors were at odds with the series' philosophical and symbolic undertones – even though advance publicity went out of its way to stress that this would be a different kind of television thriller, containing "food for thought".

That the show didn't fit the ITC mould was emphasised further by the decision to curtail the very expensive production early with a compromise package of 17 episodes. By the time *The Prisoner* ceased production, its ITC stablemate *Man In a Suitcase* had been completed on time and more or less within budget with 30 colour episodes. Unlike Tribune, Everyman Films made only one production, and the company was wound up in 1974 with debts of over £63,000.

The Prisoner may have broken the mould of the action adventures series but commercially it was a failure, the benchmark that all ITC shows were primarily judged by. It was ironic, then, that a production bedevilled by controversy and cut short prematurely would, over time, become one of ITC's best remembered and most respected programmes. In particular, the quality of the cinematography and direction would be one of its greatest legacies, easily standing comparison with feature films, and fully realising the potential of the ITC action series as cinema for the small screen.

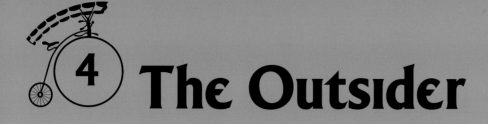

The Outsider

4

MCGOOHAN HAS SAID THAT THE issues *The Prisoner* tackled had been a lifelong preoccupation: "It was in my mind from the very early days, since maybe about seven years old. The individual against the establishment, the individual against bureaucracy, the individual against so many laws that were all confining. The church, for instance: it was almost impossible to do anything that was not some form of sin."

As a film-maker, McGoohan was something of a magpie, borrowing fron a rich variety of sources. The basic scenario of *The Prisoner* comes from Bridget Boland's play of the same name, which he starred in for the BBC in 1962 with Alan Badel and Warren Mitchell. The play was the fictionalised account of the imprisonment of the Hungarian activist Cardinal Mindszenty, with McGoohan playing the interrogator to Badel's cardinal, mercilessly needling his prisoner's Catholic guilt to undermine him. The real-life situation the action was based on was also the first recorded instance of modern brainwashing techniques, such as sleep deprivation and starvation. An episode of the historical adventure series *William Tell* (1957) was also entitled 'The Prisoner', featuring a very young Michael Caine as a member of a road gang; he is actually referred to as 'Number 6' throughout the story – a striking coincidence.

Literature had dealt with the individual versus the establishment many years before. Franz Kafka's *The Trial* was another influence, with a man accused of a crime by an elusive authority which resists all his attempts to escape its power, as was George Orwell's *Nineteen Eighty-Four* (1949). Its vision of a totalitarian state, keeping its citizens under 24-hour surveillance and enforcing its rule through psychological warfare and propaganda, formed the basic structure of the series. The all-seeing Village control room, the medical conditioning of inmates, the Village authorities' attitude of seeing rebellion as an illness to be cured and oppressive slogans - "Questions are a burden to others, answers a prison for oneself" - are all sixties upgrades of the grim elements of Orwell's world.

The dystopias of Aldous Huxley's *Brave New World* (1932) and Anthony Burgess's more recent (and influential) *A Clockwork Orange* (1962) were also to be found in the mix – respectively, a compliant, sometimes drugged population given the illusion of freedom, and social outcasts brainwashed into being acceptable citizens. It was also no surprise to find the bizarre world-view of Lewis Carroll reflected in *The Prisoner*'s depiction of a fairy-tale community with undercurrents of menace. There are games of human chess, first seen in *Through the Looking Glass*, and echoes of Carroll's reverse logic: the President in the final episode, 'Fall Out', declares, "Guilty! Read the charge!" during the trial of an inmate. Philip Purser, when reviewing *The Prisoner*'s first episode for the

Right: "I am not a number, I am a free man!" McGoohan as Number 6 in *The Prisoner*'s title sequence

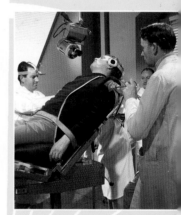

Experiments on human subjects was a constant theme of the series. The Prisoner undergoes a (faked) lobotomy in 'A Change of Mind'

Before becoming Script Editor on *The Prisoner*, George Markstein had been producer of *This Week,* a current affairs programme. Following his work with Everyman Films, he moved to Thames Television, scrpit editing the 1969 series of *Special Branch*, before that series' production team made the two colour series of the spy thriller *Callan*, in 1970 and 1972. After this assignment, Markstein moved on to Euston Films, acting as uncredited script adviser on the *Armchair Cinema* series of television films, including the pilot for *The Sweeney, Regan*. In later years, he became a successful novelist. He died in 1987.

John Lennon as Corporal Gripweed in Richard Lester's anti-war polemic *How I Won The War* (1967)

Sunday Telegraph, was immediately struck by its varied pedigree: "Is it by Kafka out of *Cards of Identity* or an extension of the Lime Tree café for broken rebels in Orwell's *Nineteen Eighty-Four?*"

Breathless in Alphaville

In the cinema, Orson Welles had seen the contemporary relevance of Kafka's *The Trial* (1962), updating it to the modern day to produce a nightmare new world for Anthony Perkins' Joseph K. It took place in a nameless city that was deliberately disorientating due to the mixture of architectural styles of Zagreb and Paris: an anonymous urban landscape comparable with the enigmatic toy-town that would confuse Number 6. John Frankenheimer's adaptation of Richard Condon's 1959 novel *The Manchurian Candidate*, made in the same year as *The Trial*, first brought to a wider audience many of the themes that *The Prisoner* would deal with: mind control, conspiracies, brainwashing, and the blurring of political ideologies. Particularly striking was the hallucinatory feel Frankenheimer brought to the direction. Stylised, idiosyncratic camera work symbolising altered states of consciousness would be common to *The Prisoner*'s visual vocabulary, as would the predominant idea that what the audience was watching should not be taken at face value.

1965 saw the realease of the French New Wave director Jean-Luc Godard's film *Alphaville*. The film blended together different film genres, importing Eddie Constantine's hero Lemmy Caution from a series of conventional crime thrillers to a science fiction setting. This combination of genres creates a third form, distilling the best elements from each to produce something new and unsettling, a technique *The Prisoner* excelled at. Caution's transplant from one genre to another is also comparable with McGoohan's John Drake persona graduating from the conventional, but well crafted, spy thrillers of *Danger Man* to the complex mind games of *The Prisoner*. Intentionally or not, the series followed Godard's lead in combining the tough-guy thriller with the trappings of the science fiction and conspiracy genres, with an incorruptible hero willing to use words as well as his fists as weapons.

There are more detailed similarities between the two. In *Alphaville*, wall mounted slogans are used throughout by the city's administration, and the residents have their own ritual greeting – "I'm very well, thank you, you're welcome"; compare this with *The Prisoner*'s own "Be seeing you". Caution is constantly told he "asks too many questions," a common criticism of the Prisoner by his fellow Villagers, and he is the first hero in paranoia fiction to destabilise the rigid *status quo* rather than be destroyed by it, another similarity with Number 6.

By 1966, Godard's hallmarks of hand-held camera work, sudden jump-cuts and a free-flowing, open-ended narrative style, honed in *A Bout de Souffle* (1959), had filtered into the work of British director Richard Lester. This modern approach was ideally suited to the two anarchic Beatles vehicles Lester directed, *A Hard Day's Night* (1964) and *Help!* (1965), and were developed further in *How I Won The War* (1966). As the film director allied to the world's most famous pop group, his work was dominant in the 'swinging sixties' zeitgeist, and a like-minded approach to visual story-telling can be found throughout *The Prisoner*'s 17 episodes.

Produced by
David Tomblin

David Tomblin began his career as assisstant director on seasons one and two of *Danger Man*. Following *The Prisoner,* he wrote 'Reflections In The Water' and 'The Long Sleep' for Gerry and Sylvia Anderson's *UFO* (1970), also directing 'The Cat With Ten Lives', with Alexis Kanner and Colin Gordon, for the same series. He helmed five episodes of the Andersons' *Space: 1999* in 1975, including 'The Infernal Machine' which featured Leo Mckern. He graduated to feature film production with the assisstant director's post on Kubrick's *Barry Lyndon* (1975), followed by *Gandhi,* (1982), *Empire of the Sun* (1987), and *Braveheart* (1995), which co-starred Patrick McGoohan. He worked in the same capacity with George Lucas on the latest instalment of the *Star Wars* saga, *The Phantom Menace* (1997).

The Kubrick connection

During production on *The Prisoner*, McGoohan asked film librarian Tony Sloman to source films by movie directors, in order to help define his own approach to film-making. A significant influence on him as a director was *Paths of Glory* (1957) by Stanley Kubrick, the visceral story of French soldiers court matialled as scapegoats for the incompetence of their high command. "The way Stanley shot those sequences in the trenches really affected him," Tony Sloman recalls. "The soundtrack to *Paths* also helped dictate the way music was used in *The Prisoner*." The style in which sequences in 'Free For All', 'A Change of Mind' and 'Fall Out' were shot by McGoohan show how much of an influence Kubrick's cold, objective eye was.

The series' connection with the New York-born director went futher than just inspiration. His then latest film, *2001: A Space Odyssey* was in production in adjacent studios at MGM Borehamwood while *The Prisoner* was being made. The production personnel used the same facilities, and this led to a photographic plate commissioned for *2001* appearing in *The Prisoner*. "I was looking for a night sky shot for the scene in 'The Chimes of Big Ben' where Pat's using the triquetrium," Sloman explains, "and had drawn a complete blank. Stanley's boys were using the photographic lab at Borehamwood, I saw this night sky they

had, which was ideal, borrowed it and shot it with a rostrum camera. Needless to say, they were sworn to secrecy." Curiously, however, the scene was cut from the finished version of the episode and only survies in the first edit.

Kubrick's production designer on *Dr Strangelove* (1964), Ken Adam, became the most influentail production designer in the sixties with his seminal work on the James Bond films. His designs for *Strangelove* were a definite influnce on *The Prisoner*'s production designer Jack Shampan, as can be seen in the recurrent use of circular imagery, gigantic wall-sized maps and cavernous sets that dwarf the human cast.

The Stanley Kubrick films *Dr Strangelove* (far left) and *Paths of Glory* (left) influenced McGoohan as a director and the programme's visual style (top)

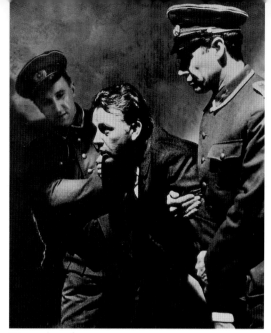

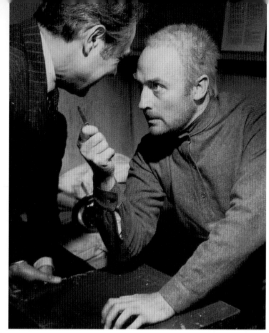

Before coming to *Danger Man* and *The Prisoner*, Don Chaffey was an established feature film director, with credits on movies such as *Jason and the Argonauts* (1963) and *One Million Years B.C.* (1966). Once involved with television, he directed episodes of *Man In A Suitcase* (1967), *TheAvengers* (1968) and *The Protectors* (1972). His film career continued throughout the seventies and included the psychological thriller *Persecution,* with Ralph Bates and Lana Turner, in 1974.

The Manchurian Candidate had a major influence on *The Prisoner*, with its portrayal of human subjects as laboratory specimens and its use of mind-bending psychotropic drugs

Right: Together with *Danger Man, The Avengers* was the most internationally successful British spy series of the sixties

No more heroes

John Drake's reinvention took place in 1966 when spy fiction was at a crossroads, as both the cinema and literature had caught up with the grim reality of intelligence work. Although the hi-tech, brightly coloured fantasies of the James Bond films and their many imitators remained popular, the film version of John Le Carré's *The Spy Who Came in From The Cold* (1965), filmed in a gritty black and white, caught the authenticity of real espionage. Featuring Richard Burton as Alec Leamas – near alcoholic, middle aged and world-weary – he was as far as it was possible to get from the flippant 007 superman depicted by Sean Connery, or Michael Caine's fashionably working class, laconic Harry Palmer. His was a murky, cerebral world full of double agents and double crosses, of false identities and friends revealed as enemies – and vice versa. *The Spy Who Came in From The Cold* was a critical and commercial success, and the implication that the public wanted a more human take on their fictional spies, as well as a more sophisticated treatment of fictional espionage, was also reflected on television.

The relaunch of *Danger Man* in 1964 partly pre-empted this change of direction into cynicism and *ennui*. An audience-winning penchant for Bond-style gadgetry aside, John Drake's world, while shot in a tough, *film noir* monochrome, was far from black and white in its depiction of intelligence work. Strong supporting casts with the ambivalence of Le Carré's characters were common, and the stories were often downbeat. 'Don't Nail Him Yet' was an absorbing character study of a man who might or might not be a traitor, relegating the Drake-catches-the-villains plot to

the last few minutes. 'That's Two of Us Sorry', in particular, sees a move towards the morally complex spy fiction prevalent during the late sixties. It concerned a one-time traitor who has been living undiscovered for 20 years, is mistakenly implicated in a new theft of sensitive material and arrested. Ironically, he is cleared of the new crime and arrested for the old one, and Drake's attitude at the end of the story makes it clear that he doesn't approve. Direct antecedents of *The Prisoner* during *Danger Man*'s run were 'Colony Three', the story of a fake English village behind the Iron Curtain used to train spies, and 'The Ubiquitous Mr. Lovegrove'. This latter story used surreal camera work and direction to visualise a nightmare, adding a fresh twist to the more conventional stories in the series' run, (and pre-empting the dream-like *mise-en-scène* of *The Prisoner* itself). By April 1966, however, with only two episodes of a proposed fourth series made in colour, it was clear that *Danger Man* had run its course. 'Koroshi'

and 'Shinda Shima' were nothing but low-budget retreads of the Bond novel *You Only Live Twice*, lacking the subtleties of the one-hour black and white stories. Turning *Danger Man* into a po-faced clone of *The Man from UNCLE* clearly wasn't for McGoohan; Norman Hudis, the writer of the two colour episodes, was a script writer on the MGM super spy saga.

It was at this point that the production team split. McGoohan and story editor George Markstein defected to McGoohan's new project at Everyman Films. Various members of production personnel went with them, including second series production designer Jack Shampan, director of photography Brendan J. Stafford and prolific director Don Chaffey. Meanwhile, producer Sidney Cole retained most of the *Danger Man* writers on his new project, *Man In a Suitcase*. Both shows were to premiere in the same week of September 1967, and in different ways, explored the dilemma of moral, if flawed, men trapped in an amoral profession.

Man In a Suitcase starred Richard Bradford as McGill, a discredited, homeless American agent who made a precarious living doing jobs for money, frequently coming off worse in his assignments. Bradford described McGill as "a flesh and blood hero with faults — not an emotionless, celluloid figure.... He makes mistakes in his job. That shows he's human." By necessity, McGill was also a loner, a trait he had in common with McGoohan's new *Prisoner* persona, a man who resigns from a highly secret job as "a matter of conscience" and is imprisoned against his will. ABC's *Callan*, launched in July 1967, ahead of the two ITC offerings, featured the first of 1967's three espionage anti-heroes. David Callan, another man with a

conscience, is blackmailed into working for the security services, and his series was the first on British TV to recognise that the West's intelligence methods were as ruthless as the opposition, involving "eliminating people, framing, extortion, death." *The Prisoner* followed up this precedent with the uneasy implication that the West could be the side that ran the Village. Interestingly, the only alternative Callan is given to his seedy career is imprisonment.

There were clearly two routes for the morally centred spy. On the one hand, realistic drama/action adventure, with fallible lead characters, or on the other, with *The Prisoner*, a move towards allegory and fantasy; a nameless and incorruptible, almost superhero, anonymous jailers, and the inmates of the prison only referred to as numbers. However, the core idea of the series – of ex-intelligence agents imprisoned in a holding facility indefinitely – was based very firmly on fact, thanks to the series' script editor George Markstein.

The encyclopedic man

Markstein was born in Berlin in 1929. His family fled to England as refugees when the Nazis came to power, and he carved out a career for himself in journalism. He returned to Europe to work for the US forces as a military correspondent on their paper *Stars and Stripes*, which suited him as he could speak German fluently. While working for the military, he became fascinated by espionage. Moris Farhi, a writer who would later work on *The Prisoner*, describes Markstein as a man with an "immense background in intelligence and spying. He was almost an encyclopedic man. If you suggested something, he could give you five examples of when it had happened." On his return from Europe, Markstein became a crime reporter, before moving into television in the early sixties to work on the Associated Rediffusion current affairs programme *This Week*.

Mid-sixties loners and anti-heroes. From top clockwise: Richard Burton as Alec Leamas in *The Spy Who Came In From the Cold*; Edward Woodward as *Callan*; Richard Bradford as McGill in *Man In A Suitcase* and the Prisoner

After *The Prisoner*, Bernard Williams became Executive Producer on *The Battle of Britain* (1969), *A Clockwork Orange* (1971) and Associate Producer on *Barry Lyndon* (1975), a post he also took on *Flash Gordon* (1980) and *Manhunter* (1986). He became a fully fledged producer on the Steve Martin and Michael Caine film *Dirty Rotten Scoundrels* (1988). In 2001, he was the Associate Producer on *The Score* (2001), which starred Robert De Niro, Edward Norton and Marlon Brando.

UNUSED SCRIPT 1:
DON'T GET YOURSELF KILLED
by Gerald Kelsey

The Prisoner is invited to join the Village Escape Committee, where he learns about a miner who is rumoured to be digging an escape tunnel. Number 6 goes to the man's cave and discovers that he is, in fact, mining gold. They do a deal; the Prisoner accepts half the gold in return for developing an escape plan... Number 6 considers a job in the Village establishment. Suspicious, Number 2 puts the Prisoner forward for a loyalty test at the Faculty of Environmental Adjustment. There, he meets the Head of Faculty and brokers another deal: gold in exchange for a means of escape, which the Faculty's leader devises through the acquisition of a helicopter. He visits the miner, intending to double-cross Number 6, but is accidentally killed when the miner thinks the Head of Faculty is stealing the gold. Loading sacks of the mineral into two stolen Mini Mokes, the Prisoner and the miner head for the helicopter launch pad, but Number 2 uses Rover to stop them. He confiscates their cargo, only to be told by Number 6 that it is iron pyrites - 'Fool's gold'.

An artist's impression of how the introduction of the original Rover in 'Arrival' might have looked

George Markstein had a cameo role throughout *The Prisoner*, as the ex-agent's un-named superior in the title sequence of fourteen of the seventeen episodes. He reprised the performance in the last episode he worked on, 'Many Happy Returns' (above)

Out of necessity, he opted for a career change: "He couldn't see all that well any more and wore really thick glasses," Farhi recalls, "so he couldn't follow up the scoops as he once could. That's why he became a scriptwriter." Markstein initially used his background experience as script editor for the US forces series *Court Martial* (1965-6) before being introduced to McGoohan through Lewis Greifer, by now a script editor at ATV and an old friend from Markstein's formative days as a cub reporter. "Pat was working on *Danger Man* and wanted to start writing himself," Greifer says, "and needed someone to edit his stuff; a personal story editor, if you like. I recommended George and he started working on *Danger Man*." Markstein became script consultant for some episodes in the third series – his background in espionage added

authenticity to the scripts – before becoming story editor on the aborted fourth season of the show.

While McGoohan maintained that he had been thinking about the idea for *The Prisoner* all his life, it was Markstein who fleshed out the concept of a man held against his will and defined the new series for the actor. Justifiably, he saw himself as the show's creator. As Greifer recalls: "We were discussing *The Prisoner* long before it started. George had worked on the *Stars and Stripes* and had discovered the existence of these camps where they kept people they didn't want wandering around." Specifically, Markstein had learnt about Inverlair Lodge in Scotland, an establishment controlled by the Special Operations Executive during World War II, where agents thought to be a security risk were held. "They were sent on 'holidays' and were

WHAT WAS THAT..??

WAIT!!

ROVER

30

The Outsider

extremely well treated," Markstein explained. "They had excellent wine, salmon cooked in season.... That was the birth of *The Prisoner*, people being sent somewhere and isolated.... The other reason was that *Danger Man* was coming to an end and another series was needed for McGoohan, who wanted nothing more to do with Drake. It would cash in on a secret agent who wanted to get out and 'they' wouldn't let him. Stir, boil ten minutes and hey presto!"

The Prisoner's title sequence ingeniously linked the real-life situation to the fictional one, showing a publicity photo of McGoohan from his former series relegated to the 'resigned' drawer. He would always maintain that "there is no connection with *Danger Man*. You won't see a continuation of that series." Even though Markstein's writer's guide for the series – which mapped out the details of the fictional community, gave it a name, the Village, and indicated how the action was to work – presented the hero as nameless, he was in doubt about the Prisoner's identity. He considered the anonymity of McGoohan's new character to be primarily a legal consideration: "*Of course* he was John Drake, but it's cheaper to have a number so you don't have to pay royalties."

The avoidance of royalties aside, from the outset it seemed that the production team and star didn't agree on the provenance of the main character: Tony Sloman remembers that on the continuity sheets for the early episodes, the protagonist was indeed called 'Drake'. This difference of opinion anticipated how McGoohan and Markstein's views on the direction of the *The Prisoner* would diverge as production of the series progressed.

Everyman for himself

The other-worldly influence of the main location, Portmeirion in North Wales, built on the enigmatic elements already present in the series' format. The decision to film there was McGoohan's as he remembered the place from a location shoot for the first series of *Danger Man* in 1959. Tellingly, the location's varied styles of architecture had doubled for Italy, Switzerland, the Middle East and China – in fact, anywhere in the world. The use of the location, as itself, would as McGoohan noted, be "beautiful enough, mysterious enough and confining enough to be the base for our man in isolation."

McGoohan was without doubt the prime mover behind getting the series made. The first Markstein knew about *The Prisoner* going into production was when he read about it in his evening paper. Exercising his influence with ITC chairman Lew Grade, McGoohan sold him the idea. Famously, the TV mogul declined to read the outline and agreed to the series on the strength of McGoohan's passion for the idea alone. "The great thing about working for Lew Grade was that he left you alone," McGoohan says. "I never even had a contract with him, it was all done on a handshake." With the series sold by the actor's singular personality and to be made by his own company Everyman Films, it was clear that McGoohan was very much the boss: "Pat was the producer, star, and on some director, too," property buyer Sidney Palmer points out. "He was the number one man." Fittingly, he was referred to as 'Sir' or 'guv' by members of his production team.

An early indication of the effect of the uncompromising stance McGoohan adopted was the early departure of the original co-producer, Leslie Gilliat, from the production, although he did attend some of the location shooting in North Wales. An experienced film producer, Gilliat had worked on *Two Left Feet* (1965) and *The Great St. Trinians Train Robbery* (1966), and was charged with recruiting key members of the production team. The old catch-all of 'creative differences' is cited as the reason for his departure, but it is clear that even at the beginning, Gilliat realised very quickly he did not wish to be associated with the direction in which *The Prisoner* was heading.

McGoohan was much more comfortable working with his former *Danger Man* associate David Tomblin, today considered the best first assistant director in the world, having worked on high profile films such as *Superman* (1978), *Gandhi* (1982) and *Braveheart* (1995). Now sole producer in the absence of Gilliat, Tomblin brought an intricate understanding of film-making to the project and was on McGoohan's wavelength regarding the content of the series. He directed two episodes, wrote the outline for two others – 'The Girl Who Was Death' and 'Living In Harmony' – and co-authored the pilot script, 'Arrival', with Markstein. Crucially, the appeal of the series for him was primarily as an adventure series in the ITC style, and he deferred the creative decision making to McGoohan: "The style of the series was really his baby... I was used to action adventure things, which I like very much, and his more imaginative ideas came into *The Prisoner*."

The script for 'Arrival' doesn't mention the famous pennyfarthing insignia or the distinctive dress of the

Inverlaır Lodge ın Scotland, the real-lıfe Vıllage durıng World War II

Regular characters: Angelo Muscat as the Butler (top) and (above) Peter Swanwick as the Supervisor

Villagers. Both are attributed to McGoohan himself. He decided on the pennyfarthing after art director Jack Shampan submitted some initial ideas that McGoohan rejected. Although with hindsight he claimed that the old-fashioned bicycle represented "an ironic symbol of progress", during production he refused to explain its significance. While it remains an elegant, quirky and eccentric symbol in its own right, it also reflects those particular aspects of the Portmeirion setting, helping to embroider the fantasy. As McGoohan was the boss it was simply accepted by the production team. "Patrick is a very secretive man in many ways," Tomblin offers, "so he would come up with these weird and wonderful ideas and never explain them – so you just had to work them into the context of the stories."

At an early stage, however, McGoohan's involvement would encompass more than the cosmetic look of the show. He was responsible for the original design of the Village guardian Rover, bypassing Shampan's art department and commissioning its construction by an external contractor. Originally described as a 'vehicle' in the 'Arrival' script, the prop consisted of a dome mounted on a go-kart chassis. (The prop was remarkably similar in design to Dr. Noah's personal hovercraft in the Bond spoof *Casino Royale*, in production at the same time as *The Prisoner* in Borehamwood). McGoohan's decision proved to be misjudged: Once in Portmeirion, it was found that the Rover machine could only function on flat concrete, and the noise of its engine made the recording of dialogue inaudible. At this point, however, he was able to salvage the situation by sanctioning the use of meteorological balloons as replacement Rovers. The substitution of the enigmatic balloon in place of a device that was recognisably mechanical was typical of McGoohan's instinctive approach to film-making; if it looked or felt right it was done, regardless of the implications for narrative clarity.

This oblique stylisation continued with the Villagers' costumes. Catherine Williams, assistant to wardrobe mistress Masada Wilmot on the Portmeirion location shoots, explains the reasoning behind the clothes' design: "They had to be ageless. Everything had to be a uniform. They couldn't use drainpipes or flares, it all had to be neutral – no age. And the colours had to be the same. That was the one thing the wardrobe had to be very careful of." This left the costumes themselves open to interpretation. Markstein has stated that the

distinctive piped blazers were a dig at organised, regimented holiday camps, "suggesting a holiday atmosphere and a take-off of the Butlins redcoats." However, with the addition of straw boaters and scarves they could just as easily be a pop art take on the British public school system or Oxford and Cambridge. Again, McGoohan wasn't saying, and neither were the scripts.

The individual look of *The Prisoner* was further enhanced by the use of a customised version of the Albertus typeface. Incorporating classical as well as modern qualities, it was the ideal font to complement this hyper-real world. It gave an all-encompassing, corporate feel to the Village through its use on food stuffs, books and signs, further eliminating any sense of a contemporary place or time. The illusion was completed by the inspired production designs of Jack Shampan. The main sets, at McGoohan's suggestion built around one stage that could be redressed as various rooms, were all circular in shape. They built on the circular theme that was emerging in the production's design: the pennyfarthing, the balloon, and the exterior location in Portmeirion chosen for Number 2's office, (the primary set the stage would be used for). Their futuristic and minimalist qualities heightened the schizophrenic feel of the Village compared with Portmeirion's fey, old world charm. The sets' circular design - further reflected in Number 2's command chair - were an articulation of the idea of a highly advanced prison. "When we came indoors, it was all way out, futuristic," Shampan explained. "Everything was stylised and symbolic. For example, [Number 2's] living space... all those lines going upwards which symbolised a cage." More so than in *The Prisoner*'s nearest television contemporary, *The Avengers*, with its merry England of evil masterminds, the detail and minutiae of the series gave it a disconcerting sense of being one step removed from reality.

We're all pawns, m'dear

While the production's look, with McGoohan as the driving force, gave *The Prisoner* a striking and unsettling *milieu*, it was the scripts that ultimately made it memorable. Writers Markstein employed on the series have nothing but praise and respect for him. "George was an inspirational script editor," Vincent Tilsley says unequivocally; Gerald Kelsey remembers him as "a great ideas man," while Moris Farhi would commend his editor's attitude of 'anything goes': "George was like a juggler; he could work several themes all at the same time." Farhi says that for him, at the time, *The Prisoner* was "the only show in town. It allowed you so many variations, you could do anything." The overriding theme of people as expendable pawns, to be manipulated and sacrificed due to the imperatives of some higher hidden agenda, one of the key images of *The Prisoner*, was undoubtedly Markstein's doing. This idea came from his experience of the real world of espionage, which he saw as an intricate game of chess for Whitehall mandarins and CIA and KGB controllers. He would elaborate on the theme in his work as script editor for the third and fourth seasons of *Callan* and in several novels he would subsequently write. His first novel, *The Cooler* (1974), takes a hard, cynical look at Inverlair Lodge, (renamed Inverloch) during World War II. Inmates are encouraged to form sexual relationships with each other and cultivate drink and drugs dependency, possibly indicating how Markstein's undiluted version of *The Prisoner* may have developed.

Ultimately, Markstein was more interested in a realistic spy series with philosophical overtones than the symbolic fantasy McGoohan favoured, and this is where the rift between the two men developed. "George's conception of *The Prisoner* was entirely realistic and Pat's was fantastic," Lewis Greifer explains, "and George questioned the changes that Pat made to it because he thought it was cheapening his idea. It was a paradoxical situation because I was friends with both of them. They were at loggerheads over *The Prisoner* fairly early on and I often found myself acting as a pacifier, trying to smooth things over." Markstein clearly didn't approve of McGoohan's intrusion into areas of production he had no experience of, particularly when it started affecting his work as story editor.

Markstein commissioned two scripts, 'Don't Get Yourself Killed' by Kelsey and 'The Outsider' by Farhi, which were cancelled at McGoohan's insistence. 'The Outsider' even got as far as pre-production before the axe fell. Typically, the reasons McGoohan gave for abandoning Farhi's script were idiosyncratic rather than there being anything inherently wrong with the writing. "The script opens with the Prisoner trying to determine where in the world he is through birds' migratory patterns," Farhi relates. "When McGoohan saw this, he said, 'heroes don't bird watch.' Later on, the Prisoner is captured and put in a non-gravitation chamber and tortured. There's a close-up of his face sweating and then the sweat becomes ice. Again, McGoohan said, 'heroes don't sweat.' Those were the two points it failed on."

PAWNS AND PLAYERS

The diminutive Angelo Muscat, the Village Butler, appeared in 15 episodes of *The Prisoner*. He was cast by McGoohan himself, replacing the conventional henchman figure described in the 'Arrival' script. Before *The Prisoner*, Muscat had been a professional wrestler and played one of the 'Chumbley' robots in the 1965 *Doctor Who* story 'Galaxy Four'. Coincidentally, he also played a moustachioed butler in Jonathan Miller's *Alice in Wonderland* (1966). Speaking about *The Prisoner* in 1967, he said: "My part is such a mystery, I don't even know yet whether I'm a goodie or baddie". Indeed, many of the production crew speculated that the silent butler was the elusive Number 1. Muscat died in October 1977, aged 49.

The other regular cast member, Peter Swanwick, who played the Control Room Supervisor Number 28, appeared in nine episodes. His other work included the TV version of the radio comedy *Educating Archie* (1959), as well as two episodes of *Danger Man*, 'The Key' (1960) and 'The Paper Chase' (1965). Swanwick underwent major surgery in 1959. Aware he might only have a few years left to live, he nonetheless continued to work up until his death in November 1968 (he was 46). His last film, *The Looking Glass War*, was released posthumously in 1969.

McGoohan chats with the production crew. "He got on fine with the rank and file," Cinesound effects librarian Angela Marshall remembers, "it was the bosses he always fell out with"

From left: McGoohan directs Alexis Kanner's scenes during the filming of the final episode, 'Fall Out'.

Kelsey also attributes the rejection of his script down to elements that McGoohan disliked: "I think if anything it was too realistic, and I don't think Pat liked it because the action was shared among too many other characters."

A change of mind

The increasing workload required to complete *The Prisoner*'s first season, for such a perfectionist as McGoohan, meant additional stress on his personal resources, and this situation did nothing to alleviate the growing conflict with Markstein. It's noticeable, too, that Don Chaffey, director of four of the first five episodes made, suddenly disappeared from the production team, having helped define the show's visual look. Film editor John S. Smith remembers that the two men had a disagreement over 'Dance of the Dead', with the result that the episode was shelved for some time.

As production wore on, McGoohan became more insistent, making major production decisions. The directors of three episodes, 'It's Your Funeral,' 'A Change of Mind' and 'Many Happy Returns' were replaced at short notice by McGoohan himself. Only Peter Graham Scott and Pat Jackson, trusted directors the star had worked with earlier in his career, would stay the course, with even Scott, by 1966 an experienced producer/director, finding McGoohan incredibly demanding. "One of the actors came up to me and said, 'I really don't understand this,' and I said, 'Forget it, just say the line,' " he remembers. "Of course, a voice booms out behind me: 'You haven't done your homework.' I snapped back, 'Give me a chance, I only got the script two days ago!' "

By January 1967, the atmosphere at the MGM studios in Borehamwood was very different from when Gerald Kelsey handed in his script for 'Checkmate'. His impression then had been of a production team enthusiastic about their new project and pulling together. "They were thrilled about the script. George opened the door and called out to Patrick. He came in, shook my hand and said, 'Wonderful script! Great!' It was a very complimentary meeting." By 'A Change of Mind,' the ninth story made, McGoohan's attitude to Markstein, and the writers he employed, was decidedly cool: "I think George introduced us," Roger Parkes, the author of 'A Change of Mind' remembers. "There was a curt shake of the hand and that was it. Patrick was very offhand, very casual. I think writers to him were fairly dispensable." By the filming of the next story, its author Anthony Skene recalls that "George was in disfavour by 'A.B. and C.', but still doing writing in his office." With the completion of the last story of the first production block, 'Many Happy Returns', Markstein felt that the programme had moved so far from his original intentions – particularly with the semi-hysterical, absurdist theatre of McGoohan's own 'Once Upon A Time' – that he left the production. He was bitterly disappointed: "I felt very strongly that the full potential of the series was not being realised," he said years later, "and that there were further dimensions we could and should have explored further."

Number 1's the boss

The loss of his script editor was a further diminution in the talented team McGoohan had gathered around him. The irony was that the tension between the two men had produced something unique: a genre series that addressed weighty, serious issues formerly the preserve of literature, theatre or *avant garde* cinema. The loss of Markstein is not to be underestimated; McGoohan asked members of the production team for story ideas to use in the remaining episodes. It's significant, too, that out of the four remaining stories made, two, 'Living in Harmony' and 'The Girl Who Was Death,' were made up primarily of action sequences and feature a reduced amount of dialogue. The final scenes in the last episode, 'Fall Out', have no dialogue at all.

It was somehow inevitable that the series would end prematurely with the revelation that the Prisoner himself was Number 1. McGoohan had manoeuvred himself into the position where he had complete creative control, but with the series expensive and time consuming to produce, and with its proposed second season already behind schedule by Autumn 1967, continuing was simply not an option. The final episode's revelation of Number 1 as the hysterically deranged alter ego of the series' star ironically foreshadowed Sidney Palmer's comment that his boss was "the number one man." In production terms and within the fiction of the series,

The Prisoner was a spiral that ultimately led back to McGoohan/Number 6. It was artistically satisfying – and, as ever with the series, more by accident than design – that fiction fused with reality as Number 6 destroyed the Village and McGoohan killed the series. The show had begun almost every week with an allusion to Drake/Number 6/McGoohan's resignation and ended in the same way, with the actor fused with the character he played – his on-screen credit in the final moments was, simply, 'Prisoner'. The biggest irony is that an ending that so outraged audiences, and changed forever the perceptions of what television was capable of, was only possible because of Markstein's decision to quit, unshackling completely McGoohan's raw, uncompromising creative energies. The ex-script editor, would, however, describe 'Fall Out' with characteristic candour as "nonsense".

Lewis Greifer, the man who brought McGoohan and Markstein together, still considers *The Prisoner* to be a career highlight. "It was the most outstanding series... It had a bit of *The Avengers* to it but the social observation was what it made it special. That's why it became a cult in its own right. I'm very proud to have worked on it." The following pages look at the 17 stories in detail, elaborating on Greifer's great affection for a series he unequivocally describes as "the *Pennies from Heaven* of its day."

Phyllis Townshend (14, 15, 17)
Set Dressers
Kenneth Bridgeman (1-12, 16)
Colin Southcott (13)
John Lageu (14,15,17)
Theme Music
Ron Grainer
Editors
Lee Doig (1, 9, 10, 12, 16)
Spencer Reeve (2)
Geoffrey Foot GBFE
(1,** 3, 4, 5, 7)
John S. Smith (6, 8, 11)
Eric Boyd-Perkins GBFE
(13, 15, 17)
Noreen Ackland GBFE
(14, 17)
Sound Recordists
John Bramall (1-12, 16)
Cyril Swern (13-15, 17)
Sound Editors
Wilfred Thompson
(1, 2, 4, 6, 7, 12-17)
Peter Elliott (3)
Stanley Smith (5, 8)
Ken Rolls (6, 10, 11)
Clive Smith (9)
**Incidental Music/
Musical Director**
Albert Elms (3-8, 10-17)
Music Editors
Eric Mival (1-6, 8, 10-17)
Robert Dearberg (1,9)
John S. Smith (7)
Sound Effects*
Cinesound
Make-Up
Eddie Knight (1-12, 16)
Frank Turner (13-15, 17)
Hairdressing
Pat McDermot (1-12, 16)
Olive Mills (13-15, 17)
Wardrobe
Masada Wilmot (1-12, 16)
Dora Lloyd (13-15, 17)
**Wardrobe Assistant,
Portmerion***
Catherine Williams
Film Librarians*
Tony Sloman (1-12, 16)
David Naughton (13-15, 17)

*Not credited on screen
**Edited the alternate 'Arrival'

1: Arrival

Written by George Markstein and David Tomblin   Directed by Don Chaffey

A man resigns from a top-level job, is gassed by unknown assailants and awakes in an Italianate village. The community's chairman, Number 2, reveals that the Village is a top-secret security establishment where people with access to sensitive information are held. The man - the Prisoner - refuses to divulge the reasons for his resignation. He walks out of a probing interview at the Labour Exchange, and a ploy by a bogus maid to win his confidence also fails. Attempting to escape, the Prisoner falls foul of Rover, the Village's balloon-like guardian. Waking up in hospital, he meets an old colleague, Cobb, another abductee, who later commits suicide. Assigned the number 6, the Prisoner follows Cobb's funeral procession and sees a woman crying. She knew the dead man and they had both planned to escape using the Village helicopter. Number 6 and the woman, Number 9, agree to try Cobb's scheme, but she is being manipulated by the new Number 2. She refuses to go with him and, alone, the Prisoner takes flight in the helicopter. However, it is under remote Village control and brought back. In a final twist, Cobb is revealed to be still alive and leaves for a rendezvous with his "new masters". For Number 6, though, the ordeal is just beginning...

The new Number 2
(George Baker)

Who is Number 2?: In *The Prisoner*, authority has multiple faces, yet is fundamentally faceless: early in the episode, we are introduced to the first of the Village administrators, who is then arbitrarily replaced by another man.

Both epitomise the Village's approach, by turns charming and ruthless. The first has an old Etonian air, advising the Prisoner to "be reasonable, old boy", about his incarceration. The second is business-like and coldly to the point, telling his new charge that he's interested in facts, and that "if you won't give them to me, I'll take them."

You are Number 6: The character of the Prisoner as a symbolic man with no name is something of a blank canvas, acquiring skills as the stories require. Here, his background is broadly sketched in: he worked for and resigned from a secret government department where he had access to highly sensitive information. Shortly before his abduction, he was due to meet Chambers, "about to become late of the Foreign Office", and had recently been in Singapore. He had also known Cobb for some time prior to his imprisonment. He is skilled in hand-to-hand combat, drives a Lotus 7, registration KAR 120C, likes lemon tea and has two eggs with his bacon. The Village authorities have a comprehensive dossier on him but were unaware he was born at 4.31am, 19 March 1928. He is possessed of a deeply-

felt personal outrage at the restraint of his liberty and the intrusion into his private life. The Prisoner also has no trouble resisting the charms of female Village agents.

One? Two? Three? Four?: The original transmission order was jumbled and this section will address the episode-to-episode inconsistencies, based on the original UK and US transmission orders. However, in both production and screening order there can be little argument that 'Arrival' is the first episode!

Information: Originally entitled 'The Arrival', the opening episode was one of script editor George Markstein's favourites: "It's the germinal script, which sets up the situation and launches us into the Village, the admission ticket to the world of Number 6." Patrick McGoohan had equally high praise for the story, considering it "the best pilot script I have ever read". It was sweated out between producer Tomblin and Markstein in the course of a month; on its completion, the star added personal touches of his own. "We just went a little further in certain areas - the political area, for instance," McGoohan says, "and that great banner I was always waving around: 'I will not be pushed, filed, stamped, indexed, briefed, debriefed or numbered!' I wouldn't have done it if I couldn't have written that in."

In line with McGoohan's drive for more political input, one of the slogans on the Labour Exchange wall

Guest Stars

Guy Doleman

Number Two

George Baker

The New Number Two

Virginia Maskell

The Woman

Paul Eddington

Cobb

with

The Taxi Driver

Barbara Yu Ling

The Maid

Stephanie Randall

The Doctor

Jack Allen

Welfare Worker

Fabia Drake

Shopkeeper

Denis Shaw

Gardener/Electrician

Oliver MacGreevy

Ex-Admiral

Frederick Piper

Waitress

Patsy Smart

Labour Exchange Manager

Christopher Benjamin

Attendant

David Garfield

1st Croquet Player

Peter Brace

2nd Croquet Player

Keith Peacock

Rover's First Victim*

Seamus Byrne

First Maid*

Jill Hennessy

*Uncredited. Seamus Byrne
was the third assistant director
on the Portmeirion shoot.
Jill Hennessy was the
assistant accountant.*

The first Number 2 (Guy Doleman) gives the Prisoner a guided tour around his new home from home

The Prisoner gets his first sight of the hi-tech sophistication behind the Village's *olde worlde* facade

"I will not be pushed, filed, stamped, indexed, briefed, debriefed or numbered. My life is my own"

THE PRISONER

VILLAGE SLOGANS

Walk on the grass

Questions are a burden to others, answers a prison for oneself

A still tongue makes a happy life

Of the people By the people For the people

The Prisoner uses the Village's 'Free Information' map and summons a Mini Moke taxi driven by a Chinese girl (Barbara Yu Ling)

- "Of the people, by the people, for the people" - is adapted from the Gettysburg address, Abraham Lincoln's famous speech of 19 November 1863: "This nation under God shall have a new birth of freedom, and that government of the people, by the people and for the people shall not perish from the Earth."

Production: The Lotus 7 used in the title sequence was chosen in place of the proposed Lotus Elan after McGoohan spotted the vehicle while visiting the company's head office; he felt that the 7 better reprsented the prisoner's idiosyncratic character. The runway the 7 drives along in the opening sequence was part of Elstree aerodrome, not far from *The Prisoner*'s Borehamwood studios.

Scenes in the opening title sequence in central London were shot the weekend before an advance party from the production team departed for Portmeirion, on Saturday 3 September 1966. The ramp into the under-

ground car park is situated in Abingdon Street but the interiors were shot in Park Lane. 'Arrival' was the first time that members of the production team were used in minor roles. The man behind the desk who accepts McGoohan's resignation is George Markstein – David Tomblin thought he was ideal for the part as "he looked like a bureaucrat". The Prisoner's journey finishes outside his home, No.1 Buckingham Place.

Location scenes for 'Arrival' were slated for filming in Portmeirion between 5 and 9 September. The mechanical Rover taken there proved unworkable, and 2m (6ft) diameter meteorological balloons filled with a mixture of French chalk, helium and air were used to represent the Village guardian. The balloons were more manoeuvrable as they worked on land and at sea. Rover's distinctive sound effect was synthesised by sound editor Wilf Thompson from sources as diverse as the inner tube of a tyre filled with shotgun pellets, a

Above and below: The first appearance of the Village guardian, Rover, in the Village's main square

recording of a man screaming and a monks' chorus.

The two stunt men credited as '1st Croquet Player' and '2nd Croquet Player' are the assailants in the Mini Moke who attack the Prisoner on the beach. A scene involving dialogue for them and showing them playing was scripted, and their credit shows that the scene was filmed. It was later decided to drop the sequence after one of the actors, Keith Peacock, was later killed working on the BBC police series *Softly, Softly*.

Following the unforeseen early departure of Guy Doleman from the shoot, his scenes were restructured. A stand-in was used on the Village square's balcony - his face obscured by a megaphone (and also as he alights from the helicopter). A scene also shot but dropped showed two men fighting by a pond. They fall in and are subsequently 'arrested' by two gardeners, or, as Number 2 calls them "PMCs – Public Minded Citizens". Local man Will Parry played one of the offenders and remembers the unfortunate aftermath of that particular shoot. "There were all these wonderful £100 carp in there and they all died after we did it! There was a terrible fuss about that."

The Alouette helicopter, piloted by Charles James, arrived on 13 September and remained for three days. It

was filmed every time it took off or landed to maximise the amount of footage available. A particularly happy accident was the discovery that the down draft of the rotor blades made the Rover balloons bounce along the water.

The distinctive livery of the Mini Mokes used in *The Prisoner* is attributable to a company called Barton Accessories which specialised in moke conversions. These revamped models were referred to as "beach buggies", the description of the Village taxis given in the 'Arrival' script.

Filming on the interior sets designed by Jack Shampan and his team began at the MGM studios on Monday, 3 October 1966. The main circular set, Number 2's office within the Green Dome, was designed to be redressed as other rooms, and in 'Arrival' became the Labour Exchange. It also doubled as the Control Room throughout the series. The stage was built over a system of trap doors to allow for the rise and fall of various chairs, including Number 2's revolving command seat - a prototype of the famous sixties globe chair designed by Eero Aarnio. It also included mechanisms for the centre-mounted rotating scanner arm and camera eye in the control room. Other sets that would be used over the coming weeks were

PAWNS AND PLAYERS

Guy Doleman played Harry Palmer's superior Colonel Ross in the three film adaptations of Len Deighton's espionage thrillers *The IPCRESS File* (1965), *Funeral in Berlin* (1966) and *Billion Dollar Brain* (1967), produced by Bond mogul Harry Saltzman. Doleman was also cast as the villainous Count Lippe in 1965's 007 adventure *Thunderball*, the first of four Number 2 actors to appear in the cinematic adventures of James Bond. His successor, George Baker, was another, appearing as Sir Hilary Bray in *On Her Majesty's Secret Service* (1969). The ex-RSC actor had a distinguished career for over 40 years on television; he appeared in series as varied as *The Goodies* (1970), and *I, Claudius* (1976). Virginia Maskell had played the title role of the colonel's daughter in the *Danger Man* episode of the same name in 1964; her life was cut tragically short when she committed suicide in 1968. Paul Eddington's first major role on television was as Will Scarlet in *The Adventures of Robin Hood* (1955-60). In later years he starred as the put-upon Jerry in the sit-com *The Good Life*, (1975-8), and the bumbling politician Jim Hacker in *Yes Minister* (1980-4) and *Yes, Prime Minister* (1986-8).

In the first of *The Prisoner*'s action sequences, Number 6 tackles two guardians and Rover on the beach

Filming the Prisoner's first fight with Rover, with Jack Lowin behind the camera

Number 6 has his first tour of the Village hospital, courtesy of the doctor (Jack Allen)

Number 6's cottage – which also stood in as his London home – and various Hospital rooms.

The music for *The Prisoner* has a chequered history. The first attempted composition of the show's theme was handled by Robert Farnon, composer of the film score for the feature film *Shalako* (1968) and memorable themes for the TV shows *Colditz* (1972) and *Secret Army* (1977). Farnon's theme was however deemed unsuitable and he left the production. His original signature tune can be heard briefly at the start of the first episode of *The Champions*, 'The Beginning'. Some of the other work he completed for *The Prisoner* entered the Chappell's Music Library and would, in the end, be used on 'Arrival', as well as in the final episode.

Wilfred Josephs was the next composer employed. He wrote a wild, erratic orchestral theme tune, which suited the programme's paranoid mood rather than the tempo of the on-screen action, and incidental music based on the main theme's melody. Early prints of 'Arrival', and the second episode, 'The Chimes of Big Ben', were struck with his compositions. However, the main theme was again dropped, with Josephs' only surviving music in the show being incidental tracks in the

final cut of 'Arrival'. (Josephs later produced distinctive theme tunes for *The Pallisers* (1974) and *I, Claudius* (1976), as well as the title music for the film version of *Callan* (1974).

In December 1966, Chappell's recommended Ron Grainer to compose the third version of the theme and Albert Elms to compose incidental music and select stock compositions for the series (both were acting in the same capacity on ITC's *Man In A Suitcase*). Grainer had composed singular, idiosyncratic TV themes for *Steptoe and Son* (1962), *Doctor Who* (1963), and the film score for *To Sir, with Love* (1963). This time around, his version of the theme, which perfectly matched the energetic pace of the title footage, was accepted, and Elms stayed with the series throughout its run.

The signature tunes were recorded in quick succession. The session for Farnon's theme took place on 20th December 1966, with Josephs' following on 2nd January 1967. The recording of Grainer's composition took place shortly before work commenced on Albert Elms' incidental music on 21st March 1967. The final choice was a disappointment to music editor Eric Mival: "I thought Bill Josephs' was the better tune; it was a distinctive, original and idiosyncratic. However, the powers that be decided they wanted something that sounded more like an action theme, which they got with Ron's."

The Village Band was recorded without any music in mind; the extras mimed silently on location in Portmeirion. Film librarian Tony Sloman suggested the Radetsky march that was ultimately bcame the musicians' accompaniment: " I had this *Reader's Digest* compilation with the music on it, suggested it to Pat and that's what we used."

There were several changes between script and screen. The opening storm was to begin with "jagged lightning" and the sports car was originally silver. Originally four undertakers got out of the hearse in the title sequence, rather than just the one eventually seen. A ring on the doorbell was to have followed and the Prisoner was to have been gassed as he answered the door. An elevator scene in the underground car park was also removed, as was a computer

The Prisoner attempts to escape using the Village helicopter but the remote controlled aircraft is brought back

sorting through cards for the Prisoner's ID. The electronic Village map that summons the taxi is not present in the script; as written, the Prisoner approaches a taxi rank of "beach buggies" and summons the Chinese driver by pressing the horn. Most significantly, the Butler was originally scripted as "a man who would look at home in an E-type Jaguar", a formal-looking, athletic type who also had dialogue.

In the initial exchange with Number 2, one of the Prisoner's hobbies is revealed as chess and the time of his birth is not given when the comment is made that it is missing from the file; the time and birth date supplied on screen are McGoohan's own. Rover's second appearance revealed a major change from the script: the confrontation between the Prisoner's Moke and Rover originally occurred in open woodland, where the car is forced into a tree by the machine; on location it was moved to the beach in the Treath Bach estuary. The machine was also to have featured at Cobb's funeral, but with the substitution of the balloons this idea was dropped. The tour of the Village by helicopter, with the tall Butler changed into overalls, has Number 2 commenting on water skiers and that a "quite brilliant journalist" runs the newspaper.

During 'Arrival's' first UK network repeat in 1983 on Channel 4, the slamming bars animation, and the disassembling and assembling pennyfarthing 'bumpers' used to signify the beginning and end of each act, were missing. They were reinstated when the series was repeated in 1992.

The alternate 'Arrival': An early cut of the episode, which somehow found its way into syndication in the US, the alternate 'Arrival' is interesting for showing how the version eventually used is more tightly and more smoothly put together. There are several minor differences in the camera angles and editing but the scenes dropped or changed were clearly amended either because they weren't up to scratch technically, or because they were considered unsatisfactory artistically. For example, the animation of bars slamming together over the Prisoner's face at the end of the

episode before the credits is paced a lot slower, lacking impact. The concluding end titles animation, marrying together the pennyfarthing and images of the universe and Earth, overcooks what was already a rich mixture of styles and symbols and was replaced by footage of Rover moving across the sea.

Victims of the editor's scissors include shots of McGoohan looking particularly manic as he is gassed in his apartment and later as he gazes out at the Village for the first time. They were understandably replaced as they don't portray the countenance of a man constantly in control. His taxi tour around the Village is edited differently and is longer, and was presumably cut to omit his comment that being a taxi driver "is an unusual job for a girl". The sound effect and attack method of Rover is also a lot cruder. The noise is obviously someone breathing through an oxygen mask, rather than the carefully synthesised sound the beast usually makes, and when Rover assaults the Prisoner on the beach, there is no smothering effect showing the balloon's membrane stretched over a victim's face.

Tally Ho: *"We're all pawns, m'dear. Your move."* The skill of 'Arrival' is that it retains the staples of the mid-sixties spy thriller - the powerful man in charge, the hired muscle, the traitors, even a helicopter - and subtly and disconcertingly peels away the certainty of what we are witnessing. The first sight of the stylised interior of Number 2's residence; the appearance of the Rover balloon, with the Villagers freezing into robot-like immobility; the Villagers at the Labour Exchange monotonously humming 'Boys and Girls Come Out To Play' all take the story of an abducted ex-spy into a bizarre new area. The atmosphere of uncertainty and unease is enhanced, too, by the anonymity of the protagonist and the Village controllers, and the large amount of location filming that adds to the authenticity of this strange new world.

All the acting is excellent, but it is McGoohan, with a simmering, righteous indignation, who holds the attention. He was the star, and right from the outset it looked like the Executive Producer's series was going to be a new departure for televised entertainment.

Scenes from the rough-cut edit of 'Arrival'

2: The Chimes of Big Ben
Written by Vincent Tilsley   Directed by Don Chaffey

A new prisoner, Nadia, is brought to the Village and installed as Number 6's neighbour. Following an escape and suicide attempt by the girl, the Prisoner agrees to co-operate by joining in the Arts and Crafts Competition if Number 2 leaves her alone. Correctly guessing that Nadia knows the location of the Village – in Lithuania, 30 miles from the Polish border – he enlists her help... Number 6's sculpture for the Arts Competition converts into a boat and, using a tapestry bought from Number 38 as a sail, they both escape on it at night. Using Nadia's contact Karel, the pair are sealed in a crate and on a journey by ship, plane and truck head for the Prisoner's H.Q. in London. Once there, he is reunited with his old colleagues Fotheringay and Colonel J. Promising to negotiate asylum for Nadia, the Colonel says he can't do the same for Number 6 until he knows the reasons for his resignation. As he is about to reveal all, he notices that the chimes of Big Ben relate to the same time on the watch he was given by Nadia's accomplice in the Baltic – there should be one hour's difference. Searching the office, the Prisoner discovers it to be a Village mock up and that the Colonel and Fotheringay are both traitors. Nadia herself turns out to be another Village agent.

Scenes from the alternate edit of the episode

Who is Number 2?: Alternating between good-natured bonhomie and threats, this Number 2 relishes crossing intellectual swords with his prize prisoner: "I am glad you're here... We must play [chess] sometime." He accepts his fate as one of the Village's "lifers", but equally believes in the pioneering spirit of the community. At the end, it is revealed that he didn't think the plan to deceive the Prisoner would work.

You are Number 6: The Prisoner has been experiencing nightmares and developed the nervous habit of twiddling his thumbs. His concern for Nadia, an attractive and vulnerable young woman, reveals "an obvious weakness". When she later asks him if he has a wife in England, he says no; when pressed if he's engaged to anyone he doesn't reply. Again Number 6 proves to be a man of varied talents: aged 15, he was top of his class in woodwork and is able to manufacture stone-age style tools which he uses to construct a modern art sculpture convertible into a boat.

One? Two? Three? Four?: 'The Chimes of Big Ben' was the fifth script to be produced, and its composition suggests it was intended to be broadcast a lot later than the second episode. The softening of the Prisoner's attitude, as well as the apparent success of his escape, has much more impact if screened after four episodes featuring his uncooperative stance and an aborted run of breakouts.

Information: The deception practised on Number 6 has similarities with the Harry Palmer thriller *The IPCRESS File* (1965). In the film, Palmer is made to believe he is behind the Iron Curtain by means of a mocked-up interrogation centre staffed with East German guards just as the Village replicates the Prisoner's London office. Coincidentally, the second episode of *Man in A Suitcase*, 'Brainwash', broadcast the same week as 'The Chimes of Big Ben', features its anti-hero McGill imprisoned in a fake country house inside a warehouse.

During judging for the Arts and Crafts Competition, Number 2 refers to Number 6 as "our very own Epstein". Sir Jacob Epstein (1880-1959) was born in New York and studied sculpture at the École des Beaux-Arts in Paris. In 1905, the artist settled in London. He became a British subject in 1910 and was knighted in 1954. A primitive, rough-hewn realism and vigour distinguish Epstein's sculpture. He also did figurative work, including portrait busts of George Bernard Shaw, Albert Einstein and Winston Churchill.

Production: Between Wednesday 28 and Friday 30 September 1966 a minimal amount of location footage for 'Chimes' was shot at Portmeirion. When the Alouette helicopter was present, film of Nadia being brought to the Village was shot, with Helweun Vaughan Hatcher used as a stand-in for Nadia Gray on the stretcher attached to the aircraft. When 'Chimes' began production at Borehamwood in late November 1966, it was the first episode

Number 2 (Leo McKern, top) and Nadia (Nadia Gray, above) involve Number 6 in an elaborate deception plan

"What has in fact been created is a perfect blue print for world order. When the sides facing each other suddenly realise they are looking into a mirror, they will realise that this is the pattern for the future."

NUMBER 2

CAST

Guest stars
Leo McKern
Number Two
Nadia Gray
Nadia
Finlay Currie
The General
Richard Wattis
Fotheringay
with
Colonel "J"
Kevin Stoney
Assistant
Christopher Benjamin
Karel
David Arlen
Number 38
Hilda Barrie
1st Judge
Jack LeWhite
2nd Judge
John Maxim
3rd Judge
Lucy Griffiths
Double for Nadia Gray*
Helweun Vaughan Hatcher

Uncredited on screen.

The Prisoner explains the reasoning behind his sculpture, 'Escape', to the judges of the Arts and Crafts Competition

Above: the Prisoner about to reveal the reason for his resignation to Colonel J (Kevin Stoney)

Right: Leo McKern awaits his cue to enter the beach set constructed at the Borehamwood studios

extensively to use studio-mock ups of the Portmeirion location, primarily Number 6's cottage and the front of the Old People's Home. Painted backdrops also give a sense of perspective to the studio-bound sets. As Nadia Gray had not been present in North Wales, a beach set complete with cliff top and a pool for the water's edge were used for scenes of her sunbathing then being retrieved by Rover. The studio tank was also used for close-ups of Gray swimming. These were intercut with footage of Helweun Hatcher, who again doubled for the actress, in long shots done on the beach and in the sea at Portmeirion. Doubles were also used for long shots of the Prisoner and Nadia in their makeshift boat.

A back lot set available at the MGM studios was used extensively for the first time, standing in for Portmeirion. Left over from the filming of Robert Aldrich's *The Dirty Dozen* (1967), this set consisted primarily of a courtyard based round a tree surrounded by dummy buildings, including a large structure that in 'Chimes' became the Exhibition Hall. The interior of the Hall was again the versatile Number 2 set redressed. The studio-bound woods were also used for the first time.

McGoohan's reluctance to play romantic scenes with his leading ladies substantially affected one scene. The change did not please author Vincent Tilsley: "He made a nonsense of that scene with Nadia. There were loads of cameras about, watching them, and it was supposed to be a fake love scene so they could pass on information. But it became a bit of hair fondling and they even used a double who was shorter than the actress playing Nadia!" The scene had already been toned down, in accordance with McGoohan's views on family viewing; in an earlier draft, Nadia and the Prisoner exchange information lying intimately on Number 6's bed. The original script still features the mechanical Rover. The earlier draft also dilutes the suspense by implying that Number 2 knew about the deception plan. McGoohan dropped a section of dialogue from Number 6's speech about his sculpture, as it offended the actor's religious convictions: "Our escape leads us back to discipline, faith, organisation. In fact, religion."

The Prisoner realises that he has been tricked and discovers that his London office is a Village replica

Leo McKern's first story initiated a fractious relationship with the series' star. Meeting in a bar before production began, McKern remembers McGoohan said, " 'You're a funny little fucker, aren't you?", and I thought, 'It's going to be *that* sort of relationship!' "

Prison writers: Like David Tomblin and George Markstein before him, Vincent Tilsley was not a regular ITC writer. He had worked on plays as well as series, including *The Road* (1963) as script editor, and *Jury Room*'s 'The Traitor' (1965). Following *The Prisoner*, he worked on the experimental Second World War drama *Manhunt* (1970). He created a sympathetic

Close-ups of Nadia and Number 6's escape by sea were shot in the studio and used back projection of a coastline

German character for the series, and included interrogation scenes up to 15 minutes in length – two innovations for TV drama at the time. Disillusioned with television after his last play *The Death of Adolf Hitler* in 1973, he gave up writing to concentrate on a career in psychotherapy.

The alternate 'Chimes': A rough cut exists of this episode which contains several differences. The Wilfred Josephs' version of the theme music is again used on the beginning and end credits, and snatches of the composer's incidental music can also be heard throughout the story. A sequence dropped when the titles were finalised has Number 6 being chased by

Rover from the beach. Another scene, previously seen at the end of the rough cut of 'Arrival', shows him being smothered by Rover outside the Old People's Home.

One major scene is completely absent from the final cut. Nadia discovers the Prisoner working on a device called, as he explains, a "triquetrum, a makeshift Greek device for discovering one's whereabouts" by plotting the position of the stars. A line of dialogue cut from the transmitted version, but kept here, indicates that Number 6 and Fotheringay were "at school together" as well as work colleagues. Christopher Benjamin's voice is his own – in the final cut it is dubbed.

The end titles feature another variation as the production team still clearly hadn't decided on their final form. The wheels of the bike vanish to become the Earth and moon, but instead of being linked by a ghostly cycle frame, (as on the alternate 'Arrival' titles), the camera zooms in on the Earth until the word 'pop' fills the screen.

Tally Ho: *"We're off to the woods" "Naughty, naughty."* Viewers were getting their first taste of inconsistencies in *The Prisoner*'s screening order with 'Chimes', which did not help the public reaction to an already radical series. From the Prisoner's point of view, Nadia's first experiences in the Village reflect his own and she is clearly meant to be the first person he really trusts. Placing the episode second rather undermines this, although because of the story's superb twist ending – one of the best in the series – its impact is still powerful.

'Chimes' is a rich brew, encompassing a philosophical discussion on the Village, a clever satire of modern art – "It means what it is" – a dramatic escape by sea and an underplayed love story. With so many elements in the mix, the story could have easily congealed to a standstill. That it balances all its elements so effortlessly and, if anything, more accessibly than 'Arrival', is a testament to both Vincent Tilsley's skill as a writer and the strength of George Markstein's original brief for a spy series with a satirical edge. The story also calls into question the provenance of what the viewer is witnessing on screen, a concept *The Prisoner* would play with and build on in the coming weeks.

PAWNS AND PLAYERS

An experienced film and television actor, Leo McKern had featured as the cynical Bill Maguire in Val Guest's gripping *The Day the Earth Caught Fire* (1961). Nadia Gray (real surname: Kujnir-Herescu) spoke six languages fluently, enabling her to enjoy a varied English-speaking and European film career. She featured in Federico Fellini's landmark movie *La Dolce Vita*, in *Candide* (both 1960) and *The Naked Runner* (1967) with Frank Sinatra. The Scottish actor Finlay Currie was associated with many memorable films. He narrated the seminal Ealing comedy *Whisky Galore!* (1949), appeared in the Roman epic *Ben-Hur* (1959) and John Schlesinger's classic *Billy Liar* (1963). He also played an unlikely Mafia Don pitted against Simon Templar in 'Vendetta for the Saint' (1969). Richard Wattis played John Drake's NATO contact Hardy in the first series of *Danger Man* (1960–61). He was perhaps most well known as Eric Sykes' pompous neighbour Mr Brown in the comedy *Sykes* (1960-61), and the seventies revival (1972-–74). Kevin Stoney played two memorable *Doctor Who* villains in the sixties: Mavic Chen in 'The Daleks' Master Plan' (1965-66) and the cyborg Tobias Vaughn in 'The Invasion' (1968).

3: A.B. and C.
Written by Anthony Skene   Directed by Pat Jackson

Number 6 is taken unconscious to an underground complex and undergoes a process that manipulates his dreams and visualises them on a screen. (While there, he briefly wakes and sees the doctor in charge of the process, Number 14.) Number 2 has surmised that if the Prisoner were to sell out, it would be to one of three people – A, B or C, – who attended Madame Engadine's Paris parties. 'A', a defector, is inserted into the Prisoner's dream. They meet, banter and fight; Number 6 wasn't selling out to him. Requiring rest, he is returned to his cottage. He spots an injection wound on his wrist and recognises Number 14 from his dream. Realising that the Prisoner is suspicious, Number 2 brings the next session forward. Number 6 meets B, a female spy, and Number 14 manipulates her into asking him questions. He spots the deception and repels the interrogation. The next day, he follows Number 14 and infiltrates the complex. He replaces the last dose of the mind-bending drug with water. That night, Number 6 meets C – of whom no visual record is available. It turns out to be Madame Engadine herself, although she takes him to meet yet another conspirator, 'D'. Removing the man's mask, Number 2's own face is revealed. On the screen, Number 6 hands Number 2's dream counterpart an envelope containing holiday brochures; he "wasn't selling out".

The Prisoner meets A (Peter Bowles), an "old friend", at Madame Engadine's latest Paris soirée

Who is Number 2?: An intense, worried man with an ulcer, if his milk drinking is anything to go by. This is the first Number 2 to be afraid of his masters: "Yes, sir. I know I'm not indispensable." He is bullying towards Number 14, telling her he'll have the drug proved on her if she doesn't do as he says. As the red phone bleeps at the end, it seems an unpleasant fate awaits him because of his failure.

You are Number 6: The Prisoner is described as "not conventional." In his sleep, he constantly dreams about his resignation, "an anguish pattern". He attended Madame Engadine's parties in Paris with the defector A, the female spy B and the anonymous C. His life proceeds in his dream how it would had he not been abducted to the Village, beginning with a holiday. He describes B as "an old friend". He has a formidable mental resistance to the drug and is able to dictate the direction of his own dreams, although the effort required pushes him to the limit and he collapses.

One? Two? Three? Four?: "I am Number 2". The introductory voice-over of 'A.B. and C.' was the only one to be worded in this way, indicating that this was to have been Colin Gordon's second televised appearance as Number 2. The Prisoner again appears relatively settled and mentions the attempts of Number 2's predecessors to extract information from him. The episode was the tenth to be filmed; access to Portmeirion was minimal, explaining the inventive shift away from the Village location.

Information: The trio of opposition agents, A, B and C are a possible allusion to the spy triumvirate of Burgess, MacClean and Philby. Number 14 says that A "made world news when he defected six years ago":

"I see you still overrate absolute truth. Whatever way you look at it, we both want to conquer the world."

'A'

TALLY HO HEADLINE

Is Number 2 fit for another term?

CAST

Guest stars

Colin Gordon
Number 2

Katherine Kath
Engadine

Sheila Allen
Number 14

with

"A"
Peter Bowles

Blonde Lady
Georgina Cookson

"B"
Annette Carrell

Flower Girl
Lucille Soong

Maid at party
Bettine Le Beau

Thug
Terry Yorke

Thug
Peter Brayham

Henchman
Bill Cummings

Above: Engadine (Katherine Kath) in her party dress and (below) Jack Shampan's design for Number 14's laboratory

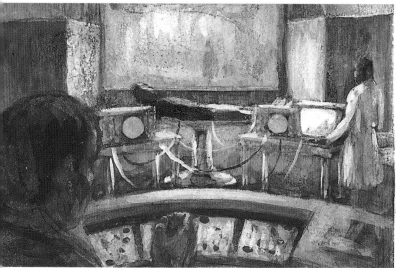

The Outsider: A.B. and C.

47

A scene cut from the final version of the episode featured Number 14 and Number 2 (Colin Gordon) in conversation on Number 2's office set

Number 6's night time drive with Engadine and (top right) filming the scene at Borehamwood. Studio mock ups of the Portmeirion hotel, also used in the story, can be seen in the background

At the end of the episode, Number 2 receives an ominous call on the red phone

Philby's defection to the Soviet Union in 1963 had the same effect. The origins of 'A.B. and C' lie in Anthony Skene's first script for the BBC science fiction series *Counterstrike*. The series concerned the efforts of an extra terrestrial, Simon King (Jon Finch), to stop the take-over of Earth by a race called the Centaurans. Although the series was not transmitted until 1969, *Counterstrike* had a long development – the initial scripts were written in 1966. Skene's script, 'Nocturne', was rewritten for *The Prisoner* when the production of *Counterstrike* stalled.

In 1994, The crime thriller *Killing Zoe*, directed by Quentin Tarantino cohort Roger Avary makes a specific reference to *The Prisoner* and 'A.B. and C.'. Film buff Oliver enthuses about the series as his gang enjoy some chemical recreation. "What I was telling you... the final conflict between 6 and Number 2 to find out who was Number 1, Number 6 realises he is Number 1... It's like we're all prisoners of ourselves, you know... but the best episode is 'A.B. and C.' where [sniffs cocaine] he takes three drugs and he realises three different alternative realities and... This is really good gear, isn't it?"

Production: Michael Truman, who had made 15 episodes of *Danger Man*, was the original director but he became ill and was replaced by Pat Jackson. Titled 'Play in Three Acts', then '1, 2 and 3' and finally 'A.B. and C.', filming began on 13 February 1967. Studio mock-ups of the Village were again used, with the MGM back lot used for exterior shooting – this time for Number 6's night time drive and fight with A's men, and D's "impressive offices". Location inserts were shot at Portmeirion, beginning on 5 March 1967, with rear views of Frank Maher as Number 6 following a stand-in for Sheila Allen. Number 14's laboratory was again a redressing of Number 2's office set, complete with the large screen. The episode required many scenes to be shot prior to the lab sequences so they could be back projected on to the screen, a complex task that required the presence of *Prisoner* film librarian Tony Sloman on the set throughout shooting. New sets originated included the house for Engadine's party, the garden and the arbour. The episode also marked the first use of the red, curved phone that connects Number 2 with his unseen master, an ominous symbol of authority that the direction emphasises.

Number 6 reveals the face of the fourth conspirator, 'D', to Number 2, turning the tables on the Village chairman

The story was another which was dictated by budgetary restrictions. "Tomblin wanted to do an episode using lots of stock shots he knew about," Anthony Skene remembers, "with lots of back projection of Morocco, or somewhere. I thought that was a crappy idea, so I put on my wellies and tramped over MGM's backlot. I wrote it around the church door, the street from *The Dirty Dozen* and other bits, too, which were all leftovers. And people think writers spend their lives on a *chaise-longue*!" Ironically, 'A. B. and C.' was to become David Tomblin's favourite episode. The episode built around stock footage was ultimately made as 'Do Not Forsake Me Oh My Darling'.

An alternative version of the episode, under its original title of 'Play in Three Acts', is held in the Carlton International archive.

In the 1983 screening on Channel 4, the scenes where Number 14 manipulates B's speech were missing. They was reinstated for the 1992 re-run.

Prison writers: Anthony Skene was an accomplished writer of both television plays and series, with scripts

The crew shooting the "dreamy party" sequence

for *Armchair Mystery Theatre* and *Saturday Night Theatre* as well as series like *Haunted* (1967) and *Couterstrike* (1969). He epitomised the fresh writing talent George Markstein wanted to attract to *The Prisoner* and it was to be the only ITC series he worked on. Skene had a fascination with female characters, both in his three *Prisoner* scripts and the work he did afterwards. In 1970, he scripted three plays under the title *Wicked Women*, about fictional female criminals in the nineteenth century. His love of classic literature also saw him adapt Alexander Dumas' *The Three Musketeers* for the BBC in 1966. Skene worked with Markstein again on *Frontier* (1968) and *Special Branch* (1969). In 1968, his anti-racism play *Love Thy Neighbour* was broadcast at 9.00pm on the Midland channel, the same day as the last episode of *The Prisoner.*

Tally Ho: *"We mustn't disappoint them, the people who are watching"*. Anthony Skene's scripts are some of the best in the series – clever, literate, unpredictable fantasies. 'A.B. and C.' is also self-aware, as shown by the nocturnal thunderstorm at the beginning, traditionally the backdrop for scientists up to no good in horror films. The Paris sequences follow this lead, playing with their function as a play within a play, and some of their knowing winks to the audience are very funny. A says "I'm saving myself money", when, in the absence of his henchmen, two doormen unaccountably grab Number 6 for him. The Prisoner's straightening of the mirror, which straightens the room as it becomes "a dreamy party", is also a piece of sixties psychedelic madness at its best. The script is beautifully constructed: both stories run parallel then, when Number 6 enters the lab in his dream, and lies on the table where his body is reclining in the real world, the plots dovetail and conclude. One of the finest examples of *The Prisoner* "exploiting the possibilities in film for playing with its own nature as illusion", as *The Observer* put it in 1969, 'A.B. and C.' showed that the programme was about far more than the Shangri-La qualities of its principal location.

4: Free For All

Written by Paddy Fitz   Directed by Patrick McGoohan

The new Number 2 challenges the Prisoner to run against him in the annual Village election. He agrees and is given the services of Number 58, a maid who speaks no English. He confronts the town council, is found in contempt and subjected to the Truth Test to determine whether his desire to run was genuine. He leaves the test brainwashed into continuing the election. However, the conditioning breaks down. He attempts to escape in a speed-boat and is brought back by Rover. The election continues. Lapsing into paranoia in the Cat and Mouse club, Number 58 takes the Prisoner to a cave with a hidden alcoholic still (where he finds Number 2). He is able to drink genuine alcohol but this proves to be another ruse to drug him. Polling day arrives and a landslide victory is declared for Number 6. He is taken to Number 2's control centre and shown the mechanics of power. Coming to his senses, his pleads with the Villagers to leave but they ignore him. He tries to escape again but is brutally beaten and brought before Number 2, now revealed as the fluent English-speaking Number 58.

Examples of McGoohan's nightmarish direction. A full interview with the Prisoner appears in the Village newspaper minutes after he has agreed to stand; his prepared election speech; the Rover watchers in the cave behind Number 2's office

Who is Number 2?: The grey-haired, senior holder of the post has an almost benevolent manner, but he proves to be one of the most skilled manipulators of the Village yet seen. He is in control from the start and with his drunken act in the Therapy Zone cave, successfully manages to fool Number 6 into believing he is on his side. The revelation that the incomprehensible Number 58 was really Number 2 all along reinforces the overwhelming influence the Village has during the election.

You are Number 6: 'Free For All' sees the Prisoner at his most helpless, manipulated and brainwashed by the establishment. He is also at his most suspicious, self-righteous and paranoid, haranguing the Council – "this twentieth century Bastille which pretends to be a pocket democracy" – and snapping angrily at Number 58 and the other Villagers. In contrast to his Herculean resistance to the drug in 'A.B. and C.', the lapses in his conditioning are momentary. For the most part, he becomes the perfect Village stooge. Some biographical details about him emerge; he gave up taking sugar three years and four months ago on medical advice and he is partial to an alcoholic drink. He also shows himself to be a proficient speed-boat pilot.

One? Two? Three? Four?: 'Free For All' was the second episode to be filmed. Number 6 is new to aspects of the Village such as the Council and the fact that the community apparently has annual elections. He doesn't know his way to the Town Hall and consults the electronic map to find it. His aggressive manner also indicates he hasn't been in the Village long. His first conversation with Number 2, saying that he's going to run "like blazes, the first chance I get", therefore seems odd in the transmission order when, as far as the viewer is concerned, he has already mounted an elaborate escape in 'The Chimes of Big Ben'.

Information: British TV became more politically literate in the 1960s. This episode was written and made in a British election year. Political thinkers at this time were beginning to question whether elections brought about a change in policy, as people recognised that individual politicians were subject to the party machine and that the government was controlled by an unelected body of civil servants. This was an issue examined by cabinet minister Richard Crossman, and developed in political drama such as Dennis Potter's *Vote, Vote, Vote for Nigel Barton* and the series *The Power Game* in 1965. Similarly, in 'Free For All', the panoply of Village democracy is exposed as a sham, devised and manipulated by the forces that control society. To underline the Prisoner's election to a position where he is still ultimately powerless, the incidental music ironically references the song 'For He's a Jolly Good Fellow'.

Production: Location shooting for 'Free For All' was done in Portmeirion between Saturday 10 and Thursday 15 September 1966, with McGoohan directing the majority of the action. Some problems occurred; guest

"I intend to discover, who are the prisoners and who the warders. I shall be running for office in this election"

THE PRISONER

TALLY HO HEADLINE
Number 6 speaks his mind

CAST

Guest Star
Eric Portman
Number Two
with
Number 58
Rachel Herbert
Labour Exchange Manager
George Benson
Reporter
Harold Berens
Man in Cave
John Cazabon
Photographer
Dene Cooper
Supervisor
Kenneth Benda
Waitress
Holly Doone
1st Mechanic
Peter Brace
2nd Mechanic
Alf Joint

Peter Swanwick appears, but is uncredited, as this episode reuses film of him from 'Arrival'.

The Prisoner accepts his election as the new Number 2 outside the Town Hall

The Outsider: Free For All

Filming Number 6's election campaign. McGoohan's personal assistant, Jimmy Miller, can be seen looking on in the background, next to his boss

The cut scene from the Cat And Mouse night club: Number 6 entertains the Villagers

star Eric Portman had difficulty remembering his lines so prompt boards had to be held up for him out of shot. There was also trouble with the local accent: the election chant of "6 for 2!" by the extras at first sounded like "Sex for 2!"

A Doughty Jet Drive, which belonged to local man Brian Axworthy, was used for the speed boat chase. He was required to pilot the boat in the long-shot sequences and join in with the on-screen action: "When I saw the helicopter I was more interested in that, and I hit the stunt man, Frank Maher, full in the face! I couldn't believe the pain... He said 'That's the last time I'm working with amateurs', but they were shouting from the helicopter, 'It looks great! It looks great!' " Studio work commenced around Monday 17 October with McGoohan again in charge of directing. The Town Hall and Labour Exchange sets were again the main Number 2 set reconfigured; the Therapy Zone cave was a new set.

Two sequences shot for 'Free For All' were excised from the programme's initial UK broadcast. The first, a scene showing a drugged or drunken Number 6 singing an odd election song – *"Vote for me/I'm for you/Let me see/And be, tra la"* – was dropped completely, never to be reinstated. The second, where he is given a nasty, explicit beating by stuntmen Alf Joint and Peter Brace at the story's climax, fell foul of regional TV network censors. Thought too graphic for *The Prisoner*'s early evening time slot, the scene was cut, leaving scene-to-scene continuity badly disjointed: after being grabbed by two henchmen in Number 2's office, the Prisoner's blazer suddenly vanishes and blood appears at the corner of his mouth. Channel 4's transmission of the episode in 1983, after the 10p.m., restored the sequence in full.

The peculiar, invented language spoken by Number 58 presented actress Rachel Herbert with something of a problem. "In the end I recorded a conversation with a Yugoslav friend of mind, played it back and transposed the rhythm and consonant sounds of her voice to the words Pat had written. That was that. I could speak McGoohan."

'Free For All' was also the first episode where regular voice-over artist Robert Rietty recorded the introductory Number 2 dialogue instead of the actor playing the role; a standard voice-over may have been considered to save production time. This version is also heard

Rachel Herbert outside the Town Hall in a break between takes

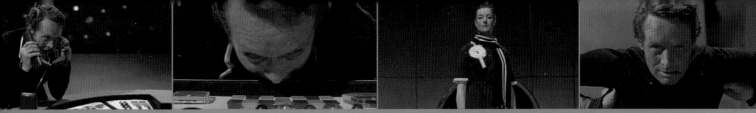

on episodes 5, 7, 10, 11, 12 and 15.

The photographs of Number 6 used in the election parade are another reuse of Patrick McGoohan's *Danger Man* publicity photo, previously seen in the programme's title sequence.

Filming of the studio sequences at Borehamwood saw a major difference of opinion between McGoohan and Don Chaffey. " 'Free For All' started out with Chaffey directing," film librarian Tony Sloman remembers, " but he and Pat had a huge disagreement and it ended up with Brendan J. Stafford and Pat shooting all the interiors." McGoohan's input into the direction was so great that the finished episode was credited to him alone.

Tally Ho: *"You are free to go! Obey me and be free!"* Bleak in a technicolor way, there's not a lot of hope in this story. The first script written by Patrick McGoohan (under a pseudonym borrowed from his mother's maiden name, Fitzpatrick), 'Free For All' declares the Executive Producer's obsession with the conflict

between the individual and the demands of society. His conclusion, that those who literally gain the seat of power are no more in control than the people they govern, is incredibly pessimistic and places *The Prisoner* firmly in the same league as such seminal dystopian visions as *Nineteen Eighty-Four* and *Brave New World*.

'Free For All' is also the best use of the Village location as a nightmarish wonderland, with the Prisoner led through a confusing series of stage-managed events and traps by a succession of ambiguous characters. McGoohan is being a disturbing dramatist, and his direction establishes an edgy, dream-like atmosphere. *The Saturday Review* defined this particular aspect of the production as "fast, ambiguous cutting, minimum of dialogue [and] free handling of time and space" when *The Prisoner* was first broadcast in the USA in 1968.

A dramatic statement of intent from a man who clearly saw himself in control of *The Prisoner*, 'Free For All', powerful though it was, clearly tipped the balance of the programme in favour of allegory, with any refer-

PAWNS AND PLAYERS

In 1967, film actor Eric Portman commented that "I would like to do more television but, fortunately or unfortunately, I seem to get involved in so many long-running stage plays." He suddenly found himself available again, appearing with Peter Wyngarde in the Algerian Civil War play *The Cross-Fire* by Maurice Edelman in February, eight months before his *Prisoner* guest spot. The versatile Rachel Herbert was semi-regular in the business drama *The Power Game* (1965–67) as Justine, daughter-in-law to Caswell Bligh (Clifford Evans). In 1968, she co-starred in the underrated but influential London gangland drama *Spindoe* as Renata, opposite Ray McAnally. George Benson enjoyed a great variety of parts on television, stage and film; his noteworthy movie appearances include *The Man in the White Suit* (1951) and *The Private Life of Sherlock Holmes* (1970), as Inspector Lestrade. Harold Berens had originally been a music-hall comic before moving into acting, and knew Patrick McGoohan from the TV play *This Day in Fear* (1958), in which they appeared together. McGoohan enjoyed his company and the actor stayed on at Portmeirion after 'Free For All' was finished.

Jack Shampan's stunning production design for the Town Hall Council Chamber

"THE PRISONER"

5: The Schizoid Man
Written by Terence Feely   Directed by Pat Jackson

The Prisoner is co-operating with a girl called Alison in her attempts to compete in the Village festival. This includes an ESP recognition test using zenner picture cards. She accidentally bruises one of his fingernails when she knocks over a soda siphon. Undeterred, she takes a picture of Number 6 holding the cards. That night, on Number 2's orders, he is hypnotised... Waking apparently the next morning, he now finds himself known as Number 12 and changed in appearance – he has a moustache, different coloured hair and has become left-handed. He is told he has been recruited to impersonate the Village's "prize prisoner" – himself. Beaten by the ersatz Number 6 at shooting, fencing and hand-to-hand fighting, the 'twins' are taken before Number 2. The real Prisoner says he can prove his identity by remounting the ESP test with Alison.

However, he fails on all the questions and Alison insists the fake is the real man. That night, the Prisoner shows signs of cracking. When he wakes up, he finds Alison's photograph, which shows his damaged fingernail and the date the picture was taken. He sees that the bruise has changed with the growth of the nail. Gradually, he remembers his reconditioning as Number 12 and uses an electric shock to break his left-handed bias. He goes to see his double, they fight and he discovers that the man is called Curtis. As Curtis flees, Rover accidentally kills him. Having learnt the real password from Curtis, Number 6 persuades Number 2 that the real Prisoner has been killed and uses the imposter's identity in an attempt to escape. Unfortunately, Number 6's ignorance of his double's background betrays him.

Right: Number 6 posing for Alison and (above) the end result

Who is Number 2?: Smooth, charming and officious, he knew Curtis, the Prisoner's impersonator, well before his secondment to the Village. Appears to be British, resenting being "stuck in admin" and talks disparagingly about Curtis's superiors, who "screamed as if I were taking their pensions away." His friendship with Number 6's double undoes the Prisoner's escape attempt.

You are Number 6: The Prisoner has a telepathic empathy with Alison, which is indicated by her correctly naming the images on the cards he chooses. He has a "strong sense of territory" in his own home, drinks scotch and smokes white cigarettes and cigars – although this is the only story in which he does. Among his other accomplishments, he is a consummate sportsman; his pistol shooting has a 90 per cent average and he was on the Olympic teams for fencing and boxing.

He also has a fondness for Shakespeare and says that he trusts humans more than machines. Not surprisingly, he is a very light sleeper.

One? Two? Three? Four?: 'The Schizoid Man' was the seventh story to be filmed. The episode is one of the few to give specific dates, with the action beginning on 10 February. Number 6 is again fairly settled, co-operating with a fellow resident. Made after a run of scripts that established the Village location and had included four failed escapes, 'The Schizoid Man' takes the action in an interesting new direction with its psychological emphasis.

Information: For a long time doubles had been a common element in fantasy and science fiction, particularly on TV when it was a chance for the main actors to play another side to their regular roles. Series such as *The Avengers*, *The Baron*, *The Man from UNCLE* and *Doctor Who* had already used the idea. Typically for *The Prisoner*, the idea was given a serious twist. Terence Feely delivered a story "about a man who was programmed to be another man, and then a second man played him," following the discovery that he had a doppleganger. The fantasy cliché of the 'evil double' becomes a compelling psychodrama as the Prisoner literally becomes his own worst enemy.

"Do you know, I never realised I had a freckle on the side of my nose... when they come to film my life story, you've got the part"

THE PRISONER?

CAST

Guest Stars

Anton Rodgers
Number Two

Jane Merrow
Alison

with

Supervisor
Earl Cameron

Number 36
Gay Cameron

Doctor
David Nettheim

Nurse
Pat Keen

1st Guardian
Gerry Crampton

2nd Guardian
Dinney Powell

The telepathic Alison
(Jane Merrow)

The Outsider: The Schizoid Man

When 'The Schizoid Man' was written, there was considerable interest in the paranormal. A TV series called *Margins of the Mind* was screened in May 1968 and investigated such phenomena as water divining, clairvoyance and telepathy. To determine instances of possible telepathic connection between people, the psychologist Chris Evans employed the same zenner card recognition test that Alison and Number 6 use.

Production: 'The Schizoid Man' commenced production on 19 December 1966, there was a break for Christmas then the story was completed with another week's work in January 1967. It was to be the first of four *Prisoner* episodes that Pat Jackson directed. He remembers very clearly his first acquaintance with the script: "I read it through in one session and I was absolutely thrilled. I didn't know what the hell it was all about, mind you, but I thought it was fascinating, an absolutely wonderful idea. So I rang up at once and said, 'Pat, I'd love to do it.' "

Number 6 and Number 6 attempt to settle a matter of identity in the Village shooting gallery

Pretending to be his double Curtis, the Prisoner visits Alison

The production was shot mainly on interior sets owing to the time of year. The interior of the Recreation Hall was another modification of the main Number 2 set and the MGM backlot was again used for exteriors, including the Recreation Hall (previously the Exhibition Hall from 'Chimes') and some other shots of the Village.

To produce the scenes of Number 6 and his double, a technique called split-screen was used. This required half the film to be exposed with McGoohan present then re-shot with the star in the other half of the frame. Frank Maher was used as a stand-in when these scenes were being filmed; by getting Maher to speak McGoohan's dialogue, Pat Jackson was able to get the timing of the scenes correct. A production photograph shows both men wearing the Prisoner's black blazer with white piping, although in the finished episode the fake Number 6, Curtis, wears a white jacket with black piping. Having the twins totally identical may have been considered too confusing for the audience, so the double was given a strong branding that would distinguish him from his counterpart. This would certainly explain Number 2's otherwise odd comment that once the plan is put into operation, "even I won't be able to tell you apart". However, this change made filming 'The Schizoid Man' even more confusing for the participants, as Maher remembers: "It was crazy. A nightmare. 'Are you wearing the white jacket or the brown one?' 'White one.' 'Oh no you're not, you're in the brown one.' Unbelievable." From being a production headache, the change of jackets became a clever visual touch as the fake's blazer was a negative reflection of the Prisoner's usual one.

The card recognition test was introduced after Terence Feely's original idea that the Prisoner and Alison should be lovers, and she would be able to tell the real man from the double by kissing, was dropped at McGoohan's insistence.

Prison Writers: Terence Feely had the distinction of working on some of television's best remembered series. These included the first season of *The Avengers*, *The The Persuaders!* and *The New Avengers*.

The above photographs show how it was possible for Patrick McGoohan to appear opposite himself; Frank Maher stood in for the star as his double, also speaking the actor's lines

He was associate producer on the first series of *Callan* in 1967 and worked as a story editor on *Armchair Theatre*, along with George Markstein, during the same year. "My brain's always been slightly off key", he once said. "I've always seen things that other people don't see." This talent served him well with 'The Schizoid Man'; on the strength of the script, he was invited to join Everyman Films by McGoohan and Tomblin.

Prison Governors: Director Pat Jackson beagan his career with the wartime films *Ferry Pilot* (1941) and *Western Approaches* (1944). He gave Patrick McGoohan his first screen test. Before moving into television, he directed feature films such as *The Feminine Touch* (1956) and *What a Carve Up!* (1962). He worked with McGoohan on the *Danger Man* episode 'The Hunting Party' and directed 'The Revolution Racket' for The *Saint*, both in 1965, and three episodes of *Man in A Suitcase* in 1967, including the excellent 'The Bridge', which also featured Jane Merrow. He was reunited with Terence Feely on *Arthur of the Britons* in 1972, directing the writer's 'The Gift of Life' and 'The Duel'.

Tally Ho: *"I take it I'm supposed to go all fuzzy round the edges and run off into the distance screaming 'Who am I?' "* 'The Schizoid Man' takes the Prisoner's greatest asset, his "strong sense of identity", and turns it into a weapon against him. The mind-bending premise is brilliant. Number 6 is made to believe he is impersonating himself and the real impostor is treated as the genuine article. (The title is a great joke – this must be the worst case of schizophrenia ever recorded.) McGoohan is excellent in the dual role, exhibiting just enough smugness for the audience to know that the white-jacketed version is "the economy pack" and the intense, perspiring model the genuine article.

For such a complex and tightly plotted script, the clues to the Prisoner's conditioning seem so obvious and careless that it is almost as if he's meant to find them. However, overlooking the details cuts both ways, as he discovers when his lack of knowledge about the death of Curtis' wife Susan lets him down at the end.

'The Schizoid Man' is another triumph, particularly notable for the remarkable ingenuity of the writing that produces one of *The Prisoner*'s best stories.

PAWNS AND PLAYERS

Anton Rodgers started off as an adult actor playing dangerous and irresponsible overgrown juveniles, for example in *Gideon's Way* (1966), and later reinvented himself as a cuddly middle-aged comedy actor in series such *Fresh Fields* (1984-6) and *May to December* (1989-94). Jane Merrow was a successful international actress, featuring in well known action and fantasy series on both sides of the Atlantic, including *Danger Man*, in which she made three appearances over 1964-5, *Mission: Impossible* (1970) and *The Six Million Dollar Man* (1974 and 1977). She received a Golden Globe nomination for her role in the 1968 film *The Lion in Winter*, which depicted the domestic squabbles at the court of Henry II in 1183, and was once mooted as Diana Rigg's replacement in *The Avengers*. Earl Cameron, a Jamaican actor living in Britain, was kept busy by TV and film work for over 40 years. Amongst his credits are the TV series *The Buccaneers* (1956), four appearances in *Danger Man* between 1960 and 1966, and the films *Guns at Batasi* (1964) and *Mohammed, Messenger of God* (1977).

6: The General
Written by Joshua Adam   Directed by Peter Graham Scott

Posters around the village advertise a new process, Speedlearn, endorsed by the anonymous 'General', showing the photograph of a man known as the Professor. On the beach, the Prisoner finds and hides a tape recorder with the Professor's message that the General should be destroyed. He returns to his cottage where the Speedlearn process is broadcast via the TV. Apparently co-operating again, the Professor tells the Villagers about Speedlearn - a three-year university course subliminally learnt in three minutes. Following the 'lecture', Number 2 arrives in search of the tape recorder. Failing to find it, he questions the Prisoner, who realises that he knows the historical details just broadcast word for word. Returning to the beach, he finds Number 12 who gives him the recorder. He then infiltrates the Professor's house and discovers that the older man is being kept sedated, away from his wife. Number 12 gives Number 6 the means to broadcast the Professor's warnings about Speedlearn and infiltrate the Town Hall. Apprehended, he is taken to meet the General - a super computer. As Number 2 is about to use the machine to determine Number 12's guilt, the Prisoner asks it a question. The machine overloads and destroys itself, killing the Professor and Number 12 in the process. The question was unanswerable: Why?

Number 6 shows off his illustrative skills (top) and (bottom) finds himself a subject for study

Right: Preparing to film the scene where the Prisoner meets the Professor's wife for the first time. Betty McDowell can be seen standing on her 'marks' – positions on the studio floor where actors stand to allow for positioning of the cameras

Who is Number 2?: A man who is assured and arrogant, with a messianic zeal for the General. As in 'A.B. and C.' he drinks milk, but compared with the frightened man of the previously transmitted episode, he is almost dismissive of his superiors. He is no fool – suspicious of Number 12 and wise to the value of media manipulation, he uses the Professor to sugar the pill of Speedlearn. "It's the image, you see, that is important. The kindly image". Over-confidence proves to be his downfall.

You are Number 6: The Prisoner again exhibits a variety of abilities, from being an accomplished portrait artist to being *au fait* with Village technology. Like the rest of the Villagers, he yields completely to Speedlearn

but is seriously worried about the moral implications of the process. Number 2 describes him as "a trained conspirator, a very hard man". Although he has one arm in a sling, he can still beat up security guards and also knock them out with one punch. Is there nothing this man can't do?

One? Two? Three? Four?: 'The General' was recorded directly after 'A.B. and C.' It was the eleventh story made and Colin Gordon was asked to stay on as Number 2. The rewording of the Number 2 dialogue in Gordon's first episode indicates that an attempt was made to impose some retroactive continuity in the light of Number 2's implied fate in 'A.B. and C.' (somewhat ruined by being shown first). The end of the script was also rewritten so Number 2 doesn't die, suggesting even more strongly that 'The General' should have been transmitted first.

Information: "'The General' was a blast of rage against rote learning," Lewis Greifer confesses. "It was quite angry. I had children at school and there was no room for any imagination or innovative thinking in what they were doing.". 'The General' mixes Greifer's educational concerns with ambivalence about the supposed benefits of new technology. Significantly, Village slogans and posters emphasise the efficiency and time-saving features that the General offers, but ignore the

CAST
Guest Stars
Colin Gordon
Number 2
Peter Howell
Professor
John Castle
Number 12
with
Announcer
Al Mancini
Professor's Wife
Betty McDowall
Doctor
Conrad Phillips
Buggy Man
Michael Miller
Waiter
Keith Pyott
Man at Café/First Top Hat
Ian Fleming
Mechanic
Norman Mitchell
Projection Operator
Peter Bourne
1st Guard
George Leech
2nd Guard
Jackie Cooper

The Prisoner meets a fellow conspirator in Number 12 (John Castle)

The Outsider: The General

VILLAGE SLOGANS

**It can be done.
Trust me.**
THE GENERAL

**Our aim:
one hundred
per cent entry
one hundred
per cent pass**
THE GENERAL

**Speedlearn –
a three year
course in
three minutes.
It can be done.
Trust me.**
THE GENERAL

**No homework
with Speedlearn**

**University for all
in 3 minutes**

The Addams Family money box became a security device in the Town Hall

point that while facts may be learned almost instantly through the Speedlearn process, they are not understood. The implication is that the Village establishment has discovered a new form of mind control. There is also an implied criticism of modern media industries, whereby the authorities use television and advertising to sell morally questionable resources to the community. The potentially fatal implications of smarter technology were also explored in several episodes of *The Avengers*, TV productions such as *Out of the Unknown*'s 'The Machine Stops' (1966) and Stanley Kubrick's movie *2001: A Space Odyssey* (1968).

In France, 'The General' was renamed 'Le Cerveau' ('The Brain'), in case the title was misconstrued as a reference to President De Gaulle.

Production: 'The General' went into production on 27 February 1967. Peter Graham Scott's assumption of the director's chair was a last-minute appointment as he only received the script 24 hours prior to shooting. Production was again pressured – Scott admitted that he didn't understand the script after the first day's filming, and he was advised by the cast to treat McGoohan with care owing to his heavy workload.

The garden set and Engadine's house from 'A.B. and C.' were redressed for the open-air venue where the Professor's wife teaches and the Professor's house, respectively. Studio mock-ups of the café were reused and the slightly modified Town Hall interior, previously used in 'Free For All' (another redressing of Number 2's office), had another outing. Modified again, this also became the Speedlearn projection room. A new set of futuristic metallic corridors was built for the interior of the Town Hall and was staffed for the first time by the green-suited Village military police. The studio beach used in 'Chimes' was also featured and intercut with additional material shot at Portmeirion in March 1967. This featured local man Fred Couture standing in for Peter Howell as the Professor.

The small box with a clockwork hand that grabs the entry tokens to the Town Hall was a toy commercially available at the time, The Thing Money Box, based on

the character of the same name from the gothic American TV comedy *The Addams Family* (1965-6). One of McGoohan's idiosyncratic touches, it was incorporated into the set at his request.

Prison Writers: Joshua Adam was a pen name for Lewis Greifer, put together from the names of his two sons. "Myself and George [Markstein] started out working for the same paper", he recalls. "We became great personal friends. George was the news editor on the *St Marylebone News* in those days." Moving on from journalism, Greifer worked on to radio comedy, television thrillers – including *The Voodoo Factor* (1959-60) – films, and documentaries. At the time of *The Prisoner*, he was a story editor for ATV and oversaw the *Love Story* series of plays, which ran between 1963 and 1967. He usually wrote one script a year, including 'A Merry Chinese Christmas' for the show's final run.

Prison Governors: Director, producer and writer Peter Graham Scott started in the film business at the age of 23, editing the Boulting Brothers' classic *Brighton Rock* (1947). He knew McGoohan well, directing seven episodes of *Danger Man* for the first series in 1960-1. He also screen tested 40 girls in four days for the role of Emma Peel in *The Avengers*;. In the end the role went to the last girl he tried, Diana Rigg, "who I'd met under a piano at a Christmas party". He produced *Mogul*, a.k.a. *The Troubleshooters*, for the BBC between 1965 and 1972 and was drafted in between the first and second series to work on *The Prisoner*. His greatest joy was the success of his pet project *The Onedin Line* (1971-80), about a nineteenth-century sailing company.

Tally Ho: *"That mass of circuits... is as revolutionary as nuclear fission."* It's no coincidence that Number 2 describes Speedlearn as "a military exercise". The episode is awash with warlike references – guards, European military history and a cheerful military-style tune as incidental music. The most telling allusion is the master computer's title - 'The General' was the nick-

60

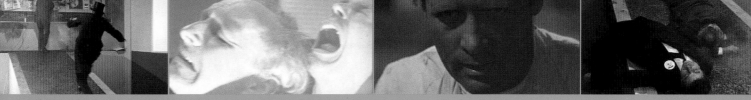

The General computer is destroyed by a simple question – "Why?" – killing the professor and Number 12 in the process

Peter Howell stands on his marks, observing the Professor's *meisterwork* – the computer known as the General

name French troops gave to their commander-in-chief, Napoleon Bonaparte; indeed, Number 6 says of the computer, "Napoleon could have used it." The machine and the learning of hard facts are just weapons in the Village's hi-tech arsenal; art and philosophy are seen as redundant and are trivialised. It's particularly satisfying, then, to see the General destroyed by philosophical reasoning in the final moments.

If this sounds heavy going, the seriousness of the point is offset by heightened satire. In places 'The General' is almost a black comedy; like all the best comedy, it works because it's played completely straight. The cast have great fun with the Village being likened

to a school, complete with references to "playing truant", "homework" and "prefects". It's a joy to watch Colin Gordon's Number 2 and the Prisoner circling each other, wittily parrying each other's moves with volleys of puns and clever remarks.

The realisation of 'The General' as a room-filling box with spinning tape spools may have dated, unlike the rest of the production design, but the best of vintage science fiction always remains relevant. The themes of 'The General' – ethical implications of new technology, and "the freedom to learn, the liberty to make mistakes" – are as just as topical now as when Lewis Greifer first wrote about his fears in 1966.

7: Many Happy Returns
Written by Anthony Skene   Directed by Joseph Serf

The Prisoner wakes to a deserted Village. Observed by a black cat, he constructs a raft, photographs the Village before leaving and carefully plots his course, recording how many days he has been at sea. Following a fight with some gun-runners who capture his raft, he swims to the nearest coastline. He discovers he is back in England and hitches a ride to London. A Mrs Butterworth is living in his house, but she believes his story. He realises that the next day is his birthday and Mrs Butterworth promises to bake him a cake. The Prisoner calls on his London office before being reacquainted with 'The Colonel' and his associate Thorpe. His superiors are suspicious of his story and photographs but they agree to co-operate in finding the Village and the Prisoner acts as navigator on an aerial search. The Village is located, but a Village agent has replaced the jet's pilot and ejects Number 6, who parachutes down to the beach. As he enters his cottage, the Village comes back to life. Finally Number 2 – Mrs Butterworth – enters the cottage with the cat and the cake she promised to make: "Many Happy Returns, Number 6".

Top: Jack Shampan's production painting of the gypsy emcampment and (above) its realisation on screen

Who is Number 2?: Mrs Butterworth, seemingly so concerned for the Prisoner's welfare, is revealed as the absent Village administrator. Her delivery of the cake to his Village home reinforces the cruel irony of the episode's title.

You are Number 6: The Prisoner is able to build a raft using felled trees and empty oil drums and create a compass out of a magnetised needle, rulers and a glass jar. He meticulously photographs the Village before leaving and keeps a daily log while at sea, sleeping for four hours out of every 24. He owes the General Stores 964 work units on departure. He gives his name as Peter Smith, and built his Lotus 7 with his own hands. The lease on his house had six months to run when he left. The estate agents, Stumbel and Croydon, organised a new lease and log book for the car. It is not surprising that Number 6 is also a qualified aerial navigator.

One? Two? Three? Four?: 'Many Happy Returns' was the last episode, the thirteenth, made in the proposed first filming block. The Prisoner is offered liberty, and having it snatched away again is a superb dramatic conceit. Anthony Skene wrote the script as a possible ending to the first series, as "Number 6 gets out, but has to be recaptured in case the show continues." Ultimately transmitted as the seventh episode, the story can be tied down to specific dates, as the events begin about 30 days before Number 6's birthday on 18 March. This makes the Prisoner's date of departure around 23 February.

Information: Script Editor George Markstein called 'Many Happy Returns' "the signpost episode for the future of the series... Both 'The Chimes of Big Ben' and 'Many Happy Returns' explored the involvement of the 'outside', hinted at the world beyond the Village and yet brought us back each time to the fundamental core of the situation. I like both episodes for their neat story telling qualities and the way they were directed." Anthony Skene mixed references to fairy tales and

The Prisoner aboard the gun-runners' boat

"We must be sure. People defect. An unhappy thought, but a fact of life. They defect – from one side to the other"
THE COLONEL

TALLY HO HEADLINE
What are facts behind Town Hall?

CAST
Guest Stars
Donald Sinden
The Colonel
Patrick Cargill
Thorpe
Georgina Cookson
Mrs Butterworth
with
Group Captain
Brian Worth
Commander
Richard Caldicott
Gunther
Dennis Chinnery
Ernst
Jon Laurimore
Gypsy Girl
Nike Arrighi
Maid
Grace Arnold
Gypsy Man
Larry Taylor

Number 6 makes meticulous preparations to escape the Village, watched by Number 2's cat

Production manager Bernard Williams keeps a watchful eye on Number 6's raft in the Irish sea

Mrs Butterworth (Georgina Cookson)

Extensive location filming included scenes at Beachy Head on the South coast

Mrs Butterworth – Number 2 – wishes the Prisoner "many happy returns"

superstition into Number 6's epic journey. Hans Christian Andersen is mentioned, and a black cat and broken plate appear, both symbols of bad luck. Showing that *The Prisoner* borrowed from all over the cultural spectrum, the Village agent who replaces the Group Captain is disguised as a milkman – just like Victor Maddern's STENCH agent in *Carry On Spying* (1965).

Production: Location shooting for 'Many Happy Returns' was carried out at Portmeirion during March 1967. Michael Truman, previously pencilled in to direct 'A.B. and C.', began work on the location shooting, but left the production after a few days work because of ill health. With time pressing, McGoohan chose again to direct, under his pseudonym Joseph Serf. The London scenes, which included work done at Stag Place, Wellington Arch and 1 Buckingham Place, were shot on Sunday 16 April 1967. Before the episode entered the studio on 10 April 1967, there was a week's gap after the filming of 'Hammer into Anvil'. It's possible that the remaining location footage was shot dur-

ing this period, with work at Beachy Head, Dover, Chalgrove Airfield – complete with a Meteor jet – and the A1 near Borehamwood, standing in for the A20. Ejector seat manufacturer Martin-Baker provided film footage of the Meteor in flight. The set used for the Prisoner's resignation put in a brief reappearance, with the majority of studio work being devoted to Number 6's London home; a library-style set previously used in 'The General' became the Colonel's residence.

During the location shoot at Portmeirion, the Breda, the boat that had appeared in 'Checkmate', the third episode shot, was reused as the gun-runners' vessel (the interior studio set was also used again). A trained diver, Brain Axworthy doubled for McGoohan in some of the swimming scenes. He also provided an additional, unused prop for the scene where Number 6 parachutes down to the Village: "I borrowed an ejector seat from the airfield, a demonstration one. It was laying on the beach but I don't think it was ever filmed. It was a pity, really, because I'd probably have lost my job there if they'd seen it!" As in Skene's 'Dance of the Dead' (the

"Be seeing you": the Prisoner gets an unexpected return trip to the Village

Although storyboarded, Number 6's investigation of the Hospital was dropped from the final version of the episode

lated as being a volcanic island that exploded while he was at sea. Two tantalising scenes of him dreaming were also deleted – in the first, he imagines that the truck he is hiding in is moving through an alien landscape, and in the second that it's still in the Village. The original ending had Mrs Butterworth giving him a present wrapped in a copy of the Village newspaper. The headline read: 'Plane Lost Over Sea. No Hope of Survivors'. Mrs Butterworth tells him to "give in and enjoy being dead"; the Prisoner screws up the paper and replies, "I'll die first."

George Markstein reprises his cameo as the Man Behind the Desk. Despite his enthusiasm for 'Many Happy Returns', and Skene's writing in general, he parted company with the show he helped create during production of the final story of the first series.

This was the first episode not to feature the actor playing Number 2 in the title sequence because of the twist ending. A shot of Rover on the beach was substituted instead.

Tally Ho: *"Nothing to do with you, my dear fellow. An escaped convict."* A story with exceptionally nasty implications, 'Many Happy Returns' indicates that the Prisoner no longer has an identity outside the Village; all trace of his previous life has been erased and his superiors suspect him of being a traitor. Tellingly, the Village only reactivates when he is returned to its embrace, implying that it exists solely for him.

With no dialogue for the first 20 minutes, the success of the episode rests squarely on the quality of its visual storytelling, and 'Many Happy Returns' has an authentic and inspired cinematic feel. The diverse location work, which takes up to some 80 per cent of the screened whole, gives the episode the panoramic feel of a feature film. The almost supernatural way in which the Village returns to life brings a disturbing edge to the realistic ambience created by the use of so many genuine locations, hinting at powerful, manipulative forces at work. The ending is a brilliant sting in the tail, with the audience's expectations of a tidy resolution once again brilliantly thrown out of kilter.

PAWNS AND PLAYERS

Patrick Cargill was the second actor in *The Prisoner* to hail from The Beatles' *Help!* in which he famously asks the Fab Four "How long d'you think you'll last?" Today, Cargill is better remembered for his comic roles, such as the humourless doctor in 'The Blood Donor', a classic edition of *Hancock* (1961), and the harassed writer Patrick Glover in the series *Father, Dear Father*, between 1968 and 1973. Donald Sinden was a distinguished Shakespearean actor who became a contract player for the Rank film organisation – appearing in the war epic *The Cruel Sea* (1952) and light comedies such as *Doctor at Large* (1957). Like Cargill, he went on to carve a niche for himself in TV sitcoms, first in *Two's Company* (1975–79) and later *Never the Twain* (1981–91). Georgina Cookson was at home in film or on TV, with roles in John Schlesinger's 'swinging sixties' exposé *Darling* (1965), and the *Danger Man* story 'The Trap' (1960). Brian Worth played the reporter James Fullalove, who comes to an unpleasant end in Nigel Kneale's benchmark science fiction thriller *Quatermass and the Pit* (1958). Jon Laurimore was the traitorous scientist Pollock in the last episode of the first series of *Callan*, 'You Should Have Got Here Sooner', in August 1967.

fourth episode made) local couple Doug and Catherine Williams' cat Tammy played the part of the Village feline on location, after a cat brought from London refused to perform.

The location shoot wasn't entirely smooth. Production manager Bernard Williams remembers how Number 6's raft nearly caused a major accident at sea; "I took it out to the Irish Channel, 30 miles off land. This raft was so heavy that the boat's engines we had pulling it caught on fire and it started pulling the back of the boat down and water was actually coming up over the edge… I had to make the decision to cut the raft loose and it disappeared in about five minutes. The Air Sea Rescue had planes and helicopters out looking for it for 24 hours but they never found it."

Several changes were made to Skene's script – these included the dropping of Number 6's attempt to escape from the Village by helicopter and his exploration of a deserted Hospital. Bizarrely, the gypsy he meets on the shore speaks Cockney, alerting him to the fact he is in England. One of the locations of the Village is specu-

8: Dance of the Dead

Written by Anthony Skene Directed by Don Chaffey

The Prisoner's latest interrogation is suspended on the orders of Number 2. As a carnival in the Village is announced, Number 6 discovers that every inmate has an observer, in his case Number 240. Refusing to settle, he breaks the curfew and discovers a body on the beach. The Prisoner finds a radio on it and refloats the corpse with details of his location and identity. While there, he is observed by one Roland Walter Dutton, an old colleague, who is being held for interrogation. Later, the Prisoner is discovered using the radio by Number 2. At the Village dance, where 240 is dressed as Bo Peep and Number 2 as Peter Pan, Number 6 slips away to investigate the corridors beneath the Town Hall. He discovers the body he found in a mortuary: Number 2 tells the Prisoner the Village will amend the corpse so the outside world will believe he is dead.

In the main hall, the Prisoner discovers he is "the cabaret", put on trial for transgressing the rules. He calls Dutton as a character witness, but the man has been brainwashed. Under sentence of death, Number 6 flees a crazed mob, and eventually reaches Number 2's inner office. Believing he has discovered the location of Number 1, the office only houses a telex machine relaying instructions.

The Doctor (Duncan MacRae, second left) attempts to use a brainwashed Dutton (Michael White) to find out the reason for the Prisoner's resignation

The dead faces of the carnival crowd

Who is Number 2?: Another female Number 2, she is confident, cultured but asexual. She believes the Prisoner will eventually be won over to the Village and has an innate sense of theatre, setting him up as the cabaret at the dance. Once again, she has an overwhelming belief in the authority of the establishment.

You are Number 6: One of the Prisoner's ex-colleagues again appears in the Village in the person of Roland Walter Dutton. Other acquaintances from Number 6's old job were "Arthur", the Colonel and the Committee. The Prisoner again shows himself to be an educated and cultured man, familiar with the judicial system in the French Revolution that sent people to the guillotine, and a connoisseur of wine though he "rarely" drinks.

One? Two? Three? Four?: 'Dance of the Dead' was the fourth episode made and eventually placed eighth in transmission order, balancing out the episodes not filmed extensively in Portmeirion, regardless of the implications for continuity; Number 6 is again markedly aggressive, unfamiliar with the community's rules and ignorant of the Town Hall's function. Although it seems the black cat from 'Many Happy Returns' reappears, 'Dance' was the first time Skene used the idea of a feline accomplice for Number 2. Had this episode been broadcast before 'Many Happy Returns', as Skene intended, the cat's appearance in the deserted Village would have had greater significance.

Information: 'Dance of the Dead' was the first Prisoner script Anthony Skene wrote and he confirms that he was given an open brief: "I saw not a single piece of paper. The show was a cosmic void. They sat there waiting for ideas, an approach, an attitude." As a result, 'Dance' was sustained very much by Skene's personal vision, and contains ideas that were revised as the series progressed: "I was allowed (such was everyone's virginity) virtually to show Number 1, even if he was an unbreakable telex... And yes, the Villagers were determined on Number 6's destruction."

The story is rich in source material from other fantasies, combining to form something new and startlingly original. Franz Kafka is a definite influence. In *The Trial* (1926), Josef K is accused of a crime he is unaware of having committed, the subject of undisclosed, ambiguous laws, just as Number 6 is; *The Trial* also ends with K's death. "I was also somewhat in love with the world of Jean Cocteau," Skene admits, "so the Orphic element is shamefully second hand. The strange voice on the radio is unashamed Cocteau, as is the beautiful young man dead on the beach and the two-way mirror." Like Skene, the French artist and film director Jean Cocteau (1889-1963) was beguiled by the Greek myths, and his 1950 film *Orphée* was a modern interpretation of the legend of Orpheus, who travels into a labyrinthine underworld to retrieve the soul of his wife. *Orphée* and 'Dance' both have the main figure lost in a similar realm – Orpheus among the dead and Number 6

The Prisoner stands trial for his ignorance of the "awful majesty of the rules", with Number 2 (Mary Morris) as defence counsel and the Observer (Norma West) as a prosecution witness

Producer David Tomblin (left) watches as Don Chaffey (centre) directs the carnival procession at Portmeirion

CAST

Guest Stars

Mary Morris
Number Two

Duncan MacRae
The Doctor

Norma West
The Observer
with

Town Crier
Aubrey Morris

Psychiatrist
Bee Duffell

Dutton
Alan White

Supervisor
Camilla Hasse

Night Supervisor
Michael Nightingale

Night Maid
Patsy Smart

Day Maid
Denise Buckley

Postman
George Merritt

Flower Man
John Frawley

Lady in Corridor
Lucy Griffiths

2nd Doctor
William Lyon Brown

Dead man on beach/*
Man in photograh
Ray Cannon

Girl in photograph*
Jill Hennessy

Uncredited on screen. Both were members of the production team: Cannon was a prop man and Hennessy the assistant accountant.

'Mr Tuxedo' and 'Mr Peter Pan' (Mary Morris) meet for a philosophical coversation on the Village beach at sunset

Skene's script was heavily influenced by Jean Cocteau's 1950 film fantasy

The Prisoner's judges

The costumed Day Maid (Denise Buckley) refuses to answer any of the Prisoner's probing questions

among the Villagers, who are symbolically deceased.

Another influnce Skene cites is William Dieterle's 1941 film *The Devil and Daniel Webster*; an interpretation of the Faust legend, in which a man sells his soul to the Devil for seven years good luck. The end of the film features a dance in which most of the guests are the dead; one of them partners a live guest and drains the life from him – a literal dance of death. Villainous characters are summoned from American history as judges, in the same way that figures from European history preside over the Prisoner. Number 6's tuxedo may also be an allusion to the secret agent genre; by 1966, the

dinner suit and bow tie had become the familiar motif of the celluloid gentleman spy. In the company of Peter Pan and Bo Peep, this turns him into another fictional (i.e. 'dead') character. Richard Condon's political thriller *The Manchurian Candidate* (1959) also has the brainwashed assassin's controller dressing up as Bo Peep at a party.

Production: Location filming at Portmeirion for 'Dance of the Dead' was allotted for the 23rd, 26th and 27th of September 1966. There are conflicting stories concerning the choice of actor playing Number 2; it has

The Outsider: Dance of the Dead

often been suggested that the distinguished film actor Trevor Howard was signed to play the Village chairman, with some sources claiming that he actually participated in location filming. Although the script was written with a man in mind – he was to play Jack the Ripper or Old Father Time at the Carnival – Skene explains the possible source of the story: "At the initial meeting, I was told 'Oh, Number 2 will be some big star – write it for someone like Trevor Howard or Alec Guinness'." Keener on getting guest actresses into the show, Skene was delighted when Mary Morris was eventually chosen. Helweun Hatcher again doubled for one of the series' actresses, singled out by Morris herself as a stand-in. Cuts made to the script included the loss of a voice-over, as Number 6 writes the message he hides on the dead body, and his encounter with two gravediggers, attending a fresh grave in the woods.

Studio shooting for the story commenced on 14th November 1966. New sets constructed included a beach, and the interior of the Town Hall; the Number 2 set was reconfigured for the dance sequence. During this scene, the Prisoner was to have danced closely with his Observer (Norma West) and questioned her. Don Chaffey felt the scene could be shot as scripted, but McGoohan's aversion to intimate scenes with his female co-stars again saw the scene amended, and recorded as finally seen.

McGoohan's attitude may explain why the episode appears so late in the running order. The story should have ended with the Prisoner acknowledging his death in the outside world, and saying that "being dead does have its advantages". He would then smash the telex machine with an ash tray, and join in a frantic dance with Bo Peep – requiring more close shots with West – and the rest of the Villagers, making the meaning of the story's title explicit. This final sequence was never shot; as a result, the original edit under ran by several minutes. Film editor John S. Smith asked McGoohan if he could try and salvage the story and was inspired by what he found, filling out the story to the required length with the material available.

Tally Ho: *"Never trust a woman, even the four-legged variety."* On paper, the plot of 'Dance of the Dead' is simple enough; its visual realisation is another matter. It has a quality that the episode's film editor John S. Smith, with great insight, defined as a unique mixture of "theatre, cinema and fantasy... That atmosphere was the essence of the series".

The script's mixture of historical costumes reflects the mixture of architectural styles in the Village, heightening the sense of unreality. Fittingly for such a visually poetic story, 'Dance of the Dead' has the most stunning cinematography seen anywhere in *The Prisoner*. In particular, the scene with Mr Tuxedo (Number 6) and Mr Peter Pan (Number 2), on the beach in front of a magnificent sunset, gives the episode an almost lyrical power. The two characters' weird, expressionistic dialogue in this sequence further enhances the surreal mood.

A parade of dream-like scenarios rather than a developing narrative, this technicolour cavalcade has a sick heart at its centre: as the Village becomes more visually outlandish, so the Prisoner is sentenced to death at the hands of a screaming mob. The symbolic death of Number 6 also ties in with 'Many Happy Returns', with the implication that the Prisoner no longer exists outside his prison.

Bizarre even by *Prisoner* standards but brilliantly made, if one episode belonged on the big screen between Jean Cocteau and James Bond, it was this one.

The telex, relaying instructions from Number 1

PAWNS AND PLAYERS

Mary Morris' decision to dress for the carnival as Peter Pan came from her own experience. In 1946 she had played "one of the most controversial Peters of all time", when she interpreted the role for the theatre as a tough gypsy boy. 'Dance of the Dead' was Duncan MacRae's last acting role; he died before the story was transmitted. A staunch Scottish nationalist, his last feature film appearance was in *Casino Royale* (1967), playing Inspector Mathis; when Peter Sellers says to him he's worried because Mathis, a French policeman, has a Scots accent, MacRae replies: "Aye, it worries me too." Norma West enjoyed a thirty-year career appearing in well-known British TV series. Her credits include *Danger Man* (1964), *Smiley's People* (1983) and *A Touch of Frost* (1994). Character actor Aubrey Morris featured in two classic cult films of the seventies; Stanley Kubrick's *A Clockwork Orange* (1971), and another tale of a community turning on an outsider, Robin Hardy's *The Wicker Man* (1974). Michael White had played Leading Seaman White in the sitcom *Tell It To The Marines* (1959-60). Bee Duffell featured as Mrs Charmer in the George Harrison sound-tracked hippy fantasy *Wonderwall* (1967).

9: Checkmate
Written by Gerald Kelsey   Directed by Don Chaffey

Number 6 takes part in a human chess match on the Village green, where he meets the Queen, the Rook and an old man who is one of the participants in the match, who lets him in on his technique for telling the guardians from the guarded. If the subject is a Village agent, questions will always be met with a confrontational attitude. Adopting this attitude, Number 6 recruits the Rook to an escape plan together with a group of Villagers whom he can trust. The Queen, meanwhile, has been brainwashed into believing the Prisoner loves her and wears a locket that acts as a tracking device whenever she is with him. Discovering the bogus locket, Number 6 and the Rook use it to complete a radio transmitter, which they then use to contact the MS Polotska, a ship cruising close to the coast. The conspirators knock out the search light in the bell tower and take Number 2 prisoner. Reaching the Polotska, Number 6 discovers the boat is a Village vessel. The Rook, certain that the Prisoner was one of the guardians due to his authoritarian manner, in turn convinces the other conspirators and they release Number 2. The Prisoner fights off the crew men, but the boat is bought back to port by Rover.

The Prisoner and the man with the stick discuss the technique of differentiating between prisoners and warders

Who is Number 2?: A charming but hard character who again regards recalcitrant Villagers as people in need of treatment: "if you have another attack of egomania, return to the Hospital at once." A patient man, he practises karate, an aggressive sport that exploits an opponent's weaknesses.

You are Number 6: The Hospital again gives an assessment of the Prisoner's personality: "Total disregard for personal safety and a negative reaction to pain..." Faking pain "would require superhuman will

power". More importantly, the Hospital discovers he used to drink in a pub called the Hope and Anchor. Number 6 is openly suspicious of the Queen – "everybody wants to help me" – but his attitude to her appears to soften although he doesn't believe for one moment that she really loves him. Skilled at recruiting and organising fellow inmates, ironically the Prisoner's self-reliance and independence prove to be his undoing.

One? Two? Three? Four?: 'Checkmate' was filmed third, back to back with 'Dance of the Dead'. As far as the audience is concerned, the Prisoner has been in the Village for several months and the psychological technique of differentiating prisoners from warders seems out of sync in an episode transmitted ninth; shown earlier, or in production order, 'Checkmate' makes more sense. As in the first four episodes made, the Prisoner is introduced to an aspect of Village life new to him. This is also the point where the UK and US transmission orders differ, with 'Checkmate' being shown eleventh in the States.

Information: The central idea of human chess had come to author Gerald Kelsey a few years before. "I had been on holiday with friends in Germany and near where I was staying was a castle that had a huge chess board. The local Baron used his retainers as the pieces and that's where the idea came from." A subconscious influence on Kelsey may also have been Lewis Carroll's

"It's like
the game. You
have to learn
to distinguish
between the
blacks and
the whites"

MAN WITH STICK

CAST

Guest stars
Peter Wyngarde
Number Two
Ronald Radd
Rook
George Coulouris
Man with Stick
Rosalie Crutchley
Queen
with
1st Psychiatrist
Patricia Jessel
2nd Psychiatrist
Bee Duffell
Supervisor
Basil Dignam
Painter
Danvers Walker
Assistant Supervisor
Victor Platt
Nurse
Shivaun O'Casey
Skipper
Geoffrey Reed
Sailor
Terence Donovan
1st Tower Guard
Joe Dunne
2nd Tower Guard
Romo Gorrara

Number 6 is invited to be the Queen's pawn in the Village's game of human chess

During the chess game, the Rook (Ronald Radd) declares his individuality by moving to 'check' and is taken to the Hospital

Top: Filming the raft sequence as director Don Chaffey looks on. Above: the scene as shot

Top right: Rosalie Crutchley as the Queen

Through The Looking-Glass (1871), which features chess pieces as characters – part of the book features the looking glass world marked out as a huge chess board. Alice is invited to be the Queen's pawn, just as Number 6 is. 'Checkmate' also synchronised with George Markstein's take on espionage: expendable human pieces manipulated and sacrificed to the dictates of a larger game.

In the wake of the Second World War, a sub-genre of action films had developed – one of the most memorable and commercially successful was John Sturges' *The Great Escape* (1962). 'Checkmate' could almost pass as a World War II escape drama, with its emphasis on the meticulous planning of the breakout. A searchlight mounted in the Village Bell Tower to look for escaping prisoners is iconography lifted straight from the visual grammar of the war film.

Number 2's reference to "Pavlov's experiments with dogs" during the treatment of the Rook refers to the technique of making animals respond to alternate painful and pleasurable stimuli, demonstrating conditioned and unconditioned reflexes. The Russian psychologist Ivan Pavlov (1849-1936) developed this process in 1889.

Production: The location work for 'Checkmate', originally titled 'The Queen's Pawn', was carried out at Portmeirion between Saturday 17 and Thursday 22 September 1966. For the chess sequence, the lawn beside the Gothic Pavilion was transformed into a human chess board. Wardrobe assistant Catherine Williams remembers how complex the shoot was: "That chess game took five or six days. Pat and Don Chaffey worked that out the night before they started it, but it really was a shambles. And I remember I burst into tears when it had finished because it was hell on earth for continuity, because every time they moved, those damn stupid capes moved. Then they'd break, somebody'd go to the loo, they'd come back and they'd got the thing on the wrong way round! The continuity woman [Doris Martin] screamed at them... And we were off again." The location work also saw the first use of the boat the Breda, rechristened the MS Polotska, hired from a local man at £10 per day, for scenes of Number 6's attempted escape at sea. The boat was recreated at Borehamwood for scenes of Number 6's fight with the crewmen when the episode went into the studio on 31 October 1966. Major sets were reused from episodes already shot, with the addition of the Bell Tower for another fight sequence.

"They'll be back tomorrow – on the chess board". Number 6's independence is his undoing, and he is brought back to the Village

Kelsey remembers that 'Checkmate' was the second script written, with plans for the series not yet completely finalised. Number 2 actor Peter Wyngarde recalls that his involvement in *The Prisoner* might have been a lot longer: "Pat had considered a permanent Number 2, which he wanted me to be. He finally decided that a change of Village administrator added to the air of mystery."

In an earlier draft of the script, the ending was significantly different. The Queen followed the Prisoner to the beach and boarded the MS Polotska with him. Once there, they discovered Number 2 on the boat. The final dialogue between Number 6 and Number 2 remains unchanged from the early draft, although it occurs in Number 2's office in the transmitted episode. In the earlier version, the Prisoner also revealed he had been in touch with another boat by radio earlier in the day. The ending was much more dramatic in the finished version, with the Number 6/Number 2 exchange incorporated in to the fight scene on the boat.

Although credited for directing the whole episode, Don Chaffey only oversaw the location shooting. McGoohan, having directed all of 'Free For All', the previous story made, continued as director for all of the interior scenes done at MGM. Chaffey may have been credited with sole directorial duties because of the large amount of location work. McGoohan's personal assistant, Jimmy Miller, played an uncredited, non-speaking role as one of the conspirators.

Prison Writers: Gerald Kelsey began his writing career for television with *Steve Hunter*, an adventure series for boys. Co-written with Dick Sharples, it premiered three weeks after commercial television began. He went on to co-author the comedy *Joan and Leslie* (1955-7), again with his writing partner – the duo parted when Kelsey wanted to concentrate solely on drama. He became a regular writer for ITC shows, with credits on *The Saint* (1962 – with Sharples), *The Champions* (1968), *Department S* (1969), *Randall & Hopkirk (Deceased)* (1969) and *The Adventurer* (1972). Between 1955 and 1976, Kelsey had a 14-year stint writing

Jimmy Miller (right), McGoohan's personal assistant, had a non-speaking and uncredited role as one of the escapees

scripts for the BBC police series *Dixon of Dock Green*. To assist aspiring television writers he wrote the book *Writing for Television* in 1979.

Tally Ho: *"Come and be the Queen's pawn."* Directed as a straightforward escape story, 'Checkmate' is a literal interpretation of George Markstein's view of espionage as a game of chess – it's almost an extension of the chess scene with the Admiral in 'Arrival'. It also reveals the powerlessness of the individual within society. The human chess game is played in the background as the conspirators plot, characters are referred to by their names on the board and covert details of the escape plan are passed on as chess moves. Unlike 'Dance of the Dead', this deft combination of symbolism and adventure doesn't alienate the audience. The cast is exceptionally strong: Rosalie Crutchley is sympathetic as the besotted Queen and Ronald Radd suitably tragic as the Rook. Peter Wyngarde, one of the best Number 2s, is the epitome of sinister charm.

The success of 'Checkmate' can be judged by the way its imagery became a visual shorthand for the whole series. Its definitive iconography is always used by video directors, advertisers and documentary makers when characterising *The Prisoner*. The final scene, where the Butler replaces a pawn representing Number 6 on the board while he is returned to captivity, is a chilling image and sums up the ethos of the entire programme.

PAWNS AND PLAYERS

Ronald Radd and Peter Wyngarde both played well-known parts in TV espionage. Radd became Callan's controller, Hunter, in *A Magnum for Schneider*, an *Armchair Theatre* presentation in May 1967 and in the first series which followed in the same year. Wyngarde rang the changes for ITC crime fighters as Jason King; the author turned spy/camp crusader featured in *Department S* (1969) and the spin-off, *Jason King* (1971). Alarmingly, 30,000 women in Australia voted him the man they most wanted to lose their virginity to! George Coulouris, one of Orson Welles' Mercury Players, featured in what is still seen as the greatest film ever made, *Citizen Kane* (1941) as Kane's grumpy guardian, Thatcher. This was a source of some irritation to the veteran actor; "Everybody wants to talk to me about *Citizen Kane* – bloody everybody! Best picture I ever did was *California* (1946) for John Farrow," he told Tony Sloman. Rosalie Crutchley had enjoyed a thriving movie career since the 1940s, appearing in such notable films as *A Tale of Two Cities* (1958) and *The Haunting* (1963). In 1970, she starred as Catherine Parr in *The Six Wives of Henry VIII* for the BBC.

10: Hammer into Anvil

Written by Roger Woddis   Directed by Pat Jackson

Number 2 causes the death of a young woman, Number 73, despite the Prisoner's efforts to stop him. Promising retribution, he is later forcibly brought before Number 2, who quotes from Goethe as a threat - "you must be anvil or hammer". Sensing that the man is nervous of his masters, the Prisoner embarks on a programme of disinformation to undermine him. With Number 2's suspicions aroused, the Prisoner listens to identical copies of Bizet's *L'Arlésienne* and questions the word "security" in a *Tally Ho* article. Number 2's henchman, Number 14, discovers a message apparently revealing that Number 6 is a spy for the controllers. With the seeds of insecurity sown, Number 6's campaign escalates: blank sheets of paper concealed on the Stone Boat, a cuckoo clock 'bomb', a code sent by carrier pigeon, a nonsense signal from the beach and the incrimination of Village personnel all fuel Number 2's panic about a conspiracy against him. His imagined betrayal by Number 14, his one trusted aide, causes him finally to crack under the strain. Number 14 attacks the Prisoner for discrediting him and Number 6 defeats him in a fist-fight. In the final scenes, the Prisoner visits the broken dictator, revealing that it was Number 2's fear of his own masters which caused his downfall.

Who is Number 2?: A superficial charm belies a man who is openly sadistic but who has a deep-seated fear of the Village controllers. Number 2 is clearly on edge from the beginning and cannot take criticism from his staff: "Would you like to sit in this chair?... Don't tell me what to do!" In the end he is broken by his belief in Number 14 being turned against him by Number 6: "I thought you were the one man I could trust... Traitor!" He even dismisses the bespectacled Control Room Supervisor and the Green Dome's Butler.

You are Number 6: The Prisoner's eyes are "light blue – fearless", he "knows [his] Goethe" and can translate from the German. He apparently quotes from *Don Quixote* in the original Spanish. Number 6's acquaintance with the classical arts also extends to music, with an appreciation of Bizet and Vivaldi. He also beats Number 14 at the unusual Village sport of kosho. His espionage skills again feature prominently: he can write in number code, knows Morse, can catch pigeons and use psychological warfare effectively.

Right: filming Number 2's interrogation of the Prisoner and (above) a close-up from the finished scene

The insecure Number 2 (Patrick Cargill) becomes a victim of the Village's inherent paranoia

CAST

Guest star
Patrick Cargill
Number 2

with

Bandmaster
Victor Maddern

Number 14
Basil Hoskins

Psychiatrist
Norman Scace

New Supervisor
Derek Aylward

Number 73
Hilary Dwyer

Operator
Arthur Gross

Shopkeeper
Victor Woolf

Lab Technician
Michael Segal

Kiosk Girl
Margo Andrew

Code Expert
Susan Sheers

1st Guardian
Jackie Cooper

2nd Guardian
Fred Haggerty

3rd Guardian
Eddie Powell

4th Guardian
George Leach

The Prisoner takes on number 14 in the first televised appearance of the kosho game

Storyboards showing the Prisoner's race to the Hospital to help Number 73 (Hilary Dwyer, below)

One? Two? Three? Four?: 'Hammer into Anvil' was recorded twelfth and appears fourteenth in the US broadcast order. Its late placing in both transmission sequences is attributable to the Prisoner's familiarity with the Village's security system – he now has the confidence to turn its in-built paranoia against Number 2 and successfully defeat him. He also tells Number 2 that "many have tried" to break him before. It also saw the first appearance of the bizarre kosho game. Devised by McGoohan, two combatants would engage in hand on combat on raised walkways using two trampolines with a tank of water positioned between them. The winner was the first to give his opponent an early bath.

Information: 'Hammer' is an episode that openly plays on its acknowledged classical references. The title is a quote from *Faust* by the German poet Johann Wolfgang von Goethe (1749–1832), in which the eponymous anti-hero makes a pact with the Devil. The drama itself is structured like a Shakespearean tragedy. Number 2's self-destructive insecurity is taken from the same fatal template as Othello's jealousy, with Number 6 as a nobler Iago, seizing on his opponent's weakness and ruthlessly exploiting it.

Miguel de Cervantes Saavedra (1547–1616) wrote *Don Quixote* in two parts, in 1605 and 1615. This epic satire features the adventures of a Spanish nobleman who believes he must confront the world's injustices. Prone to flights of fancy in which he imagines windmills are giants and flocks of sheep enemy armies, his world view is balanced by the realism of his squire Sancho Panza. Number 2 is clearly as deluded as Don Quixote, and Number 14, his henchman, is a quasi Sancho Panza, the only one with the insight to see the Prisoner's campaign of disinformation for what it is.

The soundtrack to Number 2's breakdown, *L'Arlésienne*, was a collaboration between the French composer Alexandre Bizet (1838–75) and the playwright Alphonse Daudet. A tale of disastrous love, it features a heroine (the girl from Arles) who never once appears on stage. Similarly, Number 2's masters are never shown, but his fear of them drives the nar-

Number 14 (Basil Hoskins) challenges the Prisoner to kosho

rative. Bizet rescored the version of *L'Arlésienne* Number 6 listens to in 1885 for a full orchestra. The composer Ernest Guirard completed a second suite Bizet was unable to finish before his death.

Production: 'Hammer into Anvil' entered the studio on 18 March 1967. Studio mock-ups for exterior scenes were again used, although the majority of the outside scenes were shot on the return visit to Portmeirion beginning in March. Director Pat Jackson travelled to North Wales to supervise the large amount of location work required, including day-for-night filming of Number 6's nocturnal visit to the Stone Boat. McGoohan himself returned and, as usual, Frank Maher doubled for the lead actor in several long-shots. Patrick Cargill, Basil Hoskins and Victor Maddern did not appear on location. Doubles were used for Numbers 2 and 14 and a close-up shot of Maddern as the Band Leader was done in the studio and edited into footage of his Portmeirion stand-in. Number 6's fight with the three stunt men Guardians was shot on location near the Borehamwood studios.

Originally, the code the Prisoner attaches to his carrier pigeon was composed of letters – Z Y P R S T V H I J P N R S – and close-up inserts were duly shot. By the time the episode was aired, the inserts had been remounted and changed to numbers – 20 60 40 47 67 81 91 80. *Spotlight* was again used as a photographic resource – the portrait of Number 2 used in the headline story on the *Tally Ho* was Patrick Cargill's publicity shot for his 1967

The Outsider: Hammer Into Anvil

The cuckoo clock thought to be a bomb by Number 2 pokes fun at his increasing paranoia

entry. The green fire bucket used by the Village bomb squad to contain the cuckoo clock was a real one from the Portmeirion Hotel. A magazine in the General Stores has as its cover star Tony Anholt, who in 1972 starred in ITC's thriller series *The Protectors.*

The overall tone of the script was originally much more melodramatic. Number 2 appeared more unbalanced earlier than on screen and Number 14 had a pronounced sadistic streak. The end of the episode as shot omits Number 2's originally scripted physical collapse and his failure is not so overplayed. The scene that would have directly followed, where the Prisoner meets the new Number 2 on his way out, was dropped completely. The final scene, where the Prisoner visits Number 73's grave following the defeat of Number 2 with "pain and pity in his eyes", was also removed, further toning down the melodramatic overtones and his status as a heroic avenger.

Prison Writers: Roger Woddis was another *Prisoner* writer with no other ITC credits to his name, before or after his contribution to the series. Prior to the 'Hammer into Anvil' broadcast, he co-wrote with Katharine Black 'To Blow My Name About', an episode of the short-lived paraormal ABC series *Haunted.* A successful writer of satirical verse as well as an accomplished dramatist, Woddis was published in the *New Statesman* and had a regular slot on the BBC Radio 4 series *Start The Week.* During the late seventies and early eighties he also had a weekly column published in the *Radio Times*, which wittily lampooned a contemporary TV programme or personality.

Tally Ho: *"You shouldn't have interfered, Number 6. You'll pay for this." "No. You will."* Taking as its model tales of tragedy, revenge and heroism by classical authors and cleverly synthesising them into the Village context, 'Hammer into Anvil' is the most successful example seen so far of *The Prisoner*'s blend of high and popular culture, showcasing the

series' sophisticated playfulness with other sources. The references to Goethe, Bizet and Cervantes are clearly signposted and determine the structure of the story. Despite the richness of its source material, though, by Prisoner standards 'Hammer' is refreshingly straightforward. A clear-cut game of cat and mouse, a battle between right and wrong, it is seamlessly made and tightly directed with nicely judged performances by both leading men.

A lot of the entertainment value comes from seeing the Prisoner turn the impregnable security system which has kept him incarcerated for so long against his Guardians, and as usual there is some dry humour mixed in with the drama. His Morse code signal translates as "pat-a-cake, pat-a-cake, baker's man", and his use of a cuckoo clock as a dummy bomb is a sly dig at Number 2's deteriorating mental state.

With more screen-time being given to the controlling administration's point of view, it was a foregone conclusion that the atmosphere of suspicion and distrust they foster would, in the end, be a trap for them as well as their captives. Clearly, anyone can become a victim of the system;

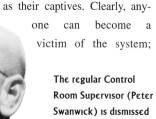

The regular Control Room Supervisor (Peter Swanwick) is dismissed by Number 2

PAWNS AND PLAYERS

Patrick Cargill later combined espionage with comedy in the TV adaptation of the Danny La Rue musical *Come Spy With Me* in 1977, as man-from-the-ministry Gribble. Playing Sancho Panza to Cargill's Don Quixote, Basil Hoskins had also appeared in *The Avengers*, in 1964's 'The Outside-In Man'. Like Patrick Cargill, he crossed over to TV comedy, featuring as Honor Blackman's husband in *The Upper Hand* in 1994. Victor Maddern was equally at home in both drama and comedy, appearing in the labour relations satire *I'm All Right, Jack* (1959) and four *Carry On* films during the sixties. He guested in television programmes as diverse as *Doctor Who* and *Dixon of Dock Green*, but his most visible role was as James Maynard Kitchener Lampwick's son-in-law in *The Dick Emery Show.* The ill-fated Number 73, Hilary Dwyer, was romantically involved with Edward Woodward's shabby spy in *Callan*, suffering a predictable fate in the 1969 story 'Let's Kill Everybody'. Victor Woolf had been well known as the regular character Derwent in the 1950s' series *The Adventures of Robin Hood*, which starred Richard Greene.

11: It's Your Funeral
Written by Michael Cramoy   Directed by Robert Asher

Number 6 is inveigled into an assassination plot through the authorities' manipulation of a young woman, Number 50, the daughter of a Watchmaker. When his watch is swapped for a faulty model by Number 2's agent, Number 100, he visits the Watchmaker and discovers the old man is preparing a trigger mechanism for a bomb. Now taking Number 50's warnings seriously, the Prisoner learns that the intended target is Number 2. Fearing that innocent people will be blamed, he warns the Village chairman and while in the Green Dome his visit is filmed. When he fails to persuade the Watchmaker of the folly of his plan, the Prisoner visits the chairman again, to discover that the younger man had been standing in for his retiring elder colleague. The old Number 2 initially disbelieves the Prisoner's warnings because of film footage, culled from his previous visit, which showed Number 6 apparently warning each previous Number 2 of attempts to kill them; the retriing chairman larer realises he is the intended viuctim of a Village plot. His credibility undermined, the Prisoner has no option but to stop the planned assassination. The Seal of Office, worn by Number 2 and handed over to his replacement at the Appreciation Day ceremony, has been swapped for a copy, concealing a bomb to be detonated by radio. The Prisoner prevents the explosion and allows the old Number 2 to escape with the trigger device securing his safe passage.

The kosho contest, with McGoohan's stunt double clearly visible

Who is Number 2?: 'It's Your Funeral' emphasises the supposed generation gap of the sixties with the "heir presumptive" Number 2 – young, charming and a study in deceit – plotting against the elderly retiring chairman: old, world weary and frightened.

You are Number 6: The Prisoner is unaware of the practice of 'jamming' – the creation of false plots to fool the observers – and reuses his "No comment" catch-phrase from 'Free For All'. He is "very active", keeping fit with a daily walk round the Village, the use of his home-made gym equipment in the woods, a semi-weekly kosho practice and water skiing. He is able to identify the trigger mechanism for a bomb's detonator and, fittingly, is "top of the list" of malcontents.

One? Two? Three? Four?: McGoohan created the bizarre kosho game for this episode, allowing it to occupy some two minutes of screen time.

'It's Your Funeral' was the eighth episode made and was obviously intended for transmission before 'Hammer into Anvil', where kosho is only featured briefly. The dummy cuckoo-clock bomb in 'Hammer into Anvil' is also a more meaningful piece of paranoia if viewed after 'It's Your Funeral', which features a disguised bomb intended for an expendable Number 2. These discrepancies were addressed in the US screening order when the two episodes were transposed, with 'Funeral' broadcast as the eleventh instalment and 'Hammer' fourteenth. The episode also sees the introduction of Number 6's private gym in the woods, consisting of a punch-bag, rope and parallel bar.

Information: 'It's Your Funeral' shows *The Prisoner* engaging less ambiguously with the real politik of the 1960s. The story is inspired by the spate of political assassinations which took place throughout the decade and the speculation about the real motives behind them, in particular the killing of American president John F. Kennedy in 1963. This event was anticipated in *The Manchurian Candidate* (1959), a book and film which had already had a considerable effect on *The Prisoner.*

The complex plot of the novel has a very specific influence on 'It's Your Funeral'. In *The Manchurian*

The Prisoner and the Watchmaker's daughter (Annette Andre) plan their next move

The wheelchair-bound artist (Charles Lloyd Pack) paints Number 6's portrait in the modern style

"We are in this prison for life, all of us, but I have met no one here who has committed a crime"

THE WATCHMAKER

CAST

Guest Stars

Derren Nesbitt
Number Two

Mark Eden
Number 100

Annette Andre
Watchmaker's Daughter

with

Retiring Number Two
Andre Van Gyseghem

Watchmaker
Martin Miller

Computer Attendant
Wanda Ventham

Number Two's Assistant
Mark Burns

Artist
Charles Lloyd Pack

Number 36
Grace Arnold

Stall Holder
Arthur White

Councillor
Michael Bilton

Kosho Opponent
Gerry Crampton

The Prisoner beats the *agent provocateur* Number 100 (Mark Eden) into submission

The Prisoner realises he has been discredited by doctored film to fool the retiring Number 2 (Andre Van Gysegham)

The computer attendant (Wanda Ventham) and Jack Shampan's original production painting for the computer room set

The new Number 2
(Derren Nesbitt)
wearing the fake
Seal of Office

Candidate, Raymond Shaw is brainwashed into trying to assassinate the Republican nominee for the Presidency so that his right-wing running mate would step in and sweep to power on a wave of anti-Communist hysteria. A crackdown by the new regime on opposition elements would ensure that a left-wing counter-revolution would then become unstoppable. The planned assassination of the retiring Number 2 serves a similar purpose: the disposal of a redundant agent and the legitimisation of severe measures against the Villagers to strengthen the authorities' control.

The structural similarities between 'It's Your Funeral' and *The Manchurian Candidate* are very striking. Each has a single parent family at the heart of the assassination attempts, but in *The Prisoner* the roles are reversed and the parent rather than the child becomes the manipulated dupe. Number 6 also takes the role of Bennett Marco, the hero of Condon's novel, as both characters attempt to stop the would-be killer. The two stories both end as a political rally unfolds, with the architects of the schemes present at the ceremony and outwitted in the final scenes.

Production: 'It's your Funeral' began filming on 9 January 1967 and the shoot was a fraught one, even though it managed to stick to its two-week schedule. Although credited on the episode, Robert Asher, an experienced film and TV professional was the first *Prisoner* helmsman to be replaced by McGoohan. Annette Andre remembers what happened: "He was a friend of Patrick's, and Patrick had insisted that he come and direct that episode and more if possible, and he just absolutely *devastated* this man. Patrick cut him to pieces, in the middle of the studio, in front of everybody. And this sweet man, who was just sitting there, wide-eyed, couldn't believe it. He just left the production, and everybody felt very, very strongly about this particular incident." By now, working on the eighth story to be made, McGoohan was increasingly involved in every aspect of production and by his own admission, "worked my way through three nervous breakdowns" during his work on the series. Mark Eden also remembers how the strain was telling on the star: "He nearly strangled me in a fight. All the veins were standing out on his forehead, and I thought, if I don't throw him off, I'm gonna black

out." The end of this fight scene, which also used McGoohan's stand-in Frank Maher, ended with Eden/Number 100 being attacked by the Villafge guardian Rover, although this scene didn't make it to the final edit. It was eventually used in 'Arrival', where Number 100's distinctive pink blazer can be briefly seen being smothered by Rover at the end of the sequence where the Village guardian corners its first victim.

The episode relied heavily on studio mock-ups of Portmeirion, with the first appearance of the studio-bound café. The brief to writer Michael Cramoy had been to base it as much as possible around existing unused footage from the first location shoot. However, additional material was shot on the return visit to Portmeirion in March 1967 for the Appreciation Day ceremony, using local extras with Maher again doubling for McGoohan and a local woman standing in for Annette Andre. The interior set of the Bell Tower was reused from 'Checkmate'. There are some strange continuity errors in the kosho fight; some close-ups of McGoohan's opponent are clearly Basil Hoskins from 'Hammer into Anvil.'

Derren Nesbitt had dyed his hair blonde for the film *The Naked Runner* (1967) opposite Frank Sinatra. He offered to return his hair to its natural colour, but McGoohan advised him to stay blonde for his part as Number 2.

Prison Writers: Michael Cramoy was a veteran of American action shows, working on four scripts for *The Saint* radio series in 1949, as well as twenty six screenplays for the police TV series *Dragnet*'s sixth, seventh and eighth seasons between 1956 and 1959. He came to England at the end of the fifties and worked on *The Invisible Man* for Incorporated Television Films, co-writing the pilot script 'Secret Experiment' with Michael Connor. For ITC, Cramoy wrote four episodes of *The Saint* between 1965 and 1967 and, before *The Prisoner*, scripted 'The Legions of Ammak' for *The Baron*. His varied experience in the action/adventure genre was more than likely why he was asked to write an episode based around already shot film sequences.

Tally Ho: *"I can think of better ways to die." "And better causes, to die for."* The idea of a conspiracy to assassinate Number 2 with the Prisoner unwittingly colluding in the plot is an excellent one. His involvement is cleverly thought out and for once the spotlight is turned on the Village's internal politics. Unfortunately, an episode bent around previously filmed sequences and affected more than most by *The Prisoner*'s inconsistent continuity, with a bias towards the behind-the-scenes orchestration of "Plan Division Q", robs the situation of any tension or surprise. It's

Number 50 with her father, the Watchmaker (Martin Miller), a dupe of the Village controllers

akin to 'Free For All' or 'The Chimes of Big Ben' beginning with Number 2 and his co-conspirators discussing how they're going to ensnare Number 6 in their latest plot: what would be the point?

The story has its plus points, though. There is another dig at modern art, some unintentionally amusing vocal affectations from McGoohan early on, and later, a sprinkling of enjoyable gallows humour. Number 2, with a disguised bomb around his neck says, "You must forgive an old man for talking, but this is a moment of great emotion for me" and his successor drily says the plan should conclude "dead on schedule".

It's left to the last-minute race to stop the assassination attempt, as well as the customary fisticuffs between Number 6 and a Village agent, to create any real excitement.

PAWNS AND PLAYERS

Derren Nesbitt was a mainstay of ITC, appearing in three episodes of *Danger Man* between 1960 and 1964 as well as featuring in *The Saint, Gideon's Way,* and *Man In A Suitcase*, nearly always as the villain. In 1969, he finally appeared on the right side of the law as Detective Chief Inspector Jordan in the first series of the Thames thriller *Special Branch*. He also appeared with Martin Miller and Mark Eden in the 1964 *Doctor Who* story 'Marco Polo', in which Eden took the title role. Annette Andre was the self confessed "most used bird in *The Saint* series", but her most famous ITC role was as Jeanie in the original series of *Randall and Hopkirk (Deceased)* (1969). Shortly before *The Prisoner*, she had appeared in the big-screen version of *A Funny Thing Happened On The Way to the Forum* (1966). Martin Miller had a played a bomb maker opposite Patrick McGoohan before, in the *Danger Man* episode 'The Lovers' (1960). Wanda Ventham played the regular role of Colonel Lake in the Gerry Anderson series *UFO* (1970). She also famously told Jason King that he was "cooling her scene" in the *Department S* episode 'The Man from X' (1969).

12: A Change of Mind

Written by Roger Parkes   Directed by Joseph Serf

The Welfare Committee – a body that investigates unmutual behaviour among the Villagers – examines the Prisoner's behaviour following his fight with two Guardians. After resisting all the Committee's attempts to rehabilitate him, he is declared unmutual. The classification means he can undergo Instant Social Conversion – a process that isolates the aggressive frontal lobes of the brain. Number 86, a female scientist, oversees the operation. Afterwards, the Prisoner is no more willing to say why he resigned, and he still resists. Correctly guessing that the lobotomy was faked, he turns the tables by giving Number 86 the drug that was keeping him pacified. He hypnotises her and gives her new orders...Visiting Number 2, the Prisoner agrees to a full confession, but feels it should be made in front of the whole Village from the balcony in the square. When the clock strikes four, Number 86 appears and declares Number 2 unmutual – the Prisoner rams the idea home by revealing that Number 2 manipulated the Welfare Committee. The defeated dictator is hounded back to the Green Dome by an incensed mob of angry Villagers.

The Prisoner's unmutual behaviour results in a faked lobotomy in an attempt by Number 2 (John Sharpe, above) to find out the reason for Number 6's resignation

Who is Number 2?: The latest Village chairman is manipulative and sly, with a thin veneer of politeness and a fondness for proverbs. He is openly contemptuous of Number 86, a highly-trained scientist, dismissing her as "a stupid woman". He positively revels in Number 6's isolation: "Let's see how our loner withstands real loneliness". Having deceived the community, he seems destined for Instant Social Conversion himself when declared unmutual by Number 86.

You are Number 6: 'A Change of Mind' emphasises Number 6's solitary side. He is seen exercising on his own in the woods yet he seems genuinely lonely when ostracised by the rest of the Village. Number 2 describes

A break in filming while make-up man Eddie Knight attends to Number 86 (Angela Browne)

him as being "as strong as a bull". The Prisoner seems fussy about the way a pot of tea is made and hypnotism is added to his long list of varied abilities.

One? Two? Three? Four?: The ninth episode to be made, it seems 'A Change of Mind' was always intended to be a late episode, occurring twelfth and thirteenth in the UK and US transmission orders respectively. It presents the viewer with a more outwardly threatening Village that does not tolerate rebels indefinitely and a decisive victory over Number 2 with the whole community turned against him. The regular Supervisor also meets the Prisoner for the first time on screen as he leaves Number 2's house.

Information: 'A Change of Mind' is another episode rich in allusions. *"The Manchurian Candidate* was a definite influence" says Roger Parkes. "My brother is a psychiatrist and I asked him all about the technological aspects of a lobotomy. It was a very obvious device to resort to. I think the macabre element of it really appealed." During the sixties, the lobotomising of aggressive mental patients in hospitals was a highly contentious issue, and this brutal treatment was criticised in Ken Kesey's novel *One Flew Over the Cuckoo's Nest* (1962). George Markstein noted the connection with real-life in another of his favourite episodes. "I think 'A Change of Mind' is a cracking good story," he enthused in 1982. "It has a sinister theme which, 16 years later, has become even more relevant. Ask any neuro-surgeon."

TALLY HO HEADLINES

Committee Hearing Continues

No. 93 confesses disharmony

No. 6 for further investigation

No. 6 declared unmutual

CAST

Guest Stars

John Sharpe
Number Two

Angela Browne
Number 86

with

Doctor
George Pravda

Number 42
Kathleen Breck

Lobo Man
Thomas Heathcote

Committee Chairman
Bartlett Mullins

Number 93
Michael Miller

1st Member of Social Group
Joseph Cuby

Number 48
June Ellis

1st Woodland Man
John Hamblin

Second Man
Michael Billington

McGoohan directs Angela Browne on the Instant Social Conversion operating theatre set

The Prisoner discovers a Villager being subjected to Aversion Therapy, a process designed to condition inmates to conform

Shooting Number 6's hearing on the Town Hall Council Chamber set

The Village recruitment drive was inspired by Lord Kitchener's World War I poster (top)

The Committee's hearings of unmutuals being televised refers to the American Senator McCarthy's cross-examination of suspected Communists in the fifties. The wave of anti-Communist hysteria inspired by these hearings became known as 'McCarthyism', leading to violent assaults on suspects.

Villagers are seen undergoing Aversion Therapy, where they are alternatively brainwashed into grateful responses to a picture of Number 2 and conditioned to be afraid of images of Rover and the damning classification 'unmutual'. Anthony Burgess' *A Clockwork Orange* (1962), a bleak tale of a future beset by violent, delinquent youths, featured the Ludovico Technique, another form of aversion therapy practised on the anti-hero Alex. Following the treatment to curb his aggressive tendencies, Alex is attacked by two of his former victims, just as Number 6 is set upon after his fake social conversion by two Villagers he had been involved in a fight with before. There is another reference to Shakespeare: the Prisoner's speech to the Villagers from the balcony in the square, where he alternately praises and denounces Number 2, recalls Mark Antony's speech to the Romans in *Julius Caesar*, where the influence of the crowd also has a decisive role. "The end was an intentional lift from *Julius Caesar*" says Parkes. "There was room in *The Prisoner* for drawing on other sources as it wasn't into profound reality or hard-edged modern real-

ism. It was a fantasy, and fantasies do that all the time."

Number 2's poster, 'Your Community Needs You', is a direct reference to a British First World War recruiting poster. It featured a picture of the military commander Lord Kitchener in the same authoritarian pointed-finger pose.

Production: Entering the studio on 23 January 1967, the shoot for 'A Change of Mind' was a troubled one. McGoohan had been dissatisfied with the work of the original director assigned to the story, Roy Rossotti, and he was replaced after half a day's work. Returning from lunch, the cast found McGoohan had taken over; one of the star's pseudonyms, 'Joseph Serf', was eventually credited as the director.

Some filmed inserts were again dropped in from the supplemental April 1967 shoot, but the episode mostly relied on studio mock-ups of Portmeirion and the woods, and footage reused from other episodes. Always keen to be experimental as a director, McGoohan proved over-optimistic in one of his ambitions. "Pat had rehearsed a very complicated tracking shot with the hospital trolleys," film librarian Tony Sloman remembers. "They rehearsed and rehearsed and couldn't get it right. Finally, at about 8.50pm, they were ready to go and they knew they could get it. They also knew that at 9pm they were booked to finish... In the middle of this very complicated shot, dead on 9pm, all the lights went out – the technicians had cut them dead. Pat was furious, said nothing and stormed off the set... They picked up again in the morning but it cost them time. That was the first time I saw a studio brought to a standstill by people who wouldn't work any extra overtime."

There was only one change to Roger Parkes' script: "The lady scientist originally really fancied the Prisoner and flirted with him a lot – all that was cut, swiftly and firmly," Parkes remembers. "Patrick would no doubt defend it by saying the character wouldn't trust anyone."

On the closing credits, the bike frame again disappears leaving two wheels before cutting to footage of Rover, evidence of the titles being recut at the last moment. This also occurs on episodes 1, 9, 10 and 16.

The Prisoner and Number 86 declare Number 2 unmutual and he is hounded back to the Green Dome by an angry mob

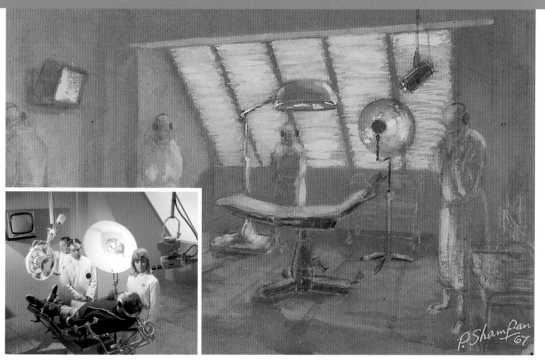

The production painting of Number 86's laboratory reveals how close the finished set (inset) was to the original design

The trailer shows an alternate take where Number 2's "Stupid woman!" dialogue occurs at the end of the sequence where he orders Number 86 to report to him after she has been drugged.

Prison Writers: 'A Change of Mind' was Roger Parkes' first commission as a professional script writer. He was in his late twenties at the time and was the trainee story editor on the BBC series *Compact*, having previously worked in journalism as crime reporter and foreign correspondent for the *Daily Express*. Following the successful sale of his *Prisoner* script, he went on to write for the other ITC shows *Man In A Suitcase*, *Strange Report* and *Return of the Saint*. Parkes has enjoyed a successful freelance writing career for over 30 years, with numerous scripts for TV and radio and over 20 published novels.

Tally Ho: *"Rebel!" "Reactionary!" "Disharmonious!"* 'A Change of Mind' is one of *The Prisoner*'s darkest stories. There is very little wit, and the usual jolly atmosphere of brass bands and cheerful announcements in the Village is replaced by ominous silences. The Villagers,

from being mostly a supporting cast to Number 6's battle with successive Number 2s, become a main character in their own right. Nothing happens that is not driven by their progressively intimidating behaviour; even Number 2 is not immune from their influence. McGoohan's direction is just right, creating a tense, unsettling atmosphere, particularly in Number 2's interrogation of the Prisoner. The scene is disorientating for the viewer as the position of the camera keeps changing during the conversation. The ambience of village-green paranoia throughout 'Change' is quintessential *Prisoner*, keeping the audience off balance with a blend of the twee and the menacing: from the Committee deciding to stop for a tea break during Number 6's interrogation to the lobotomising of Villagers.

This, then, is the true, ugly face of the Village: paying lip service to democracy and liberalism but in reality an oppressive, conformist society, completely intolerant of individual behaviour. The herd mentality of the Villagers is emphasised by references to animals – sheep, mules, lambs and "scapegoats" – and Number 2 is refereed to in the script as a "large cattle auctioneer type" and likened to "the butcher with the warmest heart [who] has the sharpest knife". Truly frightening.

PAWNS AND PLAYERS

Following *The Prisoner*, John Sharpe dropped the 'e' from his name and starred in the Granada sitcom *Her Majesty's Pleasure* (1968–69) as another custodian of the incarcerated, Prison Officer Clissit. During 1968 he was also a regular on *Coronation Street* as the head of the Clegg family, "the neurotic new owner of the corner shop". Although he had a part as the Summerisle doctor in the seminal thriller *The Wicker Man* (1974), Sharp's scenes were dropped from the released version. Angela Browne had been a regular in *Court Martial* (1965-6) as Sergeant Yolanda Perkins and appeared in *Danger Man* (1960) in the title role of 'The Girl in Pink Pyjamas'. George Pravda had played the atomic bomb specialist Kutze in *Thunderball* (1965) and went on to become the eccentric detective George Bulman's Russian compatriot in *Strangers* (1981) and *Bulman* (1985). As a result of his small role, Michael Billington was chosen to play the regular part of Colonel Paul Foster in *UFO* in 1969. Billington screen-tested three times for the part of James Bond but had to be content with the runner-up role of Sergei in *The Spy Who Loved Me* (1977).

"Do we know where Seltzman is?" Sir Charles Grover (John Wentworth) questions his advisers in the teaser sequence

In London, Sir Charles Portland and his team speculate over the whereabouts of Professor Seltzman. In the Village, Number 2 explains to a new arrival, the Colonel, that Number 6 was the last known contact with the Professor. The scientist is of interest to the Village as he has invented a machine that can swap the mind of one person into another. The Prisoner undergoes this conversion process, waking at his London home to see a new face in the mirror - the Colonel's. Realising he has to track Seltzman down, he contacts his old work colleagues, including Sir Charles. They refuse to believe his story but have him followed. Reacquainting himself with his fiancée, Janet, Portland's daughter, he convinces her of his true identity. Locating the Professor in Switzerland, Number 6 is followed and confronted by one of his own people, Potter. They fight, but are gassed by a Village agent. Seltzman and Number 6 are taken back to the village where the Professor agrees to perform the reversal operation, as long as he can be part of the process. Recovering, Number 6 reveals that the Professor has performed a three-way switch and left the Village in the Colonel's body. He is now safe to continue his work.

The reformatted title sequence used on this episode

Who is Number 2?: A cool, calculating man, he is prepared to play a waiting game while the rehoused mind of Number 6 locates Seltzman. Once again, due to over-confidence in the Village administration, and an underestimation of the Professor's abilities, he is outwitted.

You are Number 6: Ironically for an episode where the Prisoner's mind is housed in another man's body, we learn the most biographical details about him. Number 6 has been away a year to the day. A year ago, the day before his resignation, he attended a dress fitting with his fiancée Janet for her birthday party; he still has the invitation that he never used. He danced a waltz with Janet in Kitzbuhl and has a special, intimate way of kissing her. Number 6 entrusted her with a receipt for some colour transparencies that conceal the whereabouts of Seltzman, a friend he wrote to in Scotland. Details are also revealed about the Prisoner's background in espionage; his code name in the UK is ZM73, in Germany, Schmidt, and France, Duval and he names two men in his department, Danvers and Potter. His favourite dish is jugged hare. He is amnesiac when he wakes up in his apartment but remembers who he is when he looks in the mirror.

One? Two? Three? Four?: 'Do Not Forsake Me Oh My Darling' had a chequered production history. It was originally to have been the first episode of the second sea-

son of 13 stories, discernible by events being set a year after the Prisoner's abduction, i.e. the following season. When the decision was made to curtail the series, it was then scheduled as episode nine – the position it occupies in the US screening order – the idea being to intersperse three of the four episodes from the second filming block throughout the series' run. With post-production work still being carried out in October 1967, the story was unable to meet its proposed mid-November UK screening dates and was again rescheduled.

Information: 'Do Not Forsake Me...' sees *The Prisoner* dabbling in the old TV fantasy stand-by of the mind swap. As recently as May 1967, *The Avengers* had featured an episode called 'Who's Who???', where the minds of Steed and Mrs Peel were swapped with those of the villains.

It also features a references to contemporary spy fiction: The disappearance of the Prisoner for over a year without any explanation to his lover recalls a similar situation in John Le Carré's novel *The Spy Who Came In From The Cold* (1963), in which the agent Alec Leamas vanishes from the life of his lover Liz Gold for months, only to reappear with fatal consequences for them both. Seltzman's comment to Number 2 that the Village has made his device "wretched", and the mention of the scientist Rutherford splitting the atom, reflects how science had been co-opted by the nuclear arms race during

Written by Vincent Tilsley   Directed by Pat Jackson

CAST

Guest stars

Clifford Evans
Number Two

Nigel Stock
The Colonel

Zena Walker
Janet

with

Seltzman
Hugo Schuster

Sir Charles
John Wentworth

Villiers
James Bree

Stapleton
Lloyd Lamble

Danvers
Patrick Jordan

Camera Shop Manager
Lockwood West

Potter
Frederic Abbott

Cafe Waiter
Gertan Klauber

Old Guest*
Henry Longhurst

First New Man*
Danvers Walker

Young Guest
John Nolan

Undertaker**
William Lyon Brown

*Cut from finished
episode, although credited
on the end titles.*

**Uncredited*

The Prisoner (Nigel Stock) confronts the camera shop manager (Lockwood West)

The shock of seeing the Colonel's face in the mirror cures the Prisoner of amnesia after waking back in his London home

A cut scene took place in Sir Charles' office

The undertaker from the title sequence (William Lyon Brown) shadows Number 6 throughout the episode

the Cold War. Seltzman's escape at the end helps preserve the balance of power.

There are two possible in-jokes. The man who tails the Prisoner to Switzerland is called Potter, which was also the name of John Drake's contact in 'Koroshi' in the fourth series of *Danger Man* (made in 1966 but not screened until 1968). When Sir Charles asks of the photographic slides, "What's Number 6?", the reply, in the first story of *The Prisoner*'s proposed second season, is "Hopelessly over exposed"...

Production: 'Do Not Forsake Me...' was shot in August 1967, with key production staff changed with the commencement of the second filming block. Written specifically to accommodate the absence of Patrick McGoohan while he appeared in John Sturges' feature film *Ice Station Zebra* in America, the script originally had the rather better title of 'Face Unknown'. However, writer Vincent Tilsley felt the programme's integrity was being compromised by the situation he was asked to write for: "It was a very corny idea, this mind swap thing. There was no way to get any kind of an edge to it. I've occasionally thought 'Could I have come up with anything better?', but I forgive myself because I don't think I could. I didn't like it at all, and I liked what they did to it even less. I think David Tomblin rewrote it in cahoots with Patrick." The title 'Do Not Forsake Me Oh My Darling', a song from the film *High Noon* and the preferred title of Ian Rakoff's western, the next script in production, was used when the script was rewritten. A major improvement was the ambiguity of Sir Charles Portland's role; in the earlier version it was made clear he was working with the Village. The date of Number 6's resignation, 13 July, was also dropped, as was any reference to the Colonel as 'Oscar'. The most significant change from the earlier draft was the regression of Number 6's memory back to the day of his resignation. In that version, he only realises his mind has been swapped when he looks in the mirror of the office he had resigned in, stretching credibility.

Location filming again took place in London, at No.1 Buckingham Place and World Cameras on Southampton Row. The Lotus 7 used in this episode was a replacement for the Lotus demonstrator, which had been sold abroad. The stand-in car, registration LC K88D, was owned by local Borehamwood man Frank Rycroft. "I bought it from the Barnet Motor Company. It was run by a guy called Peter Warr, a friend of mine, who went on to do Formula 3 stuff, and they also supplied cars for various films. They paid me between £400-500 for using it for a couple of weeks. They damaged it a bit and when they brought it back it had new fibreglass wings on the back. After they'd used it, I sold the car on."

The Village Hearse was also a replacement, also fitted out with the appropriate number plates, and extra scenes of Nigel Stock driving the Lotus around London were shot. Stock film from World Backgrounds was again used for footage of Germany and France and the Maid of Kent ferry, with Seefeld in Austria standing in for Kanderseld, exteriors for which were shot on the Borehamwood back lot. The GCE Marconi building in Borehamwood was used for scenes of Number 6 and Villiers travelling by the unusual lifts. McGoohan's scenes were all filmed in one day on his return from Hollywood, supplemented by clips from 'Arrival', 'Free For All' and the as yet unscreened 'Once Upon A Time'. Although scenes were shot featuring 'Old Guest' and 'First New Man', they were dropped at a late stage, even though the actors are still credited on the closing titles.

Filming the ballroom scene in August 1967

The displaced Prisoner wins Janet's confidence and is able to retrieve the slides which reveal Seltzman's hiding place

The sumptuous design for Sir Charles Portland's office by Jack Shampan

'Do Not Forsake Me...' has another classic *Prisoner* in joke: Seltzman's letter is addressed in McGoohan's handwriting and gives the Professor's residence as '20, Portmeirion Road'.

The episode trailer features an alternative take of the scene where the Prisoner and Janet meet in the garden at her birthday party. The line "Nobody but you" is spoken by Nigel Stock; in the finished episode the dialogue comes from Zena Walker.

Tally Ho: *"Who else could have given you that message?" "Nobody but you."* Exploring the intriguing theme that your identity is only as real as what you look like, 'Do Not Forsake Me Oh My Darling' is a qualified success, the serious rendering of a pulp sci-fi idea. The cast is a strong one – it needed to be – and it's a shame we don't see more of the excellent Clifford Evans as Number 2. Nigel Stock gives a believable and engaging performance as the mentally displaced Prisoner, capturing McGoohan's brusque speech patterns and brooding facial expressions. There is a real emotional commitment from him and Zena Walker in their scenes together, and their touching reunion, with Janet half doubting, half convinced that a man she doesn't recognise is her fiancé, is the story's highlight.

In the end, though, 'Do Not Forsake Me...' is something of a curate's egg, the very human story at its heart undermined by a production reliant on the obvious reuse of footage from other episodes, library film and some poor dialogue. It's also an interesting and slightly ominous glimpse of what the series might have been like if it had pushed ahead into another full production block. The reformatted titles hint at the possible redefinition of the Prisoner's role as a globe-trotting Village agent by dropping the standard "Where am I sequence?" for aerial views of the Village and scenes of the helicopter in flight. While this may have been a cosmetic face-lift for the aborted new season, it is also another instance of *The Prisoner* playing with the conventions of its genre. The only episode to have a teaser sequence in the style of other ITC shows such *Man In A Suitcase* and *The Saint*, the prologue sets up a story that (despite fantastical overtones), is a straightforward secret agent adventure. In doing this it foreshadows further stylistic experimentation in the remaining three stories to be made.

This atypical story remains significant because for one story only the conflict in *The Prisoner* changes. Contradicting the rest of the series, the fight becomes a crusade to protect an established identity rather than the usual battle to defend a private, almost mythical one.

14: Living in Harmony

From a story by David Tomblin and Ian L. Rakoff   Written and Directed by David Tomblin

A sheriff resigns, turns in his gun and badge, is ambushed and taken to the township of Harmony. There the ex-sheriff, the Stranger, meets three Old West characters: the corrupt Judge who runs the town, his psychopathic gunfighter, the Kid, and Kathy, the saloon whore with a heart of gold. The Judge pressurises the Stranger to stay on as sheriff but he refuses. He tries to escape but is brought back and Kathy is imprisoned for helping him leave. To obtain her release, the Stranger accepts the job of sheriff but refuses to wear a gun. Even after a savage beating he still refuses, despite the Kid's provocation and the Judge's gang killing of a resident who had supported him. Planning to escape again with Kathy, the Stranger is finally provoked into using a gun when the Kid strangles her. The Stranger kills the Kid in a gun fight, but is killed himself in a shoot-out with the Judge's gang... The Prisoner awakes in a facsimile Western town. The action has all been a hallucinogenic trip organised by Number 2 (the Judge). Events repeat themselves. Number 8 (The Kid) and Number 22 (Kathy) enter the Harmony set and the Kid's real-life counterpart strangles Number 22. Number 8 commits suicide.

Above: the psychopathic Kid
(Alexis Kanner)

Here comes the Judge: The Judge controls Harmony totally through his gang and the Kid. He says he knows all about the Stranger and has every exit from the town guarded. As Number 2, he underestimates how involved Number 8 and Number 22 have become in the illusion, identifying completely with their fictional alter egos.

The man with no name: The Stranger is an accomplished horseman, a hand-to-hand fighter and quick on the draw. He quits his job as sheriff for a reason that is never disclosed and has an emotional attachment to Kathy. Once the illusion is broken, the Prisoner is able to differentiate fantasy from reality quickly. His presence in Harmony when Number 8 murders Number 22 suggests he was just as involved in the illusion as the others.

One? Two? Three? Four?: 'Living in Harmony' was made fifteenth, the second story of the second production block. It was originally to have been screened as the twelfth episode, between 'Checkmate' and 'A Change of Mind'. It was not ready for its UK transmission in time, and was originally banned during *The Prisoner*'s first US screening because of its pacifist stance in a country conscripting its young for the Vietnam War. It was subsequently shown twelfth in America in syndication when the ban was lifted.

Information: As *The Prisoner* progressed, various ideas were considered that could be fitted into the series' format. "Pat was a great fan of Westerns," Frank Maher recalls. "One night we were talking after playing squash and I said, 'This series is going nowhere. By now, the audience know there's no way you're ever gonna get out of this joint. You're stuck in this place and you can do anything' ... His next question was 'Are you thinking what I'm thinking? Something about the Old West?' We sat there and talked about it and that started it." With the absence of a story editor, members of the production team were also encouraged to submit ideas. Ian Rakoff, who had been working as an assistant film editor, was also a fan of Westerns. "I read a *Two-Gun Kid*, or *Kid Colt Outlaw* comic in which the unfriendly town was named Harmony," he says. "The opening sequence comes from a Gene Autry comic, and the story begins with Gene Autry walking across sage bush with no horse and a saddle on his shoulder. Suddenly, out of nowhere, six guys attack him and he wakes up in a town." Rakoff, McGoohan and Maher's ideas gelled and Rakoff developed the story, with Tomblin handling the final treatment of the screenplay. The story was also inspired by Rakoff's experiences as a militant activist against the apartheid regime in his native South Africa, when he was discouraged from carrying a gun by his black colleagues.

Other Western references abound throughout the story. Apart from the three main characters all being deliberate archetypes from Western fiction, Alexis Kanner remembers that the Kid replacing his gun in his holster after being shot was a conscious steal from Robert Aldrich's 1954 Western *Vera Cruz*, where the Burt Lancaster character does the same thing. Tomblin's

The Stranger (Patrick McGoohan) is kidnapped by gunmen and taken to the "exclusive" town of Harmony

"I agreed to wear the badge. But not the gun"

THE STRANGER

WANTED POSTER

The Bishop is coming!

CAST

Guest Stars

Alexis Kanner

The Kid

David Bauer

The Judge

Valerie French

Kathy

with

Town Elder

Gordon Tanner

Bystander

Gordon Sterne

Will

Michael Balfour

Mexican Sam

Larry Taylor

Town Dignitary

Monti de Lyle

Horse Dealer

Douglas Jones

1st Gunman

Bill Nick

2nd Gunman

Les Crawford

3rd Gunman

Frank Maher

1st Horseman

Max Faulkner

2nd Horseman

Bill Cummings

3rd Horseman

Eddie Eddon

An insanely jealous Kid strangles Kathy in the saloon, provoking the Stranger into a gun fight

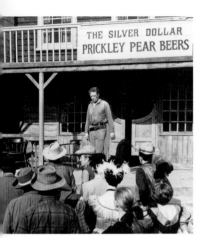

A scene dropped from the final edit of the episode. The Stranger confronts the towns folk

The doomed Kathy (Valerie French)

direction also owes a heavy debt to Sergio Leone. *A Fistful of Dollars* (1964), *For A Few Dollars More (1965)* and *The Good, The Bad and the Ugly* (1966) had changed the Western genre forever; the first film in the trilogy had its first UK release in April 1967, with the other two films following shortly afterwards. 'Living in Harmony' follows Leone's template of stylised direction and graphic violence and emerges as the most violent *Prisoner* episode by far. Both Tomblin and Leone's approaches feature a taciturn, nearly monosyllabic leading man, and the Kid could stand unchanged alongside memorable grotesques played by Gian Maria Volonté and Klaus Kinski.

A close examination of the fight scene in the square reveals assistant director Gino Marotta's young son watching the action,

The Stranger buries Kathy as dawn breaks

wearing some suspiciously 1960s-style clothes. He was originally to have presented McGoohan with his hat after the fight, another possible nod to a classic western, George Stevens' *Shane* (1953), which featured a boy who idolised the hero.

Production: 'Living in Harmony' took five weeks to shoot when the normal production time of a *Prisoner* episode was normally two. With a higher requirement of stunt work than normal, Frank Maher was cast in his only credited role as 'Third Gunman'. In addition to assembling a stunt team, as a self-confessed "Western nut" he was also charged with overseeing the authentic feel of the story. The episode was filmed over September and October 1967, with some location work on the Dunstable Downs. The MGM back lot was used again, this time redressed to resemble a Western town. David Tomblin came up with the idea for the cardboard cut-outs of the characters.

Preparation for the story was done while McGoohan was in America filming *Ice Station Zebra*. Always keen to challenge his co-stars, he sent the following telegram to Alexis Kanner: *"Am taking lessons from Sammy Davis Jnr. and Steve McQueen in quick-draw. Hope you live up to expectations. McGoohan."* "This made it incumbent upon me to go out and get a .45 Colt Pacemaker and practise," Kanner remembers. "On the day we finally shot it, a lot of bets were being placed

The Judge shoots the Stranger… and the Prisoner wakes in a facsimile Western town

around the set as to who would outdraw who… When the film came back from the lab, the editor was able to hold it up and count the frames and discover that I'd fired in nine and Patrick had fired in 11 – about a sixth of a second difference."

Owing to its exceptionally adult content, 'Living in Harmony' was the second *Prisoner* episode subject to censorship on its first UK airing. Regional TV stations again deleted five sequences – Johnson's hanging, the fight with Zeke, Number 6 being dragged back to Harmony by horses, and the strangulation of both Kathy and Number 22. Hangings, in particular, were not allowed to be shown until after the nine o'clock watershed because of a tragic incident in which a young boy had copied a scene in a Sunday afternoon Western and strangled himself with a washing line. Even with the cuts, however, three television networks – Southern,

The Prisoner's stunt arranger Frank Maher played the 'Third Gunman' in his only billed role

Channel and Westward – still opted to screen the story after 10 o'clock. The edits were smoother than those done for 'Free for All', with the exception of the last scene when Number 6 seems to appear from nowhere to tackle Kanner's Number 8. All the cuts were subsequently reinstated during Channel 4's repeat run in 1984.

Once upon a time in the West: *"I wish it had been real."* Seeing the episode in UK transmission order and sequentially as part of the second filming block, 'Living in Harmony' shows how *The Prisoner* was continuing to evolve. After the varied cultural allusions of other episodes, 'Living in Harmony' sees the series' most audacious reference yet to other genres. The remodelling of the titles in the Western style is an act of supreme daring and it's hard to imagine now the impact it must have had in the sixties. This disruption of audience expectation was a sign of things to come.

In using a Western theme, where a man is isolated from the community for his beliefs, *The Prisoner* was directly referring to the film *High Noon* (1952), itself a liberal response to Senator McCarthy's anti-Communist witch-hunts in fifties America. The sophistication doesn't stop there. The series was also incorporating elements from its own short history to make the point that the themes of *The Prisoner* could be applied to other contexts; even the title, 'Living in Harmony', is a paraphrase of "in the Village". Kathy's trial recalls a similar scene in 'Dance of the Dead', the emotional blackmail of the Stranger through a vulnerable woman has precedents in 'The Chimes of Big Ben', 'It's Your Funeral' and the Judge with a mute servant alludes to Number 2 and the silent Butler.

'Living in Harmony' reveals a refinement of a clever, self conscious film vocabulary so it's hard to square its overt violence with McGoohan's high regard for family values and wholesome entertainment. However, it still stands as perhaps the most sophisticated and accomplished example of *The Prisoner*'s manipulation of film, audience and content. You are left with the feeling that after this, the series could have gone anywhere.

15: The Girl Who Was Death

Written by Terence Feely from an idea by David Tomblin   Directed by David Tomblin

The Prisoner, 'Mr X', is on a mission to stop the mad scientist Dr Schnipps from destroying London with a rocket. He comes up against the Professor's daughter, Sonia, a born killer. He pursues her from a cricket match via his local pub to a funfair, and finally to the deserted village of Witchwood. There he escapes from a series of lethal traps and hitches a ride on her helicopter. They arrive on the coast, where Schnipps' base is hidden inside a lighthouse that is also the rocket in disguise. Mr X sabotages the armoury – killing Schnipps' henchmen – and the rocket itself, which explodes, killing Sonia and her father. In the final scenes, the Prisoner is seen telling the story – "a blessed fairy tale" – to a group of Village children. Number 2 (Schnipps) bemoans to his female assistant (Sonia) another lost opportunity for getting at the truth about the Prisoner..

Another *Prisoner* in-joke: the cast features an actor called John Drake

The photographer, an unbilled Alexis Kanner

Jimmy Miller's last uncredited appearnce, as one of Schnipps' henchmen

It's Waterloo all over again: Schnipps is depicted as a buffoon who thinks he's Napoleon; his alter ego of Number 2 is just as ineffectual. The plan for Number 6 to "drop his guard with children" comes to nothing, just as Schnipps' plans blow up in his face.

Nobody does it better: 'Mr X' dresses as a cross between John Drake, Sherlock Holmes and a ruffle-shirted and frilly-cuffed sixties pop star. He can handle a Lotus Elan, plays cricket and is proficient in the boxing ring. He can also spot a hand grenade disguised as a cricket ball. A combination of brandy, whisky, vodka, Drambuie, Tia Maria, Cointreau and Grand Marnier makes him sick (well, it would). He is skilled with a bren gun and at exploiting his immediate environment to his advantage, be it using explosive candles to escape from a sealed room or rigging the enemy's guns to fire backwards.

One? Two? Three? Four?: Sixteenth in production order, third in the second filming block, 'The Girl Who Was Death' was always intended to be screened fifteenth, preceded by 'Hammer into Anvil' (as was its US transmission). Its screening back to back with the delayed 'Living in Harmony' unfortunately dilutes the impact of again being displaced from the Village setting. It also uses the same trick twice, as the Prisoner's opponents are again revealed as Number 2 and his assistant in the final moments.

Information: In *Dr No* (1962), James Bond comments to the villain that "Our asylums are full of people who think they're Napoleon". 'The Girl Who Was Death' is this observation made flesh, and there are several other nods to Bond throughout the story. The scene where Sonia traps Mr X in a sauna is lifted wholesale from *Thunderball* (1965). In the film, it was Guy Doleman's Count Lippe on the receiving end of the same treatment from 007. The same basic story of a German madman attempting to destroy London with a rocket can be found in the Bond novel *Moonraker* (1955), in which Hugo Drax attempts the same plan and is also killed by his own invention. The similarity would have been even stronger if Schnipps had been portrayed as Hitler as originally intended; Sonia wearing a WWI-style German helmet and using German grenades is a survival of this initial concept. There is also a pointed criticism of Bond and *Danger Man*-style covert gadgets, when Potter describes the radio hidden in his shoe brush as "ridiculous". The story also recalls *The Avengers* in its depiction of a twee, stylised England with home-grown eccentric villains.

The roots of 'The Girl Who Was Death' may lie in the *Danger Man* episode 'The Ubiquitous Mr Lovegrove' (1966). The episode begins with Drake involved in a car crash. Without any further explanation, the rest of the story becomes a bizarre fantasy, with the final scenes revealing that the preceding story was Drake's nightmare as a result of his involvement in the accident. 'Girl' is a refinement of this approach, with periodic cuts showing the pages of the Village Story Book being turned and the pay-off that the story was a fantasy.

Sonia Schnipps (Justine Lord) has the Prisoner in her sights

"You may not see my face but you may know my name. My name is Death"

SONIA

HOLD THE FRONT PAGE

Col. Hawke-English murdered at cricket match 'one short of his century'

CAST

Guest Stars

Kenneth Griffith
Schnipps

Justine Lord
Sonia

with

Potter
Christopher Benjamin

Killer Karminski
Michael Brennan

Boxing MC
Harold Berens

Barmaid
Sheena Marsh

Scots Napoleon
Max Faulkner

Welsh Napoleon
John Rees

Yorks Napoleon
Joe Gladwin

Bowler
John Drake

Little Girl
Gaynor Steward

1st Little Boy
Graham Steward

2nd Little Boy
Stephen Howe

Voice of the Chief/*
Photographer at Fun Fair
Alexis Kanner

Uncredited

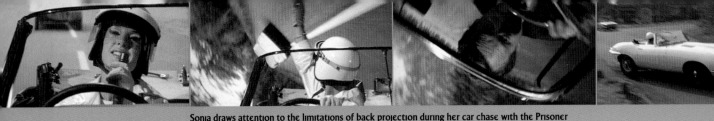

Sonia draws attention to the limitations of back projection during her car chase with the Prisoner

The illustrations in the Village Story Book which inspire Number 6's story

Number 6's taunt to Number 2, "Goodnight, children – everywhere" was the sign-off from the BBC radio programme *Children's Hour.*

Production: Based on an idea by David Tomblin, 'The Girl Who Was Death' was originally to have been a ninety minute special, although these plans didn't reach fruition. "At the end of the day Lew Grade knocked it on the head", Terence Feely explained. "He refused to put up the money, so that story is an amalgam of two scripts... what we got was a kind of compromise between the two. However, it worked perfectly well." Scenes dropped from the shortened version were Mr X's fight with two assassins in a maze and his encounter in a jungle with a murderous native.

McGoohan had to return to Hollywood for six weeks to complete work on *Ice Station Zebra*, lengthening the production period for 'Girl' to four weeks. A substantial amount of the location filming towards the end of 1967 took place with Frank Maher doubling for the star, particularly in scenes shot at the Kursaal Fun Fair at Southend; close-ups of McGoohan were shot on his return. Mr X's Sherlock Holmes disguise, not mentioned in the script, was added to allow Maher to do extensive doubling for the absent leading man. Other locations used included Meopham in Kent and Eltisely in Cambridgeshire for the cricket match, and the MGM backlot for the village of Witchwood. The exterior of the pub where Mr X gets poisoned was the Thatched Barn in Borehamwood, now demolished. Other location work took place on Shenley Road for the scenes of McGoohan on the high street and at Beachy Head for scenes of the cliffs and lighthouse. The subterranean corridor, cavern and rocket interiors were constructed especially for the episode. A model of the lighthouse, one of the few pieces of model work done for the series, was blown up at the story's conclusion. Footage of the clock counting down had been used in the Gerry Anderson productions *Thunderbirds Are Go* (1966) and *Captain Scarlet and the Mysterons* (1967-8).

Transport for the episode included a Lotus Elan and an E-type Jaguar. The helicopter had been used in *The*

Filming Justine Lord at Kursaal Fun Fair in Southend

The Prisoner with the only children ever seen in the Village

Baron episode 'Roundabout'. Jimmy Miller, McGoohan's personal assistant, again stepped into a small role as one of Schnipps's henchmen.

Schnipps' wayward heavy, O'Rourke, was originally to have been named after Griffith's great friend, Peter O'Toole. Griffith remembers: "Patrick took me aside and said, very quietly, 'I don't think we want any in-jokes, Kenneth.'" This was odd as, in an episode full of in-jokes, Griffth's playing of Schnipps as Nap-oleon was likely to have been a reference to

"Nice of you to drop in. I can see you're having a swinging time... You'll soon get the point."

his portrayal of the same role in *War and Peace* (1963). The original plan, to depict the mad scientist as Hitler, has another parallel in Griffith's career; he played the Nazi leader in the film *The Two-Headed Spy* (1958).

The correct way to kill: *"Mountaineering rope. It would hold an elephant". "I must remember that next time I go climbing with one".* 'The Girl Who Was Death' is hilarious, the Prisoner production team letting their hair down, with an excellent music score that epitomises its sixties caper movie feel. Patrick McGoohan again shows how good he is at comedy, adopting the principle that the best comedy is always played straight. Mr X is virtually his audition for James Bond, and it's easy to see why the 007 producers were so keen to have him. Indeed, 'Girl''s puns are so merrily appalling they could have been lifted unchanged from a Bond film. Despite the light, inconsequential nature of the story, the episode continues the stylistic playfulness of 'Living in Harmony', doing everything that the previous story does, but with tongue firmly in cheek.

In-jokes abound; Christopher Benjamin is recast as Potter, a role he had played in *Danger Man*, (even though the character is portrayed differently), and the episode even features an actor called John Drake. Mr X receives his briefing in a record shop, as Drake did in 'Koroshi', this time from a record that answers back. The technique of back projection, which enabled scenes apparently on location to be mounted in the studio – a staple of ITC film series and feature films of the time – is ruthlessly lampooned during a car chase when Sonia causes the back projection of Mister X chasing her to spin round.

There are also thematic links that tie 'Girl' into *The Prisoner* canon. The series had always seen women as either victims or enemies; Sonia is the ultimate conclusion of this approach. She is part Fiona Volpe, the deadly female assassin from *Thunderball*, part the femme fatale archetype of *film noir*; in effect, Bond and blonde. The adult inmates of the Village are often referred to as "errant children", so the presence of the

real thing is unsurprising. *The Prisoner* had always referenced nursery rhymes in its incidental music and dialogue and in 'Girl' it does it visually, with the butcher's, the baker's and the candlestick maker's present in Witchwood, itself a name suggestive of fairy stories. The series had alluded to Napoleon before; here, Tomblin's direction stresses that Schnipps is a very short man, implying in turn that Number 2s are nothing but small-time dictators. The Prisoner again survives a series of traps in an isolated village, and for once he is able to escape from the place by helicopter.

Still evolving, even at the eleventh hour, 'The Girl Who Was Death' shows *The Prisoner* was now being driven completely by its awareness of film, genre and imagery rather than narrative.

The professor and his daughter...

...and Number 2 and his assistant

16: Once Upon A Time
Written and Directed by Patrick McGoohan

The Number 2 from 'The Chimes of Big Ben' is brought back to deal once and for all with the Prisoner. He requests the ultimate test – Degree Absolute. Number 6 is regressed through hypnosis to childhood and both men, together with the Butler, are sealed in the subterranean Embryo Room to engage in a battle of wills for one week – to the death. Number 2 assumes the role of authority figures throughout the Prisoner's life: father, teacher, boss, judge, pilot and interrogator in an attempt to try and break him. Over time, the psychological balance shifts in favour of the Prisoner. With five minutes to go until the room is reopened, Number 2 makes a final plea for the Prisoner to divulge the reason for his resignation. He refuses and Number 2 dies. The Supervisor enters and asks the Prisoner what he desires. His answer is simple: "Number 1." The Prisoner and the Butler are led away...

'Once upon A Time''s minimal, black-draped set was suggestive of fringe theatre

Who is Number 2?: The genial figure of 'The Chimes of Big Ben' has become a tense and angry man, and has returned to the Village in a final attempt to break the Prisoner. He rejects his previous acceptance of being a "lifer" by declaring he's "not an inmate" and having Rover removed from the command chair. It is his decision to use Degree Absolute, but his respect for Number 6 proves to be his downfall as prisoner and captor change places.

You are Number 6: The Prisoner is also on edge, shouting at a fellow Villager in the square. While reliving his childhood, it transpires he has a brother, was not a snitch at school and was trained in boxing and fencing. He worked for an old established firm of bankers which was a cover for intelligence work; he resigned "for peace of mind." He was also an aerial bombardier in the Second World War – which is odd as he would have been 11 when war broke out in 1939 – even though he resists killing Number 2. The only way to defeat him is to gain his respect. He again demonstrates his knowledge of the arts, joining Number 2 in quoting from Shakespeare's *As You Like It*. Having changed places as prisoner and captor, the death of Number 2 is the symbolic death of the Prisoner's identity as Number 6.

One? Two? Three? Four?: 'Once Upon A Time' was filmed sixth, after 'The Chimes of Big Ben', and Leo McKern's contract was extended for two weeks to enable him to play the part; clips from four of the five episodes made prior to 'Once' are seen on Number 2's screen. The story was originally to have concluded the proposed first season of thirteen stories, but was held back to become *The Prisoner*'s penultimate episode.

Information: Originally titled 'Degree Absolute', the script took as its model the 'Seven Ages of Man' speech from Shakespeare's *As You Like It* (Act 2, Scene 7), and is a loose theatrical interpretation of this dialogue, following the Prisoner from childhood to adulthood. It was the first story made to acknowledge its source material in the episode itself; 'Hammer into Anvil' later followed this lead with nods to Goethe and Cervantes. The script has echoes of both Harold Pinter and Samuel Beckett, playwrights who brought an extreme and surreal edge to human relationships and the human condition. Pinter's *The Birthday Party*, first performed in 1958, features equally disturbing interrogation scenes as Goldberg and McCann, two henchmen who work for an unknown organisation, intimidate their quarry, Stanley. Beckett's *Endgame*, first mounted in Britain in 1957, contains a very similar scenario to 'Once Upon A Time', with four char-

CAST

Guest Star
Leo McKern
Number 2
and featuring
Angelo Muscat
as the Butler
with

Umbrella Man
John Cazabon
Number 86*
John Maxim

*Credited but does
not appear

The Prisoner faces the final test in an intense psychological endgame with Number 2

The Outsider: Once Upon A Time

The Prisoner is regressed to his school days and faces Number 2 (Leo McKern) as his headmaster

Angelo Muscat played a variety of supporting characters in 'Once Upon A Time'

acters confined to a single set. Two of them, Hamm and Klov, are locked in a similar oedipal struggle to the Prisoner and Number 2. Fittingly, a stage production of McGoohan's script was mounted back-to-back with *Endgame* at the 1990 Edinburgh Festival.

Art also imitates life as McGoohan draws on his own background for the screenplay. While at school, and later when acting as a stage manager at Sheffield Rep, he was an enthusiastic amateur boxer. At school he excelled in mathematics and his enthusiasm for "the numbers" saw him working in a bank for a brief period before embarking on an acting career; these significant life experiences are directly alluded to in the script. Fiction and fact become blurred as Number 6 is recruited into security work, a reference to McGoohan's first successful television role as *Danger Man*. At one point Number 2 tells him not to grow up to be a "lone wolf";

this was *Danger Man*'s original title and was changed when the series went into production.

Production: Exact dates for the filming of 'Once Upon A Time' are uncertain, although it was certainly before the cameras on 7 December 1966. Apart from brief scenes in the control room, Number 2's office and the Prisoner's house, the action was confined to the single Embryo Room set with its caged living area. The minimalist production for the story was a result of *The Prisoner* running over budget; McGoohan allegedly wrote the pared-down episode to get the series back under financial control.

The episode was the first to deviate markedly from the action/adventure format, as McGoohan was well aware: "I don't blame the property master, Mickey O'Toole, who's a wicked Irishman with a great sense of humour, for saying 'What idiot wrote this?' The name I had on it when

Number 2 runs out of time and his death marks the Prisoner's final victory over the Village

I sent it down on to the set, because I knew I would be ridiculed, was 'Once Upon A Time by Archibald Schwarz'. So Mickey says, 'This Archibald Schwarz, where did you find this guy?' I said, 'He's a good lad, Mickey, trust me.' "

Apart from stock items such as a seesaw, swing, wardrobe and child's playpen, the set was dressed with props reused from other episodes. The strange wooden 'executive toy', which had previously appeared in 'Arrival', made its last appearance. The miniature tractors that had been used in Portmeirion were reused, along with the pedal bikes from the location shoot.

The strain of the demanding acting took its toll on Leo McKern. McGoohan's attitude to his guest actor was as confrontational as it had been when they first met, as Mckern remembers: "He was almost impossible to work with, a dreadful bully – always shouting and screaming and yelling about the place... I felt a dreadful sense of pressure all the time, being shouted at. It's not a thing actors enjoy very much; they ceratainly don't do their best work... I used to get very depressed, I remember... Certainly it doesn't inspire one to anything except withdraw into oneself, which I did a great deal of." The strain was so great that the actor had to stop filming for a considerable period of time, suffering from either a breakdown or heart attack. While McKern was absent from the set, McGoohan shot all he could with a stand-in. Perhaps due to production being interrupted, there is a continuity

"You knew the only way to beat me was to gain my respect and then I would confide"

error between some of the scenes. Number 2 is wearing his left arm in a sling, after being wounded by the Prisoner fencing and when he and Number 6 play-act an aerial bombing; in the scenes prior to and after these, his arm is perfectly healthy.

Following recording of 'The Schizoid Man', Anton Rodgers recalls seeing further filming being done on 'Once Upon A Time' – presumably the remainder of the scenes delayed due to McKern's illness. A sequence with John Maxim as Number 86, although shot, was removed at a late stage, even though the actor remains credited on the closing titles.

Tally Ho: *"Why do you care?" "You'll never know".* Over the past two stories *The Prisoner* had been developing as an uninhibited cinematic fantasy. 'Once Upon A Time' is a return to the programme's original subversive intentions and sees the ITC thriller format twisted as far as it wiĺl go. In many ways, it's more unsettling to watch than the surreal coda that follows.

The Butler ringing a bell to give Number 2 the cue to enter his control room hints at the story's formal and thematic realisation as a stage play. Indeed, 'Once Upon A Time' is the only *Prisoner* episode that can lay claim to being legitimate drama, despite moments of greatness elsewhere. McGoohan was drawing on his theatrical credentials by making its success rest entirely on the strength of the two central performances, and the commitment of the actors in the intense struggle is breathtaking.

The themes of the piece, with the Prisoner confronting various forms of authority throughout his life, cut to the very heart of the series. The production is also realised as a full-blown, malevolent fairy tale, as the change of title makes clear, building on the latent theme of the Villagers as children. Number 6 is mentally reconstructed as a child and the blanket use of nursery rhymes, in the dialogue and incidental music, make the adult nature of the conflict all the more disturbing.

The Prisoner's biggest achievement – ironically, it probably convinced George Markstein to leave – 'Once Upon A Time' is the nightmare flip side to the lightweight fairy tale of 'The Girl Who Was Death'.

PAWNS AND PLAYERS

Leo McKern had appeared alongside The Beatles in 1965's *Help!*, as the bungling assassin Clang, amidst a host of British sixties comedy talent such as Victor Spinetti, Roy Kinnear and Warren Mitchell. At the other end of the cultural scale, in July 1966 he took the lead role of the Greek philosopher Socrates in *The Drinking Party* and *The Death of Socrates* for the BBC, modern productions of Plato by Leo Aylen and Jonathan Miller. *The Daily Mail* was moved to comment that "Leo McKern as Socrates made the speech on the nature of love sound as if it had been newly minted." He moved closer to the world of *The Prisoner* when he worked with Jonathan Miller and the BBC again on a production of Lewis Carroll's *Alice in Wonderland* for Christmas 1966. With great aplomb, McKern dragged up as the Duchess. He appeared with such luminaries as Peter Cook as the Mad Hatter (of course), Peter Sellers as the King of Hearts and Alan Bennett as Mouse. 'Chimes' Finlay Currie also appeared in the production.

17: Fall Out

Written and Directed by Patrick McGoohan

A bizarre scene greets the Prisoner, Supervisor and Butler in the lower levels of the Village. A cavern contains a hooded and masked Assembly of citizens, together with a huge rocket. Number 6 is venerated as having passed the ultimate test. He is given the chair of honour and is addressed as 'Sir'. As he watches, the President of the Assembly oversees the trial of two rebels - the youthful Number 48 and the resurrected, turncoat Number 2 from the Degree Absolute test. After their conviction, the Prisoner is given the option to lead the Village or go. His address to the Assembly is drowned out by repeated shouts of "I! I! I!". The Prisoner is taken to meet Number 1 and is confronted by - himself. Recognising his evil side, he sets the rocket to launch and shoots his way out with Numbers 48 and 2 and the Butler, before leaving in a truck. The Village itself evacuates as the rocket lifts off. The rebels go their separate ways - Number 48 becomes a hitch-hiker and Number 2 returns to the Houses of Parliament - while the Butler and the Prisoner arrive back at the Prisoner's home in London. As the Butler enters the house, the door closes behind him automatically. As the Prisoner drives off in his reclaimed Lotus 7, there is a clap of thunder overhead...

The one-off title sequence finally acknowledges the real-life location of the Village

All together now: The resurrected Number 2 from the previous story rejects the Village and joins forces with the Prisoner, Number 48 (speaking the language of youth that the establishment can't understand) and the Butler, the little man on the winning side. All four combine to bring revolution to the Village.

Who is Number 1? You are, Number 6: Fittingly for a secret agent, 'Sir' knows how to launch a rocket. Contradicting his previous pacifist tendencies, he shows no compunction about using machine guns to kill, but enjoys showing a policeman how to dance to 'Dem Bones'. Finally, it is no surprise to find that the mastermind behind the Village is the dark side of the Prisoner himself.

One? Two? Three? Four?: 'Fall Out' was made 12 months after 'Once Upon A Time'. Leo McKern's head and beard had been shaved in the interim for a part in a play, so a scene was included to explain his change of appearance. The ending of the episode literally brings the series back to where it started, with the last shots reusing the opening scenes from the title sequence.

Information: 'Fall Out' was written and made against a background of political turbulence. The Cultural Revolution had taken place in China in 1966, and the Vietnam war was escalating – as was the protest against it; violence broke out during the first British demonstration against the conflict in October 1967. Throughout the summer of that year, youth culture advocated the benefits of mind-expanding chemicals and the promotion of peace. The volatile elements of revolution, violence and youthful rebellion were all dealt with in McGoohan's final anarchic script for *The Prisoner*.

The Beatles, and particularly 'All You Need Is Love', had been on McGoohan's mind since the song had been recorded for the first global satellite broadcast, *Our World*, (below left) which linked 24 countries on 25 June 1967. "The Beatles epitomise the age," he said. "They parody all the things we grown-ups pay lip service to, but don't practise. In one of their latest numbers they sing 'All You Need Is Love'. Just that – over and over again. Afterwards, you realise that love is the thing we have least of." The song was also Number 1 in the UK charts in July 1967; its use in 'Fall Out' was likely to have been at least partly another in-joke.

The President's description of the Prisoner as a "man of steel" is ambivalent. While it could be a reference to DC Comics' Superman, recognising Number 6's admirable qualities of self reliance and self sacrifice, the term is also the English translation of 'Stalin', the surname of the Communist tyrant, and raises disturbing issues about dictatorship. Clearly, the Prisoner is not vindicated unequivocally.

The Outsider: Fall Out

The Prisoner, rechristened "Sir", is offered the opportunity to lead the Village. But at what price?

"He has revolted, resisted, fought, held fast, maintained, destroyed resistance, overcome coercion... We applaud his private war, and concede that despite materialistic efforts, he has survived intact and secure. All that remains is, recognition of a *man*. A man of steel. A man magnificently equipped to lead us. That is, lead us – or go"

THE PRESIDENT

VILLAGE SLOGAN
Well Come

CAST
Guest Stars
Leo McKern
Number 2
Kenneth Griffith
The President
Alexis Kanner
Number 48
with
The Delegate
Michael Miller
Number 1 *
Roy Beck

Uncredited

FALL OUTS 1

At the end of the Prisoner, the Butler and the Supervisor's walk down the corridor of jukeboxes, the butler inserts a key into a lock and the next scene shows a door marked 'Well Come' opening onto the main cavern: originally, the opening door would have led into another passage.

Frogmen on miniature tractors and cycles respond to signs on the door at the far end of this corridor as Number 6, the Butler and Supervisor stroll down the middle. The set used for this deleted scene can be seen briefly during the Village's evacuation. It was also planned to show the President escaping in a helicopter, but the scene was never filmed.

Number 48's original dialogue included references to "the bright light, Dad", but these were all cut. The original script ends with the Prisoner following the Butler into his London home, the door closing and "Now hear the word of the Lord!" rising to full volume. Variations on the final scene were also shot, with the Butler running down the steps of the Prisoner's house and waving goodbye to him as he drives away in the Lotus.

McGoohan directs his co-stars Alexis Kanner and Leo McKern on the 'Fall Out' set

Production: During the previous episode in production, 'The Girl Who Was Death', McGoohan had announced that the next story would be the last and that he would write the script, which he did in December 1967. "We were shooting 'Girl' on the Thursday, finished on the Friday," Frank Maher remembers. "Pat went into his dressing room, and at that time I was living opposite the studio. I kept taking stuff in over the weekend – scotch, a plate of sandwiches... On Monday, the whole crew were kept waiting. We had a few pick-up shots to do so we busied ourselves doing that. Tuesday, the same. Wednesday morning, he appeared, absolutely shattered, really miserable, with the script."

Among those close to McGoohan, opinion on the last instalment was divided. Maher, not a man to mince words, "told Pat exactly what I thought: Rubbish!" David Tomblin was more considered in his appraisal. "It went back to conversations right at the beginning of the series, that one obviously needed a conclusion, and naturally one needed to analyse the conclusion before you wrote the series. We had a lot of conversations and discussed various possibilities, and all these things went into the mental computer and came out at the other end, not quite as we discussed it... I understood it better than most because I know Patrick and the way he thinks. But I'm not surprised that some people found it oblique." Tomblin was the first person to discover the final metaphysical twist of the elusive Number 1's identity. "I was with David, at some tea room or something," McGoohan recalls, "and said 'You'd better read this', and gave him the script. I sat at another table and sipped tea until he finished and gave it back to me. And he said, 'I thought it might be you in the end!'" The final twist, however bizarre, made sense artistically, with the Prisoner himself revealed as the ultimate gaoler. "If you sit down and look at it and think about it, it's a man destroying himself through ego," Tomblin points out, and McGoohan succinctly explains the chaos that follows the final revelation: "Get rid of Number 1, and we are free."

The main cast had all appeared in the series before. Following his cameo in the 'The Girl Who Was Death',

Number 48 (Alexis Kanner) leads the Assembly in a spirited rendition of the Negro spiritual 'Dry Bones'

Alexis Kanner became the personification of rebellious youth. He describes the process of filming the final episode as "absolutely extraordinary. I'd never worked on anything like that. Even playing strange Hamlets at the RSC for Peter Brook was nothing like 'Fall Out'. It was an experience that took a long time to get over, but it was a great experience, working with a very brilliant man."

The story continued directly on from 'Once Upon A Time', and depended on Leo McKern's participation. He was reluctant to return to a series that had made him seriously ill, but was eventually persuaded, with Kanner interceding on McGoohan's behalf. Kenneth Griffith, fresh from his portrayal of Dr Schnipps, took on the role of the President. Production of the episode was so rushed that McGoohan allowed Griffith to con-

tribute some dialogue: "He'd seen my documentary work, knew I could write and asked me to do the speech for the President. He said, 'Look, Ken, I'm so overworked. You write the thing. You know what it's about.' So I did it over the weekend, showed him on Monday morning and he said 'Yeah, fine.' " Peter Swanwick returned for the last time as the Supervisor and Angelo Muscat made his final appearance as the Butler. Roy Beck, a crowd artist, played Number 1 before the character's unmasking revealed McGoohan's face, much to Beck's disappointment.

The location work was shot first, in December 1967. A low-loader lorry carrying the Embryo Room Cage from 'Once Upon A Time' contained Kanner, McKern, McGoohan and Muscat as it broke through dummy gates

FALL OUTS 2

With time running short, stress was beginning to affect everyone on 'Fall Out', primarily McGoohan, who by this stage was trying to oversee all aspects of the production. This led to conflict with Frank Maher. "That jump from the spiral staircase was very difficult. We did it the way Pat insisted we do it, against my advice, and I went down and hit one of the lads with the fire extinguisher, one

with my elbow, one with my foot, and I got cut up. Now, one thing you don't do on a film set is piss off the stunt men... The bar was crowded that night as everybody in the studio had heard what had happened. Pat came in, and the guys with me were quite prepared to chuck him up in the air - it was really that bad. He turned, looked at the bloke behind the counter and said 'Get me four bottles of whisky for these guys.' I went, 'Oh, alright, give me the bottle then... But don't do that again, will you?' He said 'I won't', and I replied 'I know you won't'. And that was it. We drank the whisky."

The 'Fall Out' cavern was the single biggest sound stage constructed for the series

Len Harris behind the camera filming Number 48's ascent into the Assembly cavern

The President (Kenneth Griffith) awaits the outcome of the Prisoner's meeting with Number 1

covering the entrance to a disused railway tunnel in Mayfield, Sussex, symbolising the rebels' escape from the Village. The following scenes of the lorry on the A20 were actually filmed on the A1, before the loader entered central London for scenes shot in Trafalgar Square and on the Thames Embankment; other locations used were Westminster and Number 1 Buckingham Place. A replacement Lotus 7 was again used, driven by both Lotus' Graham Nearn (as a mechanic) and McGoohan himself, but the hearse was not the car previously used, as can be seen by its different number-plate, 289 LW. The Buckingham Place sequence included another in-joke: set dresser John Lageu hung a sign for 'Lageu and Sons Estate Agents' outside the Prisoner's home. He had previously been employed by De Havilland on the British space project and found the footage of the Blue Streak rocket lifting off, which was superimposed over shots of the Village. Unused footage of extras and location filming in Portmeirion were used for the evacuation, as well as

inserts from earlier episodes such as 'Arrival' and 'The General'.

Studio production commenced in early January 1968. Sets and props were utilised from other episodes, indicating that McGoohan wrote the finale around what was available. 'The Girl Who Was Death' cavern, which occupied the sound stage used for Number 2's office, was reused, along with that story's rocket and control room, and a section of corridor from 'The General'. Clips from 'Arrival', 'The Chimes of Big Ben', 'The General' and 'Once Upon a Time' were also shown on screens throughout the story. The show's final piece of model work was the death of Rover, inspired by Kanner spooning ice into his coffee and watching it bubble.

The varied use of music in 'Fall Out' helped to make the episode particularly striking. The original idea for the jukebox corridor scene was to have six songs blending into one another. These would have been the Beatles songs 'All You Need Is Love' and 'Yellow Submarine', Sandie Shaw's 'Puppet on a String', 'Little Boxes', Al Jolson's 'Toot-Toot-Tootsie Goodbye' and 'Hello, Dolly'. In the transmitted episode, only 'All You Need Is Love' was used. Music editor Eric Mival suggested using Carmen Miranda singing 'I Yi Yi I Like You Very Much'. The Four Lads' version of 'Dry Bones' was used after McGoohan decided a version specially re-recorded for *The Prisoner* with the Mike Sammes Singers (who had recently recorded backing vocals for The Beatles' 'I Am The Walrus') was unsuitable. Memorable tracks from the Chappell Music Library included 'September Ballad' by G. Bellington and the rousing 'Rag March' by J. Arel and J.C. Petit.

The beginning and end title sequences were also different. Edited highlights from 'Once Upon A Time' were shown before the opening credits, which were superimposed over aerial shots of the Village, with a caption slide finally revealing its location as Portmeirion. The end titles omitted the slamming bars animation, and when the pennyfarthing was fully formed there was no cut to film of Rover. In the 1984

The Prisoner finally comes face to face with Number 1 and is able to break free of the Village

repeat, Channel 4 repeated the slamming bars animation three times before the credits rolled, although this was corrected for the 1992 re-run.

In the trailer for the episode, the Prisoner's dialogue when he questions Number 2 about meeting Number 1 is slightly different. Instead of asking "Did you ever meet him?", the line is "Did you ever meet Number 1?".

Free to go: *"I'm an individual?" "You are on your own."* The culmination of the second production's block's experimentation with genre and imagery, 'Fall Out' rejects conventional narrative completely in favour of bizarre images and set pieces in a loose, symbolic fantasy. Its deliberately artificial feel is a stark contrast to the careful construction of an authentic alternative reality seen in 'Arrival'.

This was the end of the line for Patrick McGoohan as a bankable ITC adventure star, and the last episode revels in it. If 'Once upon A Time' was the action thriller format twisted to breaking point, 'Fall Out' is 50 minutes of genre meltdown: the 1967 007 spoof *Casino Royale as* rewritten by Samuel Beckett and directed by Richard Lester. On a thematic level, 'Fall Out' restates even more strongly 'Free For All''s point that the man in charge still remains a prisoner. (The soundtrack even reprises the ironic refrain of 'For He's a Jolly Good Fellow' from the earlier production). Significantly, a scene towards the end shows the President sitting in the Prisoner's Chair of Honour.

Despite McGoohan's protests that he wasn't going to give the audience what they expected, namely "some James Bond villain with bald head and gold teeth", what he did do was subvert the ingredients of the secret agent genre; the cavern with its military guards, rocket and hidden mastermind bears a striking resemblance to the SPECTRE base at the climax of the 1967 Bond epic *You Only Live Twice.* However, instead of set-

Alexis Kanner takes a break between takes

piece pyrotechnics there are songs and a trial, the master villain is the hero's insane alter ego, and the main character is asked to lead the organisation he has fought for so long rather than destroy it. Ironically, the climax, with the evacuation of the installation, a shoot-out and the launch of a missile, could superficially be the climax of any mid-sixties super spy caper. The Prisoner and his gang suddenly opting for killing rather than pacifist resistance give the final scenes extra satirical bite, as does the dubbing of 'All You Need is Love' over scenes of mass slaughter.

'Fall Out'is over ambitious and that is precisely why *The Prisoner* is still argued over, written about and discussed more than thirty years after its original broadcast. (Like the episode, its title is the most ambiguous of the whole series.) Had *The Prisoner* ended in a way that made conventional sense, something that would have undoubtedly pleased the long departed George Markstein, it would probably be remembered today as a contemporary of *The Avengers* and "that one with the big white balloon". One can't help comparing the last episode with the sonic anarchy of The Beatles' 'A Day In The Life', the last song on their 1967 album *Sergeant Pepper's Lonely Hearts Club Band*. The song helped secure that LP's iconic status as the definitive pop cultural statement of the mid-1960s, if not the whole decade. Indeed, it's hard not to see *The Prisoner* doing for the film and TV medium what *Sergeant Pepper* did for popular music, even if the series was much less successful commercially.

'Fall Out' is confused, messy and inconsistent, and all those qualities make it great. It was a slap in the face for traditional viewing expectations, changing the relationship between television and audiences forever. In doing this, 'Fall Out' secured forever *The Prisoner's* reputation as a truly unique example of British film-making, at its creative, challenging and inspiring

PAWNS AND PLAYERS

After 'Fall Out', Leo McKern featured in the TV play *On the Eve of Publication* (1968) by the playwright David Mercer. He went on to carve out his own niche in TV history as the pugnacious barrister Horace Rumpole in *Rumpole of the Bailey,* which ran intermittently between 1978 and 1992. Kenneth Griffith went on to play Edward Woodward's irritating boss Waterman in the film version of *Callan* (1974). As a documentary film maker, he made a series of highly regarded films in his drive to discover "nothing but the truth" about British imperialism. They include *Soldiers of the Widow* (1972), *Sons of the Blood* (1977), *I Have Promises to Keep* (1987) and *Hang Up Your Brightest Colours* (1973), about the life of the Irish republican leader Michael Collins, which was banned by the BBC for twenty years. Alexis Kanner played Lord Tarquin Etherley in *Crossplot* (1969), another hippy character who stood for "peace against chaos".McGoohan himself starred in thirteen episodes of *Rafferty* (1977) as an abrasive medical doctor, before swashing his buckle as the deliciously villainous Fouquet in Sir Lew Grade's production of Mike Newell's *The Man in the Iron Mask* (1977).

Curiosity to cult

"You're watching Channel Number 4"

TV announcer before the broacast of 'Arrival' on Channel 4, September 19 1983

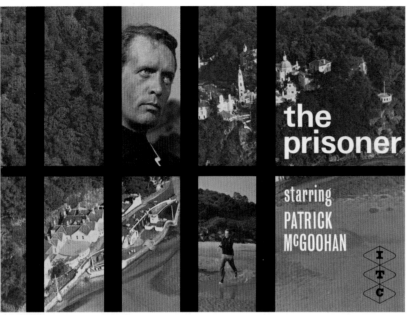

the prisoner

starring
PATRICK
McGOOHAN

ITC

Who is THE PRISONER?
He is played by Patrick McGoohan . . . in a new, startling characterisation . . . a man without a name and whose background is wreathed in mystery . . . now a captive in the most intriguing, menacing, yet beautiful prison in the world . . . a very lovely village . . . but how to escape?
THE PRISONER is the most challenging and unusual series ever filmed for television, devised by Patrick McGoohan himself. It is a series with depth: stories that will make viewers think, and, at the same time, will keep them on the edge of their seats in excitement as the Prisoner resists every physical and mental effort to break him. There is mounting suspense as each new dramatic story is unfolded . . . stories of one man's tremendous, unflinching battle for survival as an individual in a macabre world in which every move is watched by electronic eyes and in which all his neighbours are suspect.
Where is the village? Who are his captors? Who are his fellow prisoners? What country is he in? Viewing appeal which is simultaneously electrifying, controversial and gripping.
A series of one-hour dramas filmed in colour, for ITC WORLD-WIDE DISTRIBUTION.

Above: The cover and an inside spread from the promotional brochure for *The Prisoner* and (right) the story information book used to promote the series in the sixties

story information

THE PRISONER

INCORPORATED TELEVISION COMPANY LTD.
ATV HOUSE, 17 Great Cumberland Place, London, W1

ITC

THE PRISONER'S SUBVERSION OF A popular television form, its double edge of thriller and satire, and the effect its behind-the-scenes turbulence had on the series' content, meant that it was always going to get a mixed reception.

To begin with, the programme was marketed as something special, the vision of one man – "No actor has been more closely identified with a programme"– and a cut above usual thriller fare. More than anything else, the intrigue and mystery surrounding the programme was promoted: "Where is the Village?" "Who is [Number 1] and will he ever be seen?" "Who is the strange dwarf?" Significantly, the press pack firmly assures the reader that "the secrets are revealed as the series progresses." The show's sole creator (according to advance publicity), McGoohan himself, gave an encouraging response to all questions: "Wait and see!"

The Prisoner's official press launch at Borehamwood studios in September 1967 was to be indicative of the star's attitude in the coming weeks. While the hospitality may have been exemplary, McGoohan's presence at the event did nothing to answer any of the queries raised by a press screening of 'Arrival'. Indeed, he was keener on asking questions of the audience rather than giving explanations: "What about the big ball? What did it represent?... How about the old bicycle? Do you think it has any special significance?"

As the series began transmission in the UK, the response was indeed a mixed one. Bewilderment, enthusiasm for such a radical new approach to television and outright condemnation at the show's pretensions, among critics and the general public alike, was the general spread of opinion. *The Sun* saw nothing original in the programme at all, condemning the use of "every phoney science-fiction device in the book". *The Daily Mail* was more positive, commending *The Prisoner*'s skilful balance of the cerebral and the bizarre: "The withholding of the customary straight-forward narrative that moves from start to finish like a fist to a jaw makes it challenging stuff in terms of TV fiction." *The Sunday Telegraph* was equally complimentary, praising the series' artistic ambitions highly over

McGoohan in kosho outfit at *The Prisoner* press conference in September 1967, which was held during the production of 'Living in Harmony'

Above: Jack Shampan's design sketch for the 1967 press conference

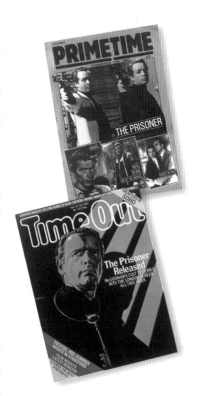

The rescreening of the series in London in 1982 was heavily promoted

the less challenging fare that could be found elsewhere in the thriller genre, claiming that *The Prisoner* "makes the average Bond epic seem as straight-forward as a child's nursery rhyme."

The key to how *The Prisoner* was received in the UK in the 1960s was the belief by the public, the media and even the programme's makers, that, come the final reel, everything would be explained. The weekly litany of questions asked by Number 6 in the title sequence seemed to make this a foregone conclusion, and ATV's press department continued to adopt this line throughout the series' broadcast. An enquiry by a 'J. Lennon' of London about the significance of the pennyfarthing symbol in the 4-10 October issue of *TV Times* brought this unequivocal response from 'a programme company spokesman': "the reason for it will be revealed later in the series." McGoohan himself remained either confrontational or tight-lipped throughout the show's run. At the eleventh hour, pushed by the *TV Times*' Anthony Davis into answering whether the final episode would explain where the Village was, who ran it and who Number 1 was he had to finally admit – "It doesn't." On the eve of 'Fall Out''s transmission, the wisely anonymous company spokesman was also backtracking: "The answers are there... but not in black and white. The viewer will have to use some imagination and read between the lines."

'Fall Out''s wild ambiguity was not received well. Any sympathy that McGoohan's experiment in film-making had in the media up until now evaporated with the final instalment's deliberate obliqueness. The gen-

eral consensus was of a sophisticated joke having been played on the viewing public; the unmasked Number 1's hysteria was taken as a good laugh at the expense of the audience. Barry Norman's review in the *Daily Mail* was typical, when he concluded, "the final episode was carried off with all the smoothness of a confidence trick." Elsewhere, *The Daily Telegraph* carried a front-page story headlined 'Angry viewers left in dark on Prisoner', with a report of ATV's switchboard being jammed due to complaints from viewers about the "incomprehensible" final episode. A few complimentary letters in the *TV Times* and *TV World* aside, the programme seemed destined for oblivion. The reaction in the US was similar to the UK's, and equally muted. While praising the artistry of the production, the American *TV World* concluded, "such murky symbolism seems unlikely to win high ratings."

The Prisoner was saved by being made as a film series for global syndication by ITC. It would always be repeated somewhere in the world, and despite its "murky symbolism", or more probably because of it, it would always find new audiences.

The Prisoner entered a late night, regional re-run slot in the UK during 1969 and into 1970. This was standard practice for film series after a first-run during peak viewing hours, and the initial repeats attracted little comment. A further batch of re-runs took place in 1976-7; when the press did notice the late-night outings of Number 6 the response still tended to be hostile. "It must be the biggest confidence trick ever played on the viewing public," Richard Afton grumbled in the *Evening News*, after catching an episode on London Weekend Television. "I didn't understand it when it was first shown ten years ago, and time hasn't changed my views.... One fortunate thing is that LWT are putting it out at 11.45 p.m., so we can go to bed and ignore it." However, the screenings inspired the first stirrings of an

THE PRISONER

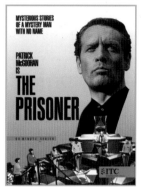

Marketing material from Bravo, ITC, Polygram and Carlton International

organised *Prisoner* fandom, when enthusiast Dave Barrie's address was given after the final episode was shown in the Midlands and like-minded individuals came together to form the Six of One appreciation society.

By the 1980s, an enthusiasm for archive television in the UK had resulted in the foundation of the organisation Wider Television Access, which promoted the past of television through events – usually screenings of old pro-grammes – and its magazine *Primetime.* In the days before affordable home videos, there was little easy access to vintage television. In 1982, WTVA helped keep the *Prisoner* flame alive by screening the entire series, between 24 and 31 of July at the Scala Cinema in London, with most of the episodes screened three times a day. For such an old series media coverage was surprisingly high-profile, with *Time Out*, London's premier listings magazine, granting *The Prisoner* a cover story for its 23-29 July issue.

Television itself was also becoming aware of the rich heritage locked away in its vaults. In the same month as the Scala screenings, ITV broadcast a late night season of archive repeats under the title *Best of British*, with *The Prisoner* as one of the highlights. Although the episode chosen was hardly typical – 'The Girl Who Was Death' – *The Daily Mirror*, rather than deriding the show, considered the behind-the-scenes story of "a mystery series that left everybody baffled" worthy of a write-up. In the absence of the elusive McGoohan, George Markstein received some long overdue media exposure and credit for his part in the series' origination.

Channel 4 began broadcasting in the UK in September 1983, with a specific policy of showing television classics. In an unprecedented move, a series that was by now seventeen years old received another primetime repeat, accompanied by the first TV documentary – *Six Into One: The Prisoner File* – to investigate seriously the pro-gramme's production and cult afterlife.

With the show's revival taking it into the iconic year of 1984, it tied into the obvious cultural interest and marketing opportunities made available by the year

coinciding with the title of George Orwell's novel. In a story titled 'The Prisoner Comes of Age' in the right-wing *Daily Mail*, Markstein, for the first time in the press credited as the show's "creator", likened the series to contemporary equivalents: "London as Ken Livingstone and his left-wingers would like it to be, per-haps even Poland with Solidarity playing the role of Number 6." The story's writer, Corinna Hollan, described the series as "timeless and ageless", and its by now confirmed 'cult' status – that is, as a programme with a limited appeal for a small but dedicated audience – was put down to the unanswered questions left by the final episode. Following Channel 4's first screening, the programme would be periodically revived by satellite stations like Bravo and the Sci-Fi Channel.

There is no little irony in the fact that *The Prisoner*'s perceived faults became its major selling points and ensured it longevity over the years. The very things that were seen as deficiencies in the programme in the 1960s – that it was confusing, weird and deliberately obscure – were now considered benefits by the programme's marketers and incorporated into its promotion. ITC pub-licity material in 1989 billed the series as "mysterious stories of a man with no name," and, nine years later, the UK thirtieth anniversary video box set made virtues of the series being "mind boggling" and "bizarre," pro-moting it as "the most acclaimed cult series of all time." In 2000, the series had its own corporate style guide commissioned by Carlton International and was the first ITC action series to be released on DVD.

How Patrick McGoohan must have laughed.

5 A Home for Fallen Buildings

T HE TIGHT, TWISTING STAIRCASES, colonnaded walkways and deceptive false perspectives of Portmeirion are a perfect visual metaphor for the equally labyrinthine plots of *The Prisoner.* It's easy to see how Patrick McGoohan's mind must have been working when he considered the architectural hotch-potch as the location for his new series in 1966. The colourful, picturesque nature of the place was also an ideal showcase for the full colour film medium ITC was just beginning to use in the making of its TV series.

Architect errant

The other-worldly haven of Portmeirion is synonymous with its creator, Sir Bertram Clough Williams-Ellis (1883–1978) and remains the best known example of his considerable achievements. He was educated at Trinity College, Cambridge and then at the Architectural Association School in London, (1902–03). A man deeply passionate about keeping the modern world in balance with nature, Clough had been looking for a site for implementing his belief that architecture could be developed in harmony with a naturally beautiful area. In 1925 he found it.

Clough originally wanted to establish his idealised township on an island, (an interesting coincidence, considering the Village's apparent location off the Coast of Portugal and Spain in 'Many Happy Returns'). However, the practicalities of building and access eventually made him abandon the idea. In the end, he found the ideal region, the Aber Iâ peninsula, five miles from his own home in North Wales. The site was purchased from his uncle, Sir Osmond Williams, for just under £5,000. Aber Iâ is Welsh for 'frozen mouth' – a forbidding title that perfectly described the "neglected wilderness" Clough found when he inspected the site.

He changed the name almost immediately; its new title was, quite simply, a description of the geographical location: Port – its position on the coast – and Meirion, from Merioneth, the county where it was situated. Seeing it as a world apart, he resolved to "keep Portmeirion free from any foreseeable enrichment – a tight little knot of controlled development, forever, as now, set in its green belt of woods and farmland".

In the village

By 1965, the main features of the village were either constructed or renovated, most of which were to form the Prisoner's eye view of his confining but beautiful environment (see side bars on the following pages). The buildings and statuary that went into the creation of the village were salvaged from all over the United Kingdom – leading Clough to dub Portmeirion "a home for fallen buildings" – and restored in a variety of Mediterranean and classical styles which deliberately contradicted each other. This architectural kaleido-

Portmeirion's founder,
Sir Clough Williams-Ellis

Left: Filming the human chess game on the lawn outside the Gothic Pavilion, in September 1966

Below: Clough's published writings on portmeirion and his life

THE CAMPANILE/
THE BELL TOWER

Built in 1928 from an initial sketch by Clough Williams-Ellis, it is designed to reflect the feel of Italian towns like Portofino. A bell tower dated back to his earliest plans for Portmeirion (below), its main function being to attract attention to the development of the site. It housed an old chiming turret clock from a demolished brewery in London that was used to mark the passing of the hour in the village. The Bell tower is visible in most episodes, but is prominent in 'Arrival', when the Prisoner climbs it to survey his new environment; in 'Many Happy Returns', when he uses the bell to try and summon the absent Villagers; and in 'It's Your Funeral', when an assassination is attempted from the Tower.

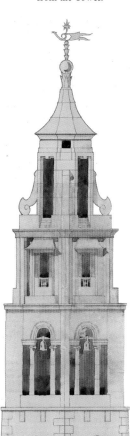

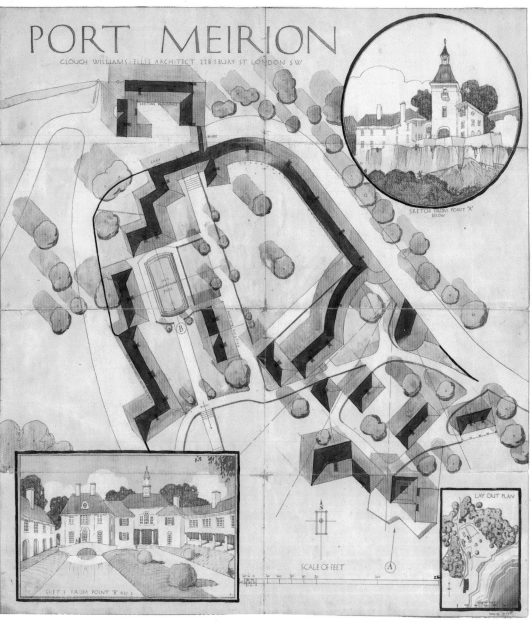

Clough Williams-Ellis' original visualisation of Portmeirion, painted in 1927

scope was always deliberate, as Clough explained: "I was aiming at winning an, as yet, uninterested and uninformed popular support for architecture, planning, landscaping, the use of colour and indeed for design generally, by a gay, light-opera sort of approach." This undoubtedly worked, with an average of over 100,000 people visiting the village every year. But there was also something distinctly disorientating about the place, as James Morris noted in the architectural journal *Horizon*. "The contrived fizz of the place is intoxicating, and we stagger through all this exuberance rather dizzily.... I can't quite define the effect of Portmeirion; I can only express my own reaction –

something between a scoff, a gasp and an ecstasy... its charm is partly the serenity of a lost society with time, money, talent and hospitality to spare." If someone opened their eyes to such a place one morning, it's easy to see how they would wonder where in the world they in fact were.

Such a unique location had a lasting impact on the direction *The Prisoner* took. As well as the obvious tactic of basing the geography of the Village around Portmeirion's best known landmarks, its striking how many other details of the place worked their way into the fabric of the show. The residents' dwellings in the series have 'Private' signs hanging outside and the warning 'Residents only' can be seen outside the Old People's Home. A closer inspection of Portmeirion today reveals identically worded signs outside the buildings. These were part of the village's original décor and seemingly worked their way into the art department's brief during a reconnaissance of the site in Summer 1966, neatly adding to the ironic nature of the stylised open prison. The circular motif, so memorably used throughout the series, occurs many times in the village's architecture, whether in arches, patterns of paving, windows or the shape of the buildings themselves. Most notably, when the domed, circular Pantheon had been chosen as Number 2's residence instead of the more conventional Unicorn cottage, the interior set became circular to reflect the proportions of the exterior location; it also formed the basis of all the major sets in the series. Significantly, Portmeirion has always been known locally as 'the village.'

Sometimes an effect resulting from the predominance of circular imagery in the location and the imagination of the production team was a happy accident. In 'Arrival', the Prisoner pauses and scrutinises the statue of Hercules, supporting a sphere that represents the Earth. There is a direct visual link made between this image and the later appearance of the balloon-like Village guardian Rover. As filmed, such a smooth com-

THE ROUND HOUSE/ NUMBER 6

A bow-fronted gate-house, built 1959-60, the Round House is one of a pair of Baroque shops, similar in style to Cornwell village hall which Clough rebuilt in 1938. In The Prisoner, it was otherwise known as the exterior of Number 6's residence. In later years, the building housed the Prisoner Shop and Information Centre, rented from the Portmeirion estate and run by Max Hora of Six of One, between September 1982 and January 1998. The shop returned to the authority of Portmeirion that year; the interior was refurbished and the frontage restored to the original design. The shop is now known, succinctly, as 'Number 6'.

Portmeirion photographed from the air in 1966 during production of _The Prisoner_

Right: Helweun Vaughan-Hatcher in her 'Dance of the Dead' costume

CASTELL DEUDRAETH/ THE HOSPITAL

Castell Deudraeth developed from an eighteenth-century cottage and a mansion known as Bron Eryri. During the 1850s it was enlarged and renamed after an original castle built around 1175. Clough's purchase of it in 1931 substantially added to his estate and his intention was always to use it as an extension of hotel rooms for the village. This has only happened recently; at the time of writing, the Castell is currently being refitted from its previous function as staff accommodation. Such a gothic edifice was entirely appropriate as the Hospital, with Number 6 and the other residents often on the receiving end of its special brand of treatment.

THE TOWN HALL

Also known as Hercules Hall as it faces the statue of the Greek hero sculpted by William Brodie in 1863, the Town Hall (right) was constructed over 1937–38 and was built to house a Jacobean ceiling, panelling and mullioned windows acquired by Clough from a demolished Emral Hall in Flintshire. It is the single most substantial building in Portmeirion and one of the most distinctive. The only building known by its own name in the series, the Town Hall is prominent in much of the fill-in footage used throughout *The Prisoner*, particularly in aerial views.

bination of iconography, recalling the sympathetic interior design of Number 2's office seen earlier in the episode, adds up to a unifying sense of strangeness.

A stay on the site also reveals an interior décor in keeping with the up-market combination of classical and modern styles seen on some of the programme's other interior sets. Portmeirion managing director Robin Llewlyn confirms that the character of the village's living areas influenced McGoohan and his keenness on their opulent clutter was passed on to Art Director Jack Shampan.

The false perspectives and deceptive sense of scale used in the construction of the buildings are also perfectly suited to the village's use as a film set. On television, this means that Portmeirion looks much larger than it actually is; sly editing and careful camera angles hide notable details like the village shop being next door to Number 6's house, and Number 2 being the Prisoner's next door neighbour.

Extra! Extra!

An integral part of the story of *The Prisoner*'s filming in Wales is the role played by the local people as extras and on-site help. The production team arrived in Portmadoc, the town immediately adjacent to Portmeirion, on Saturday 3 September 1966. They stayed in Portmeirion for four weeks in what was to be the first extensive use of the location by a film unit. Extras were recruited through the local job centre and the telephone exchange.

Helweun Vaughan-Hatcher, then a 25-year old telephonist, and until December 2000 the manager of

The Prisoner Shop, remembers the selection process.

"A member of the casting crew came to work and explained to us girls that they were looking for extras to be in a TV series called *The Prisoner*. Extras were required between the hours of 8am and 5pm (or when called) and the filming was to take place in Portmeirion. He went on to say that if we were interested, to report to the Town Hall in the village the next day for interviews. There must have been 50 or 60 people there and we were all seen separately. There were four people sitting behind a desk [one of whom was director Don Chaffey] at the far end of the room. They asked me my vital statistics, age and availability. Then they had a little discussion and finally told me I would be a Mini Moke driver and would I bring a bikini on the first day of shooting! We were then told that the star of the series was Patrick McGoohan of *Danger Man* which got all of us girls excited!"

Such was the appeal of working on the filming that most of the telephone exchange staff ended up being involved, and had to juggle their various responsibilities so they could be included. Nel Roberts, now in her nineties, remembers the hectic schedule. "It was a bit awkward as I was part of the evening shift at the Exchange from 6.00 until 12.00. We all decided to go anyway as they told us we would finish filming by 5.00. We had to be in Portmeirion by 8 o'clock, work until 5.00 and rush home to make the children's tea and go to work by 6.00. God knows how we managed it."

Of the people, by the people

For Marjorie Beer, initially taken on as an extra, the production became something of a family affair, as her relations became involved in several areas of the filming.

"My son Raymond did the dry cleaning for Patrick McGoohan. We had a dry cleaning and laundry business then and he put on a special shift in the evening. He used to come down and collect Patrick's clothes that he was wearing that day, because he used to do fights on the beach, and get all wet and sand everywhere. So Raymond used to take the clothing and bring them back for the following morning.

"They hired my husband's boat, the Breda, for two days, for £10. They rechristened it the *MS Polotska* and it also became a gunrunners' ship. Patrick McGoohan had to do the fight on board, but the scene where they rip up the inside of the boat, and smash up the galley, was done in the studio; they couldn't smash my husband's boat up – it would have cost them too much! Patrick kept saying they had to get on with it as it was costing money."

Some of the local people became involved in the more physical side of the shoot. William Parry's robust physique enabled him to take in part in some scenes that unfortunately didn't make it into the finished episodes. "I did the fighting in the pool with the stuntman [cut from 'Arrival']. Then later on I fell backwards out of a tower from quite a height into some tyres." He also pedalled a 100-year-old pennyfarthing around Portmeirion, although this footage was also unused.

The danger man

Brian Axworthy was to make a significant contribution in assisting *The Prisoner* unit during its stay. In 1966, as a young, qualified diver interested in water sports, he became a man in demand for his variety of skills. "In those days I was very keen on diving and water skiing, and I had a powerboat, a Doughty Jet Drive, that could operate in very low levels of water. And they [the production team] were interested. A guy called Eric Miles,

who ran Gwynedd Marine, contacted them and hired out my boat. So my mate Jock and I came across and met the producer and he said 'Can you water ski out there?', meaning the bay, and I said 'Sure'."

Footage shot with Brian included him doubling for McGoohan in a long shot in the speed boat chase in 'Free For All' and the brief scene with Number 6 "cooling off" water skiing in 'It's Your Funeral'. His experience as a diver led him to play a major part in the execution of one of the programme's most memorable special effects.

"Then they said 'Do you do any diving, because there's a call for divers to release charged balloons underwater?' Those Rover things were inflated under water with a compressed air cylinder and we used to hold them down with an old engine block. Jock would be at the top waiting for the signal, give us a wave that the camera was rolling and then up it would go. At other times we used to spend ages rigging up that balloon thing and getting jeeps to pull it... And then I became friendly with Patrick McGoohan. I met him when I brought my children here and he rather took to

THE PANTHEON/ THE GREEN DOME

In the late 1950s, Clough felt Portmeirion was suffering from "Dome deficiency" so the Pantheon (above) was constructed. The impressive, ornate gothic porch was in reality a huge Norman Shaw fireplace of red Runcorn sandstone from Dawpool, Cheshire. Owing in part to its position as one of the Village's most striking buildings, Clough's memorial plaque now hangs there. Referred to in The Prisoner as "the Green Dome" – since the series was made the green copper dome has faded. The Pantheon features throughout the series as the Village chairman's striking residence.

Left: McGoohan with Brian Axworthy's daughter Susan during location shooting for 'Many Happy Returns'

Home movie footage showing the filming of 'Dance of the Dead', with Frank Maher doubling for Patrick McGoohan (above)

my little daughter. He'd go along and have a chat with her. I never saw his girls, but he showed me photographs like parents do. And then it sort of escalated. I was here for about three months in all, and I nearly lost my job at the airfield!

"Whenever McGoohan went out on a boat, he wanted a diver. He had ear trouble, and hated going in the water, so I used to jump in and do a lot of the shots. He's taller than I am but we're about the same size oth-

erwise. And I also used to go out as a safety diver."

In his capacity as the star's double, Brian Axworthy stood in for the leading man during the shooting of some of the raft scenes in 'Many Happy Returns'.

The little man

A young married couple, Douglas and Catherine Williams, also had an important part to play in assisting the team from Borehamwood. "I was hauled into the

Top: In publicity shots for 'arrival', Virginia Maskell and Barbara Yu Ling pose on Portmerion's quayside and on Amis Reunis (the Stone Boat). Above: filming the Alouette helicopter coming in to land, September 1966

A Home for Fallen Buildings

wardrobe, because the original wardrobe master, Bob Smithers, didn't come," says Catherine today. "So Masada Wilmot came. A wonderful character, who became a close friend of mine. But she used to get rather irate if things went wrong. So I was put in because I didn't get so het up about things, and I was here for the whole time that the film unit was." One of her first tasks was to be responsible for costuming one of the series' most distinctive characters.

"I was on my own then as Masada had gone back to London. And we got Angelo Muscat. I looked all through *Spotlight* and couldn't find him. Now, the prop boys are notoriously naughty with wardrobe. I said to Mickey O'Toole I'd never heard of him [Angelo] and he said 'Oh, he's a great big lad.' So anyway, the next morning at quarter past five, I was standing at the far end of the wardrobe room in the corner and Pat walked in and said 'I've brought Angelo Muscat.' Well...! He needed tails, and I had nothing whatsoever that would fit. So, the only thing I could use was a black donkey jacket, so I cut the tails out of that."

In the meantime, her husband Doug also became involved in the production. As a strong swimmer, he was involved in sequences shot at sea using the Breda, doubling for McGoohan with Axworthy. He was also able to procure a stand in for one of the cast who

proved temperamental during the shoot for 'Dance of the Dead' and 'Many Happy Returns'. "The black cat was mine, because the one they brought from London wouldn't work because of the whirring of the cameras. I had a beautiful cat called Tammy, and we tried her out, and she worked perfectly, much better than their one. The best thing was, the cat was paid far more than the humans!"

The Williams have strong memories of the actor who played the diminutive butler. Catherine: "He wasn't at all good tempered. He was a wrestler and had worked in a circus. He didn't communicate very easily with anybody, really. He was a strange little person." Doug remembers he was very particular about his stature. "He was a dwarf. You couldn't call him a midget. He wouldn't like that at all. But he did what he was told, and was very good at following the director."

Who is Number 1?

Sir Clough Williams-Ellis was present throughout the September 1966 shoot. By then a gently eccentric man in his 80s, he could be seen wandering around the village in his preferred outfit of *Tin Tin*-style plus fours (which he allegedly never washed). Brian Axworthy remembers some amusing incidents concerning Portmeirion's patriarch.

THE BRISTOL COLONNADE/ THE BANDSTAND

The Colonnade (below) was relocated from Bristol, where it had originally been built in 1760 by the Quaker cooper smelter William Reeve. Damaged by bombing during the Second World War, it was removed to Portmeirion and rebuilt stone by stone by Clough Williams-Ellis' master stone mason William Davies and finally restored in 1959. The Colonnade features in 'Free For All' and 'Dance of the Dead', and housed the Village band in 'Arrival', 'The General' 'Hammer into Anvil' and 'It's Your Funeral'. In Portmeirion today, members of the local brass band can often be heard paying renditions of the *Danger Man* and *The Prisoner* themes in the same position as their sixties counterparts.

A Home for Fallen Buildings

119

THE HOTEL / THE OLD PEOPLE'S HOME

What now stands as the impressive hotel was originally the mansion of Aber Iâ, built in 1850 and expanded by Clough in 1926 and 1930. It was the first building on the site to open to the public, beginning its new life as a hotel during Easter 1926. Owing to its secluded location, over the years it played host to a distinguished clientele, including H.G. Wells, George Bernard Shaw and Noel Coward. During fine weather, guests would often take tea on the lawn, a ritual that was co-opted into *The Prisoner* when the hotel became the Old People's Home. Throughout many of the episodes residents can be seen there enjoying the view of the bay and the sunshine. Number 6 would often play chess – in 'Arrival', 'Chimes' and 'It's Your Funeral' – and Number 9 observed from there his aborted escape by helicopter in the first episode. The Hotel is adjacent to a lawn where the Village helicopter used to land, although today the area is now occupied by a swimming pool. Like the Gloriette, the front of Number 2's residence, Number 6's house and the path through to the Town Hall via the Hercules statue, the lawn and frontage of the Old People's home were recreated as studio mock-ups at Borehamwood.

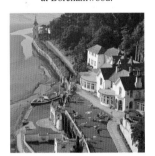

Clough Williams-Ellis observes the filming of one of the early episodes of *The Prisoner*

"We had a funny scene once down on the lawn outside the Hotel. Clough was here watching the filming, and he would get a priority place with a table and chair. He shouldn't have been in the sequence and he kept on moving. In the end, the director said 'Get that bloody man out of here!' as nobody knew who he was! They asked him to leave, and he said 'I might be asking you to leave.' When they finally realised that he owned the place, they said, all apologetic, 'Would you like to be in this film?' 'Um... Oh yes,' he said. You'll never see him, as it's all background shots."

The abiding memories of most of the local people are a mixture of bemusement and excitement at being involved with such a curious production. Leri Roberts, a long-time Portmadoc resident, remembers the experience fondly. "They were paying £2.50 – it was a lot of money then. My husband Danny was here as well, he was in the band and on the chessboard. We had fun but it was hard work as well some days. I was here for about three to four weeks in 1966 and the weather was beautiful. It was easy to get up out of bed in the morning to come here. And they treated us very well. Breaks in the morning, trays full of pork pies and sandwiches, sausage rolls and all that."

The first, major block of filming finished with two parties, one for the production team and the other for the extras. With Patrick McGoohan's renowned gen-

erosity, it was understandable, that some of the locals gave in to over-indulgence. Catherine Williams recalls: "Pat gave this wonderful unit party, it must have cost him a bomb, in this classy hotel in Tremadoc. That was for the behind the scenes people, he came to that, and then they had one for the extras that I went to and it was *horrendous*. Open bar, and people who used to usually drink pints were on whisky chasers, brandy and gin and were just ending up under the table."

Many happy returns

The unit left Portmeirion at the beginning of October 1966. Although an Everyman Films team was to return in March 1967, that visit was not on the same scale as the September shoot. Only a little work with extras was needed to complement scenes shot at Borehamwood in the intervening months and McGoohan was the only major actor to reappear. At the time, for a production team to be based in a location for so long was a luxury usually only afforded feature films. The residency of *The Prisoner* team definitely left its mark. "No one will ever recapture the atmosphere that the team brought here," says Catherine Williams now. "Some people were quite affected by it. They used to ring me up and ask me 'Have you heard if they're coming back?' A lot of the extras missed the film unit when they went; some of them had quite a gap in their lives."

Now, however, most of the people involved in the 1966 shoot are happy to be associated with the continued worldwide interest in *The Prisoner*. Portmeirion has become a predictable focus for this enthusiasm, with the official appreciation society Six of One's conventions based there. The locals are often invited along and are happy to share their memories, all bar Brain Axworthy; one of the people with the most to offer, he simply says he is "not one for reunions".

As for the philosophical nature of the series, the opinions of those involved in some of its most memorable sequences are as varied as the views of the general public. Doug and Catherine Williams describe the series' impact. "I think it was at least 10 years ahead of its time, in its thinking and the way McGoohan projected it," says Doug. "And I should think when it came round the second time, people started to realise how good it was. It was different to *Danger Man* and all the stuff he'd done before. People thought because it was all filmed in Portmeirion it was a fantasy, but it wasn't,

Local extras enjoying their involvement in the first Portmeirion location shoot in September 1966

it was really ahead of its time." Catherine analysed its appeal both as entertainment and modern parable.

"When you think about it, with all the smut and all the sleaze and all the violence you see today, there was nothing like that in *The Prisoner*. That was one rule [McGoohan] made. He wanted his children, his girls, to be able to watch it; no innuendoes, nothing. And it is today's world. We are all numbers. The other day I was ringing for theatre tickets and before I even opened my mouth they knew who I was.... And we are zombified, because you go to a hospital, or airport, you do as you're told. You follow this sign, follow that sign...." Leri Roberts echoes the view held by many people involved in the production, from Patrick McGoohan on down: "We never thought, in 1966, that for something so weird it'd catch on so much. Over thirty years and we're still talking about it!"

With Portmeirion fast approaching its hundredth anniversary, it's a certainty that interest in *The Prisoner* will endure as long as Sir Clough Williams-Ellis' glorious architecture does.

Top: Extras with Barbara Yu Ling in 1966, and (above) on a return visit to Portmeirion in May 2000

White Horses, the cottage where McGoohan stayed during location filming

The Prisoner's Village

From the files of M9, a detailed plan of
the holding facility for recalcitrant agents

1   The Recreation/Exhibition Hall
     ('*The Chimes of Big Ben*' and '*The Schizoid Man*')

2   The Ballroom ('*Dance of the Dead*')

3   The Town Hall

4   The Watchmaker's shop ('*It's Your Funeral*')

5   The Council Chamber ('*Free For All*',
     '*The General*', '*A Change of Mind*')

6   Offices, mortuary and Number 1 telex room
     ('*Dance of the Dead*')

7   The General's suite of offices ('*The General*')

8   The Old People's Home, leading to The Stone Boat

9   The Labour Exchange and Café

10   The Truth Test chamber ('*Free For All*')

11   Helicopter landing area

12   Concealed hangar for evacuation helicopters
     ('*Fall Out*')

13   Old West township ('*Living in Harmony*')

14   Balcony

15   Village Square and Free Sea

17   The Bandstand

18   Number 6

19   General Stores

20   The childrens' home ('*The Girl Who Was Death*')

21   Lowloader escape tunnel ('*Fall Out*')

22   Rover access tunnels, to the sea and inland

23   The Village Control Room

24   Concealed experimental laboratory ('*A. B. and C.*')

25   The Hospital

26   The Green Dome, Number 2's residence

27   Rover watchers' cave ('*Free For All*')

28   Number 2's living quarters

29   The Embryo room and mobile living unit
     ('*Once Upon A Time*')

30   Mobile living unit and lowloader ('*Fall Out*')

31   The juke box corridor ('*Fall Out*')

32   The Assembly Chamber ('*Fall Out*')

33   The Number 1 rocket and silo ('*Fall Out*')

I helped Patrick McGoohan escape
Now he lives next door
To the Man In A Suitcase
'I Helped Patrick McGoohan Escape', The Teenage Filmstars, 1980

The commercial afterlife of *The Prisoner* really began when the 1980s boom in home video sales helped generate a market for nostalgic television. Ironically, the amount of merchandise available now outnumbers what was on offer at the time of the programme's original broadcast. The activities of an organised fandom and periodic terrestrial and satellite re-runs also help to keep public awareness of the programme alive.

Of all the so called 'cult' shows, too, *The Prisoner* is the one most referenced by popular music, mainly due to its iconoclastic anti-establishment stance. Music video directors and advertisers have plundered its singular visual style. Its theme of the individual against the system remains timeless for the audience as well as different generations of film and TV makers, with many movies and TV programmes either spoofing or paying *hommage* to it. In short, *The Prisoner* now enjoys a cultural currency quite out of proportion to its original perception as an outlandish and short-lived experiment.

There have been five official sequels to *The Prisoner* as the series has been recirculated over the last thirty-five years; three novels, a *hommage* and a four-part graphic novel. Each one is a development of the original story, with approaches varying from the original to the enjoyably ridiculous.

ı The Novels

Stateside publishers Ace were the first company to really exploit Number 6's commercial potential. Three novels were written between 1969 and 1970, with reprints in the seventies, eighties and nineties.

All three are continuations of the series, picking up after the events of 'Fall Out' but ignoring the openess of the episode's conclusion. The Prisoner now lives in a flat in Upper Berkeley Mews and the Village Butler, now named 'Sancho', has become his full-time manservant. His car is described variously as The Locust, KAR 12060 and incorrectly as an MG. As the first novel begins, he has no memory of his life in the Village and the opening chapters act as a reintroduction to the bizarre qualities of his former prison (and also establishes the book as a stand-alone piece of fiction): "Chance and individual enterprise could not, unassisted, have created an atmosphere so uniformly oppressive; this Village was the conception, surely, of a single, and slightly monstrous, mind, some sinister Disney set loose upon the world of daily life."

The Prisoner himself is easily recognisable from his TV counterpart; a man of classical education, refined tastes, a sportsman and, of course, a highly trained agent. The second and third books state unequivocally that he is John Drake and, in the third, Janet and Sir Charles Portland reappear from 'Do Not Forsake Me Oh My Darling.' The first book includes some good in-jokes: Number 6 was planning to retire to the real Portmeirion when he resigned and, once in the Village, he finds seventeen film canisters that detail his first, televised stay there.

Reviewing an import copy of the first book in 1969, *The Observer* had this to say: "*The Prisoner* sabotaged and deranged... familiar but radical elements, exploiting the possibilities in film for playing with its own nature as illusion, setting up an unnerving identity between paranoia and conspiracy. Essential to this was that it drew on the mass culture, the symbolisms within which we actually live: but Disch's book, referring back to Kafka and Shakespeare, rather than Deighton and the Beatles, gives us a mere literary frisson."

This was entirely the point. Thomas M. Disch, one of the new wave of sixties science fiction writers that included J.G. Ballard and Philip K. Dick, was doing with *The Prisoner* in the literary medium what the series had done with film and television. His title, *The Prisoner*, has a deliberately allegorical slant, and directly references a variety of classical writers, as well as Shakespeare and Kafka, including Ezra Pound, George Eliot and Henry James. Crucially, it features a production of Shakes-peare's *Measure for Measure* that alludes to corresponding events in the novel, in a similar way to 'Hammer into Anvil''s use of *Faust* and *Don Quixote*. It also says a lot about the appeal of the series that an established novelist – with titles such as *The Genocides* (1965) and *Camp Concentration* (1968) behind him – should be employed in the adaptation of an ITC action serial.

In comparison with the first novel, *The Prisoner #2* is more conventional spin-off fare, written by David McDaniel who worked on the prolific range of *Man*

The Dobson hardbacks released in the UK. Early editions of *A Day In The Life* incorrectly credited Thomas Disch as the author on the hardback spine

From UNCLE books, with titles like *The Dagger Affair* and *The Vampire Affair* to his name. Perhaps this explains the book's conventional narrative and disappointing emphasis on hardware. It's a rather dull plod through an escape attempt involving a motorised raft, in the manner of the series' breakout/capture stories, but without the surreal gloss. *The Prisoner #2*'s straight-ahead spy adventure, which does pick up towards the end with the promise of conflict between two opposing Number 2s, recalls conventional episodes in the series itself like 'It's Your Funeral'.

The renaming of *The Prisoner #3* as *A Day In The Life* gives some indication of its obvious, but surprisingly entertaining, take on the mid-sixties zeitgeist. The author Hank Stine had been the editor of a counter culture newspaper, a film maker and counselor in a personnel agency before becoming a novelist with *Season of the Witch* in 1969. In a detailed review, he described *The Prisoner* as "one of the signal works... in the media's history" and on the strength of his enthusiasm for the series was commissioned to write the third novel. Stine's varied background is reflected in *A Day in the Life*'s distillation of sixties culture, with sometimes original, sometimes hilarious results. The book features a Number 6 who listens to *Surrealistic Pillow* by Jefferson Airplane on his car stereo, The Beatles as the Village band, characters who discuss conspiracy TV shows like *The Fugitive* and *The Invaders* and Villagers who smoke dope! The Prisoner even experiences the prose equivalent of the sonic maelstrom at the end of The Beatles' song that gives the book its title. What the novel does convey, with its raw midsixties *milieu*, is the more specific references to time and place on display in the last episode 'Fall Out'.

All three books, regardless of quality, accurately capture the articulate and philosophical nature of *The Prisoner*'s dialogue. *The Prisoner #3* is almost entirely composed of discourse between the characters and includes some thought-provoking passages: "Dignity is dead. It went out with high button shoes and honest government. It was not compatible with computers and cost accounting. When a balance book becomes more important than a human life, there is no room left for dignity."

Each book, like each episode, stands as one aspect of the programme's provocative mix of styles and issues; alle-gory, spy story and a psychedelic take on sixties society are all present and correct beneath the three covers. The approach of each novel shows the publishers cast their net as wide as possible in an attempt to capture a readership from the programme's audience. For these reasons, as well as being Number 6's only excursion into mainstream printed fiction, they are worth a read.

Top and above: the US and UK paperback releases of the novels. Left: The Salvador Dalí-inspired cover for the French hardback edition of the Disch book

The Prisoner

Thomas M.Disch

(a.k.a. The Prisoner - I Am Not A Number!)

P/b Ace Books, USA 1969;

H/b Presses de la Renaissance, France 1977;

H/b Dobson Books, UK 1979;

P/b Presses Pocket, France 1979;

P/b New English Library, January 1980;

P/b Boxtree/ Channel 4 Books 1992

The Prisoner is returned to the Village and faces more interrogation and mind games before a climatic meeting with Number 1.

The Prisoner #2

David McDaniel

(a.k.a. The Prisoner - Number Two; The Prisoner - Who Is Number Two?)

P/b Ace Books, USA 1969;

P/b New English Library, January 1982;

P/b Boxtree/ Channel 4 Books 1992

The Prisoner's car, 'KAR 1260', is brought to the Village in an attempt by Number 2 to get him to settle. Number 6 has other ideas...

The Prisoner #3

Hank Stine

(a.k.a. The Prisoner - A Day In The Life)

P/b Ace Books, USA 1970;

H/b Dobson Books, UK 1979;

P/b New English Library, April 1981

The Prisoner is sprung from the Village to assassinate the three officials who are collectively Number 1. But he suspects a trap...

N.B. The second and third books were released out of sequence in the UK.

All three novels were republished in a paperback omnibus by Carlton Books in April 2002.

11 The Laughing Prisoner

Written by Stephen Fry and Jools Holland with additional material by Rowland Rivron and Hugh Laurie

Jools Holland resigns from his job as presenter of music programme *The Tube*, is gassed and wakes in an Italianate village. The community's chairman, Number 2, reveals that the Village was founded 20 years ago with the "simple purpose of extracting information from certain show biz personalities who had inexplicably resigned their posts". There now remain two other residents, Number 6 and the totally incomprehensible Number 3. Jools – rechristened Number 7 – offers to tell all but Number 2 refuses to play his game. Pronouncing Number 7 "totally expendable", The Dream Reader is used to interrogate him, but he proves even more self-obsessed and egotistical than Number 6. Finally, a photographic competition is announced: the winner will get to leave the Village. The victor proves to be Number 3, who departs before Number 2 can hit him. Number 7 offers to tell all if he can meet Number 1, who turns out be the suited and booted version of his original self. It turns out all Jools wanted was a holiday. He returns to London to resume his career in television but ends up singing to his superiors, "We're through."

BANDSTAND

The Village band had certainly changed since the sixties. From top: Siouxsie and the Banshees, XTC and Magnum

The New Number 2: A man not all together perceptive enough to be the Village chairman. He treats Number 7's complete honesty as a ruse and is completely clueless about Number 6's continued incarceration: "Twenty years ago he resigned from a highly successful television series called *Danger Man*. Since then, he's been here, a prisoner of this Village, and no one can understand *why*." He hates Number 7 on sight and his customary Number 2 mad laughter is affected by a bad cough. He is also a complete poser, hamming up for the Village's photographic competition.

You are Number 7: Full-time presenter of the Tyne Tees music programme *The Tube*, transmitted on Channel 4. He drives a suspiciously familiar Lotus KAR 120C, and delivers his resignation to the real-life headquarters of Channel 4 in Charlotte Street, London. He also appears to be squatting in Number 6's old residence at No. 1 Buckingham Place. Skilled in hand-to-hand-combat – well, V-signs anyway. Can handle an Orange Alert (with rubber gloves) and can burst into spontaneous song, complete with backing musicians.

Production: Jools Holland, a self confessed *Prisoner* fan, often referred to the programme when he presen-ted *The Tube*, the popular music programme that ran on Channel 4 from 1983-89. In another edition of *The Tube*, he memorably sent up the famous sequence from 'The General' when he asked a computer the unanswerable question

"Why?": Without hesitating, the truculent machine replied "Why not?"

In 1986, Jools told fan club Six of One: "Hopefully, later in the year we will be able to make a wonderful *Prisoner*-based film for *The Tube*. I am very keen indeed." A spoof episode filmed on location in January 1987 was the result – XTC front man Andy Partridge remembers it was "bloody cold" – continuing Channel 4's love affair with the programme that had begun with the rescreening of episodes over 1983-84.

> **"He's known more Number 2s than the gentleman's lavatory at Waterloo Station!"**
>
> NUMBER 2 ON NUMBER 6

The Laughing Prisoner was originally shown as an hour-long segment of a regular edition of *The Tube* and subsequently repeated as a stand-alone show six years later, with a new introduction by Jools Holland. Co-writer and star Stephen Fry is also a fan. Having originally been attracted to the programme's title following his own experience of the penal system when an adolescent, he was hooked by *The Prisoner*'s individual style.

The standard title sequence was used with contemporary footage of Jools driving the Lotus and resigning. Number 6 was able to participate in the programme in clips from 'Arrival', 'Free For All', 'Dance of the Dead' 'The Chimes of Big Ben' and 'Many Happy Returns'.

Number 3 (Stanley Unwin) contemplates a game of chess outside the Old People's Home

Number 2 (Stephen Fry), Number 7 (Jools Holland) and Number 3 are joined by Rover for dinner

Number 6's entry for the Village photographic competition shows a grumpy Number 3, a jovial Number 2 and a resigned Number 7

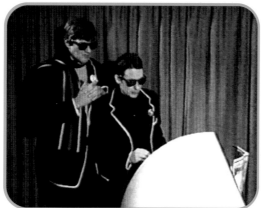

Number 2 and Number 7's meeting with Number 1 is anti-climatic: "Oh, that's not Number 1. It's a mirror. I wonder how that got there?"

Prison Writers: Jools Holland swapped channels, presenting *Later with Jools Holland* for BBC 2, as well as fronting BBC coverage of Glastonbury and regularly appearing on tour with his own Big Band. In 1987, Stephen Fry and Hugh Laurie, already a success as part of the *Blackadder* team, were the regular comic stand-ups on *The Tube*. They went on to write their own show, *A Bit of Fry and Laurie* (1989-95), as well as several solo novels. Rowland Rivron appeared with Jools Holland in *The Groovy Fellers* (1989) when he played a Martian who was introduced to various Earth institutions and social rituals. This short-lived sitcom included another Jools-inspired reference to *The Prisoner*, when the Groovy Fellers became part of their own title sequence in the last episode.

Tally Ho: Of all *The Prisoner* spin-offs, Jools Holland and Stephen Fry's witty eighties *homage* is one of the best, and certainly the most diligently researched, entertaining and affectionate. Their enthusiasm for the

subject matter shines through in every scene.

After *The Prisoner*'s dalliance with The Beatles – the epitome of sixties pop – in the last episode, it seemed entirely appropriate that following its eighties revival, the series should be fused with a contemporary music programme. Seeing Siouxsie, XTC and Magnum perform in Portmeirion has a surrealism all of its own, particularly as the Magnum singer's eighties mullet cut now has to be seen to be believed.

The use of Stanley Unwin was an inspired touch. Famous in the sixties for his trademark verbal nonsense, he provided the unintelligible narration for the Small Faces' LP *Ogden's Nut Gone Flake* (1968), a send up of self-important concept albums. In *The Laughing Prisoner* his incomprehensible language is a tribute to a series that is often seen as nonsensical itself. Full marks, too, to Siouxsie Sioux for wearing a Village-style striped top.

In short, a wonderful example of eighties TV. And it's not often you can say that.

CAST
Guest Stars
Patrick McGoohan
Number 6
Terence Alexander
Channel 4 Controller
Stephen Fry
Number 2
Stanley Unwin
Number 3
Hugh Laurie
Channel 4 Controller's son
John Peel*
Himself

And Featuring
Siouxsie & The Banshees
XTC*
Magnum

with
Drummer/Technician
Rowland Rivron
Guitarist
Chris Difford
Director (London)
Chris Cabrin
Director (Portmeirion)
Geoff Wonfor

Transmission Information
The Tube: 3/4/87
The Laughing Prisoner
(edited repeat): 1/1/93

*In the 1993 repeat, some sequences from the original transmission were trimmed. Although credited, John Peel's report on up-and-coming Welsh bands was completely absent. The Number 1 sequence originally ended with Jools setting a competition question for the viewers; the prizes were a set of Channel 5 Prisoner videos and promotional posters. Jool's talk with his film unit towards the end was also slightly truncated. On the end credits of the repeat, the 'Clips courtesy of...' credit was amended from 'Channel 5' to 'ITC'.

III The Prisoner: Shattered Visage
By Dean Motter with Mark Askwith and David Hornung

MARVEL COMICS PLANNED AN EXTENSIVE comic book adaptation of *The Prisoner* in the mid seventies. The first issue was written and drawn by Jack Kirby, with issue two scripted by Steve Englehart and illustrated by Gil Kane. However, the comics were never published and a 1979 announcement that the project was to be revived also came to nothing.

During the late 1980s, the comic format underwent something of a renaissance. *Batman –The Dark Knight Returns* (1986) began the trend, reinventing Gotham's Caped Crusader and showing that an art form previously thought trivial could deal with serious issues like the ambiguous role of vigilantes in society. *Watchmen* (1987), a melancholy tale of disenfranchised superheroes, was another watershed in the genre. DC Comics had published both titles and it was against this background that Dean Motter, Mark Askwith and David Hornung conceived a new comic strip version of *The Prisoner*.

Like the three novels, *The Prisoner* (a.k.a. *Shattered Visage* in its omnibus form) was a sequel, this time set 20 years later. Reflecting the revisionism accorded popular hero figures in comics at the time, the original Number 6 is a sad and lonely figure, who suffered a mental breakdown after the events of 'Fall Out' and has been in the deserted Village ever since. A new Prisoner – a woman security operative, separated from her husband, with one child and unnamed apart from a passing reference to 'Drake's voyage' – sets off on a round-the-world sea journey and becomes marooned in the run-down Village. There she meets the old Number 6. The Number 2 from 'The Chimes of Big Ben' has published his memoirs under the title *The Village Idiot* and returns for a final battle with his old nemesis. Meanwhile, the new Prisoner's estranged husband is involved with a covert group who want to learn the real secret behind the Village.

Shattered Visage continues the series' remit of engaging with the political climate around it by updating the story to a late eighties context. The Cold War in the eighties had cooled several degrees between East and West, thanks mainly to the aggressively anti-

Communist attitudes of the Reagan and Thatcher governments in the USA and UK, and the invasion of Afghanistan by Russia at the beginning of the decade. Tensions were further heightened by the deployment of medium-range Pershing and Cruise missiles in West Germany and Great Britain, and this was the main influence for *The Prisoner*'s shift from the sixties to the eighties.

In 1966, contemporary concerns were embodied by a hi-tech prison camp run by either side, or both, that alluded to modern Western society. In 1988, that worry had been superseded and, building on the rocket featured in 'Fall Out', the prison has become the terrestrial equivalent of a Star Wars platform, a secret arsenal of nuclear missiles: "You've got to brush away all that rococo crap and expose the truth! Power. Control. That's what the Village is all about."

Some germane topical observations are made. While the British Secret Service complains of being under-funded, the Americans, in the form of 'Lee West', are able to appropriate aircraft, weapons and a covert paratroop team at will, a reflection of how America's global profile had further eclipsed Britain's. Number 2's book *The Village Idiot* is a thinly veiled allusion to the ex-MI5 agent Peter Wright's *Spycatcher*, which was banned from publication in

Britain in 1987. The treatment of Number 2's book by the security services is identical, and has the ring of truth about it as its real secrets are deleted before publication, "so you grudgingly divulge a lesser evil in order to protect the greater one."

The new Prisoner's traitorous husband, Thomas, is clearly based on the actor Rupert Everett, who starred in *Another Country* (1984), a film based on the early life of the KGB agent Guy Burgess. A reference to George Smiley, a character who worked for British Intelligence in the novels of John Le Carré, himself a former spy, adds to the story's blend of fact and fiction.

Apart from some over-indulgence in paying homage to the 1960s – there are cameo appearances by Emma Peel, John Steed and Sean Connery's James Bond and rather too much dialogue from the original series – the writers managed to move the story on. It was still relevant to a contemporary audience, particularly as the books were drawn and inked in a style reminiscent of Frank Miller's seminal work on *The Dark Knight*.

Above all, *Shattered Visage* shows that the themes and preoccupations of *The Prisoner* still had contemporary relevance if handled carefully and perceptively enough.

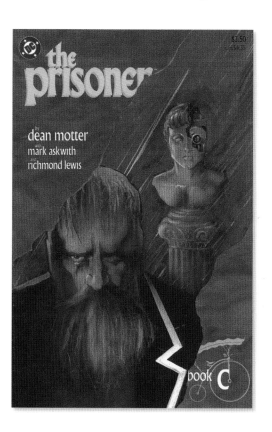

"The system imprisoned him, interrogated him, broke him, drove him mad. The man who would not bend, simply broke. Shattered and alone, he chose a number and christened himself... Number 1"

NUMBER 2 ON THE PRISONER

Written by
**Dean Motter &
Mark Askwith**

Illustrated by
Dean Motter

Colour art by
Dean Hornung

Lettering by
Deborah Marks

**The Prisoner
Shattered Visage**
Omnibus edition of all four books with a new introduction.
Paperback 1990

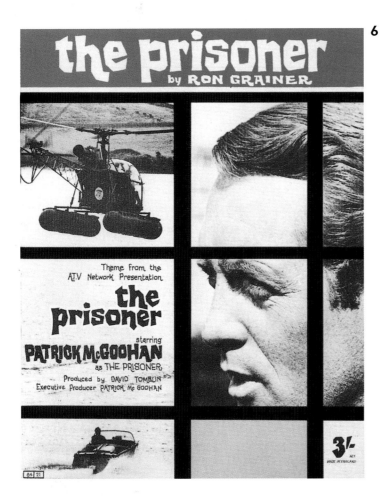

6

1960s

From James Bond through *Batman* to *The Man From UNCLE*, 1960s film and television produced many spin-offs. The makers of *Danger Man*, Patrick McGoohan's – and ITC's – first international success, were not slow to capitalise on its popularity. Throughout the early sixties, John Drake's younger fans were catered for with an abundance of toys, comic books and annuals, while the older audience was served by a series of adult novellas. (**1,2**)

By contrast, the initial broadcast of *The Prisoner* left UK merchandisers cold: how, after all, do you market something that defies categorisation? There was a tentative stab at the children's market (not, of course, the series' target audience), with a fine reproduction of the Village taxi as *The Prisoner* Mini Moke (**3**), issued by Dinky Toys in 1967, and an illustrated cover to the comic *TV Tornado* (**4**). Apart from that, and the release of a 7 inch version of the theme tune by RCA (**5**) with score sheets (**6**), no other Prisoner-related merchandise appeared in Britain during the 1960s. The USA was the first to publish *Prisoner* fiction with the three Ace novels in 1969-70.

3

5

4

1

2

1970s

The regional UK repeats in 1977 inspired the first *Prisoner*-related merchandise in 10 years to be released at Portmeirion. Three badges were available, for Numbers 1, 2 and 6 – Number 1 was, unsurprisingly, the rarest. France was the first country to reprint one of the American novels. Presses de la Renaissance published a French translation by Jacqueline Huet in 1977, with a paperback version following in 1979 by Presses Pocket. In the same year, Dobson Books Ltd reprinted the second and third novels in the UK in hardback.

The Ontario Educational Communications Authority in Canada put out two booklets as part of their media studies course on *The Prisoner* in 1978. *The Prisoner Puzzle* college booklet and *Program Guide* (**7**), although not strictly qualifying as merchandise, were accompanied by 30-minute 'working tapes' edited from the episodes; the first semi-commercial release of the series on video. The two booklets were the first publications to treat the programme seriously as a work of art.

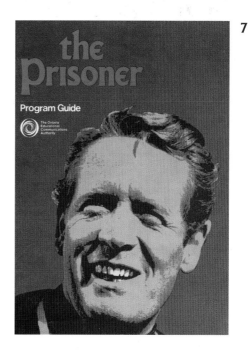

1980s

The decade saw the beginnings of a widespread interest in classic television; by its end, *The Prisoner* had been marketed in every medium from video to pop music. With the re-emergence of capitalism, entrepreneurs were looking for new markets to exploit. TV nostalgia became a profitable area, as the fans of vintage television had grown up and now had disposable incomes.

The first factual books on the series appeared during the eighties, ranging from detailed story information to the glossy reproduction of stills from the ITC picture library. *The Prisoner Files* by John Peel, produced in association with the magazine *Fantasy Empire*, were an episode by episode breakdown of each story. In 1988, *The Official Prisoner Companion* by Matthew White and Jaffer Ali was published by Warner Books Inc.(**8**), the first informed look at the development of the series - Sidgwick and Jackson republished the book in the UK in the same year with a new cover. A year later, Boxtree issued a solid episode guide to both McGoohan shows, *The Prisoner and Danger Man*, by Dave Rogers. France followed this up with *The Prisoner – A Televisionary Masterpiece* by Alan Carrazé and Hélène Oswald, (**9**) released by Editions Hutième Art, a beautifully produced coffee table edition. A translation was published by W.H. Allen/Virgin a year later in the UK and was still available over 10 years later.

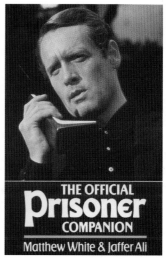

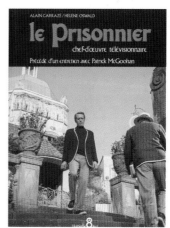

10

19

11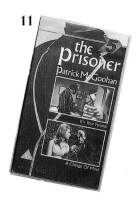

The video releases of *The Prisoner* reflect the development of the video industry itself, from an underestimation of the quality of product required by the consumer to accurate niche marketing. Precision Video released the first commercially available *Prisoner* videos, in the UK on VHS and Betamax (**10**) in 1982, primarily for the rental market: These featured two episodes edited together per tape with new, combined titles for boths stories. Channel 5 Video (**11**) released the first sell-through titles over 1986-67 with the issue of two complete, unedited episodes per tape, with 'Fall Out' available as a single release. MPI Home Video was the first company to release The Prisoner in the USA; *The Prisoner - The Lost Episode* being the first commercial appearance of the alternative edit of 'The Chimes of Big Ben'. The first digital recordings were released by MPI in conjunction with Image Entertainment on laser disc in 1988 (**12**). *The Prisoner* also debuted on video and laser disc in the Far East during the eighties in Japan.

12

13

Six of One also began releasing semi-commercial merchandise. In conjunction with Sixties specialist label Bam Caruso, the society released *The Prisoner - Original Soundtrack* in 1986 (**13**). Initially a fan club only release, it brought together the different versions of the theme tune as well as a selection of incidental music. Seeing the record's potential, Bam Caruso unofficially re-released the album for retail sale later the same year. Silva Screen oversaw its next legitimate release, on CD and cassette, in 1989.

14

15

With the eighties, popular music began to tap into TV subculture in earnest, and *The Prisoner* was an obvious source of inspiration. The first example, and probably the best, was 'I Helped Patrick McGoohan Escape', with the killer lyrics: *'We made sure that the Rovers were asleep/And that Number 2/Was at home too/Making a plan to kidnap Paul McCartney.'* Initially released in 1980 by the Teenage Filmstars, it was re-recorded in its more familiar, Beatlesque version in 1983 by The Times (**14**). Taboo's take on the series, 'Number 6' (**15**), was a semi-instrumental composition built around a chant of 'Six! Six! Six!' and featured sampled dialogue from the series.

16

18

17

T-shirt manufacturers also began to cash in on old TV. The first *Prisoner* offering appeared in the UK in the chain-stores HMV and Virgin (**16**) in 1982. The other, a tie-in to a US network screening of the series, appeared in 1986 with a rather grumpy looking McGoohan illustration.

1990s

20

Demand for classic TV continued, partly because of the growth in popularity of magazines devoted to science fiction and archive television, and the development of satellite broadcasters keen to fill airtime. The rights to *The Prisoner* passed to Polygram in 1992; as a more aggressive marketer they were keen to keep the series recirculated. The series also passed two anniversaries in this decade, two significant merchandising opportunities not lost on the company that now owned the series.

The programme's twenty-fifth anniversary was the opportunity for a third UK reprint of the first two Prisoner novels by Boxtree/Channel 4 Books in 1992. Factual books, meanwhile, became more specialised. *Be Seeing You... Decoding The Prisoner* by Chris Gregory, published by the University of Luton Press in 1997 (**17**), was an academic study of the programme. *Inside The Prisoner* by Ian Rakoff, published by B.T. Batsford in 1998 (**18**), was particularly interesting, looking at the production of the series in its original social and political context.

Video and laser disc releases continued to diversify. Two custom-made documentaries were released in 1990, MPI's *The Prisoner Video Companion*, and *The Best of The Prisoner*, primarily compilations of clips from the programme. Polygram released the first boxed set of *The Prisoner* in the UK in 1992, luxuriously packaged to appeal to the collector in the series' twenty-fifth anniversary year. France refined this approach to specialist releases with its own *Le Prisonnier* box set in the same year, with accompanying calendars (for two years), badges and postcards. The growing sophistication of releases continued with more laser discs from MPI and Image Entertainment in 1994, and a subscription-only range of videos with restored versions of the episodes, textless credits and US trailers from Columbia House and Polygram (**19**). Polygram capitalised on the superior quality of laser discs by releasing the whole series in this format in 1994. In 1998, in conjunction with Vision Video Limited, they put out another two-part box set for the thirtieth anniversary in the UK, featuring the first digitally restored versions of the episodes, branded to tie in with a range of supporting merchandise including a calendar, posters, mugs and postcards (**20**). A French box set release of digitally restored episodes in 1999, *Le Prisonnier* parts 1 and 2 (**21**), in the same style packaging, was an alternative purchase for le consumer.

21

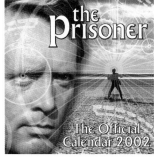

Slow Dazzle Worldwide has been releasing *Prisoner* calendars since 1997

22

23

24

25

26

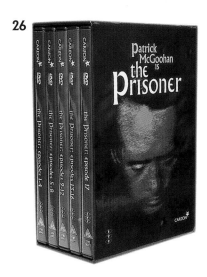

27

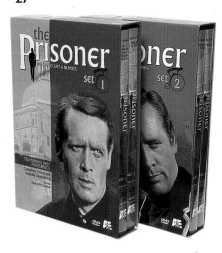

In the record and CD sector, Silva Screen released CDs 2 and 3 of original soundtrack music in 1991 and 1992 (**22**, **23**). Independent music continued to take an interest in *The Prisoner*, with Alternative Radio's *Fall Out* (**24**) in 1990 borrowing its title and sampled dialogue from the final episode. In the same year, an attempt was made to bring *The Prisoner* up to date for the House generation by releasing five dance mixes of the theme music by FAB featuring 'MC Number 6'. The various mixes were available on a club friendly 12in (**25**), as well as CD and cassette. The 'Free Man' version appeared on the album *Power Themes 90* (Telstar), alongside techno updates of other ITC favourites such as *Thunderbirds* and *Captain Scarlet and the Mysterons*.

2000s

The arrival of Digital Versatile Discs, with the capacity for superior picture quality, sound and extra features, made critical editions of films and TV programmes possible; it also enabled old material to be recirculated in a new form. At the time of writing there have been three DVD releases of *The Prisoner* worldwide, which together comprise the definitive home entertainment collection of the series.

Carlton Video's DVD release of the series in August 2000 could be purchased on five individual discs or in a box set. The discs use the same branding as another re-release of videos put out at the same time featuring four digitally restored episodes per DVD (**26**). The special features comprised a selection of old and new material, from further outings for 'The Chimes of Big Ben' and *The Prisoner Video Companion*, to the first UK exposure of 1960s trailers for the individual episodes and a selection of production paintings by Jack Shampan.

American company A&E Home Video followed up the UK editions two months later (**27**) with the first

release in a projected run of five two-disc sets. A new marketing tag line was also used - 'No man is just a number'. By contrast with the British releases, the running order of episodes was rearranged to reflect an unofficial screening order suggested by Six of One. Extras different from Carlton's offering include textless opening and closing credits and a film sequence showing filing cabinets with 'resigned' translated into different languages, which were shot for overseas sales of the programme. All the discs were re-released in a complete box set in October 2001. VHS releases ran concurrently with the DVD sets, minus additional extras.

In November 2000, the third Prisoner DVD release occurred, this time in France. Simply entitled *Le Prisonnier* (**28**), and housed in a fold-out digipak format, it includes extras unavailable on the UK and US formats. These include a 16mm film, *Prisonnier du Village*, showing a French journalist becoming acquainted with Portmeirion as it transforms into its Village incarnation, and – something of a coup – a televised phone interview with McGoohan from the sci-fi magazine programme *Destination Séries* in 1997.

Merchandising in *The Prisoner*'s thirty fifth anniversary year of 2002 shows that classic television has become an increasingly sophisticated collectors' market. Another DVD box set is scheduled for April 2002 in Australia, courtesy of AV Channel, with new extras. Finally, Carlton Books brought *Prisoner* merchandising full circle by reissuing the three Ace novels in omnibus form(**29**).

THE PRISONER SHOP

Portmeirion has hosted a *Prisoner*-related shop since 1982. Until 1998, the merchandise available there consisted primarily of material produced by Six Of One. Particularly memorable was a sticker saying 'You have just been poisoned' (inspired by 'The Girl Who Was Death') designed to be stuck to the bottom of unsuspecting drinkers' glasses. The Portmeirion estate took over the running of the shop in 1999, producing a variety of gifts that mainly feature the pennyfarthing symbol. Mugs, courtesy of Portmeirion pottery, have since been added to the items available, as well as photographic jigsaws, confectionery (below), full-size reproductions of Number 6's blazer, Village-style umbrellas and straw boaters.

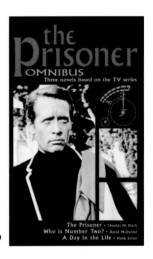

29

28

Free For All
The Prisoner and popular culture

The Prisoner is a
perennial cover star on
'cult' TV magazines

Mansun's *Six* album was
steeped in *Prisoner*
themes and iconography

Altered Images' video
for the single 'See Those
Eyes' was the first to use
imagery from the series

Away from the numbers

Music from the time of the programme's sixties heyday failed to exploit the show – regrettably, the Beatles weren't around long enough to record a tribute to their favourite TV series – and it wasn't until the mid-70s that popular music caught up with the show. *The Prisoner* was rescreened in the UK during the height of punk rock, the most enthusiastically anti-establishment, back-to-basics youth movement for some years, kicking against the icons and sacred cows of a moribund Britain. Punk's assertive individuality certainly connected with *The Prisoner*'s universal themes of oppression of the masses and plea for the rights of the individual. Coincidentally or not, The Clash recorded a b-side simply entitled 'The Prisoner' and The Jam's first b-side was the intriguingly titled 'Away from the Numbers'. On a more identifiably cosmetic level, pub rock band Dr Feelgood released an album called *Be Seeing You* in 1977 and publicity photos show Canvey Island's finest in Prisoner blazers and college scarves. *The Prisoner* has always been ideal source material for music video directors stuck for an idea, from Altered Images' 'See Those Eyes' in 1982 to Supergrass' 'Alright' in 1994. The symbolism is ready made, Portmeirion hardly needs dressing as a set – just bring your own pennyfarthing – and at least one *Prisoner* fan is guaranteed to buy the single. The best example,

though, is undoubtedly The Times' video for 'I Helped Patrick McGoohan Escape', which like the song is accurate, affectionate and very funny.

A more serious assimilation of *The Prisoner*'s themes and imagery can be found on Mansun's 1998 album *Six*: tracks about guilt, alienation and isolation, 'Six', 'Fall Out' and 'Television', are totally at home with the series' bleak world view. The cover artwork features Number 6 in the company of other famous fantasy characters, Tom Baker's Doctor Who and Winnie-the-Pooh, and one of the books in the artwork is entitled *The Schizoid Man*. Over thirty years on, *The Prisoner* is still striking chords with rock musicians outside the musical mainstream.

Children of the Village

As each generation grows up, *Prisoner* enthusiasts have entered the media and produced spoofs or referred to it in many TV shows, from rock programmes such as *The Tube* to family comedies like *2 Point 4 Children*. Virtually every travel series that visits Portmeirion is unable to resist inflating a few giant balloons and decking out eager extras in blazers and boaters. *Randall and Hopkirk (Deceased)*'s creative overseer, Charlie Higson, saw the show as "a big, escapist fantasy like *The Prisoner*, which no-one does anymore" and his enthusiasm for the series helped get the 21st-century model of *Randall* made. The second episode of the 2001 run, 'Revenge of the Bog People', featured characters called McKern, Doleman, Nesbit and Mrs Cookson, and a later episode featured a character called Danvers. Peter Bowles, Wanda Ventham and George Baker were also guest actors during the programme's run in a nod to the series' ITC heritage.

Considering *The Prisoner*'s, and therefore McGoohan's, railing against consumer culture, it's ironic that the imagery of the show has also been used by advertising. Two television adverts were made during the eighties in the wake of the series' Channel 4 revival. LBC radio (the London Broadcasting Company - 'the information station'), used *The Prisoner*'s title seq-

The Times' singer, Ed Ball, took on the role of Number 6 in the video for 'I Helped Patrick McGoohan Escape'

Clockwise from top: the Lombard Business Finance hoarding campaign, the press ad for the Renault 21, LBC's TV commercial and Number 6 as played by Ronnie Corbett in the BBC series *Sorry!*

uence, intercut with scenes of eighties London and contemporary news events. The programme's 'What do you want?'/'Information' dialogue fitted neatly with the station's remit to produce up-to-the-minute news coverage. The ad for the Renault 21 car was altogether different. It was a direct spoof of the series, featuring 'Number 21', who shows "independent tendencies", escaping from Portmeirion in the Renault 21. The thirty-second commercial cost £250,0000 – the cost of three episodes of the original series. Impressive Rover effects and a convincingly updated Number 2's control room aside, the concept of individuality was being co-opted as just another tool to sell products to baby boomers. A text-book example of how not to use an old

TV show in advertising was the 1996 campaign for Lombard Business Finance. Not only was it cheaply done in terms of its colour scheme, but McGoohan had obviously not allowed his likeness to be used (the visuals substituted a silhouette that clearly wasn't him). With the absence of the programme's title and its star, all the general public had to go on was the headline – "Who is Number One?". As a result, the campaign would only have made sense to people with an intimate understanding of 1960s television.

Members Only

Six of One, the officially recognised fan body, was formed on the 6th of January 1977 by Dave Barrie, a

Car magazines have often covered *The Prisoner* as it features classic cars. *Performance Car* even went to Portmeirion for their July 1987 cover shoot

"Why can't they catch him?": (Renault) Number 21 escapes from the Village in a big budget, thirty second remake

Six of One founders Dave Barrie, Judy Adamson, Ray Binns and Roger Goodman outside Number 6's house on April 17 1977

Patrick McGoohan and members of Six of One on the 1968 edition of *Television's Greatest Hits* in 1982

The Prisoner has been sold profitably all around the world. Above: a still from the French title sequence

few months behind the *Doctor Who* Appreciation Society, the other longest running UK-based, TV related fan organisation. With some amazement, Barrie saw his name and address transmitted after 'Fall Out' on his regional ITV station, ATV, in December 1976. "I went to bed and was awoken by a knock on the door at half past one. It was four *Prisoner* fans from Sutton Coldfield. Then later two more arrived from Oxford".

In the days before easily accessible videos and DVDs, Six of One's initial motivation was to get the series rebroadcast. Since then, it has organised semi-annual conventions in Portmeirion – the first, one-day event was held in April 1978 – and its members have done sterling work in keeping *The Prisoner* in the public eye and investigating the programme's development and production. Between 1983 and 1999, Max Hora was the proprietor of *The Prisoner* Information Centre in Portmeirion, which was based in Number 6's house. Steven Ricks, in particular, has done valuable work in uncovering little known historical information. In 1993 he discovered home movie footage of the original Rover prop, previously thought to have sunk without trace in Portmeirion's estuary. For over twenty

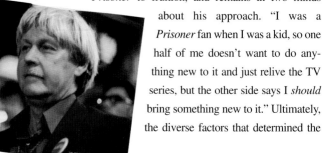

years, Ipswich-based Roger and Karen Langley have been committed to keeping the administrative side of Six of One ticking over.

In 1985, Bruce Clark became the society's US co-ordinator. His major contribution to the series' afterlife was the discovery of the alternate version of 'The Chimes of Big Ben', which premiered at the 1986 convention, as well as designing and maintaining the Six of One website.

The society has produced a variety of magazines over the years, featuring material as varied as interviews with the cast and production team to Number 6's horoscope. Six of One has also acted in an advisory capacity on several professional projects, including *Six into One: The Prisoner File*, *The Laughing Prisoner* and video, book and DVD releases. The society was also the first organisation to release the theme music by Ron Grainer (below).

Of the original founders, Judy Adamson sadly died young in 1978; a plaque and a tree commemorates her in the Portmeirion grounds. Roger Goodman has moved on, with only Dave Barrie still active in *Prisoner* fandom; his annual 'Brain Bash' is a forum for discussing issues and topics associated with the series.

McGoohan has been Six of One's honorary president since day one, but he must see a certain irony in the dedicated annual recreation of the human chess game and election parade at the Portmeirion conventions. It could be successfully argued, though, that the freedom to dress up in *Prisoner* costumes, and recreate the series' set pieces, is an example of the individual exercising freedom of choice.

Endgame

In 2000, British feature film director Simon West was commissioned to bring a big-screen remake of *The Prisoner* to fruition, and remains in two minds about his approach. "I was a *Prisoner* fan when I was a kid, so one half of me doesn't want to do anything new to it and just relive the TV series, but the other side says I *should* bring something new to it." Ultimately, the diverse factors that determined the

XTC performing 'The Meeting Place' in Portmeirion for *The Tube*, which trailed the programme's *Prisoner* special, on 6 February 1987

development of the original series can't be duplicated, and the unique, erratic nature of the original remains its most enduring quality. West undoubtedly has a tough job on his hands in attempting to catch lightning in a bottle twice, but Patrick McGoohan's reported attachment to the project is a positive sign.

There will always be a place for a conspiracy thriller that incorporates contemporary social and political comment. *The Prisoner* wasn't the first to do this – the cinema had already been there – but it remains unique in having done so in a genre seen as entertaining but essentially disposable. It has remained appealing because of its sixties gloss and the ever more relevant emasculation of personal freedoms. It also used experimental film techniques to challenge both the perceptions of the audience and, in a small way, the constraints of television itself. Its spirit lives on in media anarchists such as *Brasseye*'s Chris Morris, who spoofs current affairs programmes to draw attention to the hypocrisies and double standards of contemporary Britain.

The diverting gimmicks of Mini Mokes, homicidal balloons and human chess pieces are all very well, but media subversion, a social and political conscience and, essentially, polished and exciting entertainment are what really defined *The Prisoner*.

Be seeing you. I hope...

From left to right: Six of One's first fanzine, the photocopied *Alert*, the badge for the 2001 convention, examples of fan publishing and the human chess game recreated at Portmeirion in March 2001. Below: *In The Village*, the latest journal of the society, now edited by David Healey

Lew Stringer's cartoon strip for *In The Village*, *Rover One*, shows that *Prisoner* fans do have a sense of humour

Original Transmission Information

Arrival
Friday 29 September 1967: ATV Midlands/Grampian 7.30–8.30; Sunday 1st October 1967: ATV London/Southern Television/Westward, Channel/Tyne Tees 7.25–8.25; Thursday 5 October 1967: Scottish 7.30–8.30; Friday 6 October 1967: Anglia 8.00–9.00; Thursday 19 October 1967: Border 7.30–8.30; Friday 27 October 1967: Granada 8.00–9.00

The Chimes of Big Ben
Friday 6 October 1967: ATV Midlands/Grampian 7.30–8.30; Sunday 8 October 1967: ATV London/Southern Television/Westward, Channel/Tyne Tees 7.25–8.25; Thursday 12 October 1967: Scottish 7.30–8.30; Friday 13 October 1967: Anglia 8.00–9.00; Thursday 26 October 1967: Border 7.30–8.30; Friday 3 November 1967: Granada 8.00–9.00

A.B. and C.
Friday 13 October 1967: ATV Midlands/Grampian 7.30–8.30; Sunday 15 October 1967: ATV London/Southern Television/Westward, Channel/Tyne Tees 7.25–8.25; Thursday 19 October 1967: Scottish 7.30–8.30; Friday 20 October: 1967: Anglia 8.00–9.00; Thursday 2 November 1967: Border 7.30–8.30; Friday 10 November 1967: Granada 8.00–9.00

Free For All
Friday 20 October 1967: ATV Midlands/Grampian 7.30–8.30; Sunday 22 October 1967: ATV London/Southern Television/Westward, Channel/Tyne Tees 7.25–8.25; Thursday 26 October 1967: Scottish 7.30–8.30; Friday 27 October 1967: Anglia 8.00–9.00; Thursday 9 November 1967: Border 7.30–8.30; Friday 17 November 1967: Granada 8.00–9.00

The Schizoid Man
Friday 27 October 1967: ATV Midlands/Grampian 7.30–8.30; Sunday 29 October 1967: ATV London/ Southern Television/Westward, Channel/Tyne Tees 7.25–8.25; Thursday 2 November 1967: Scottish 7.30–8.30; Friday 3 November 1967: Anglia 8.00–9.00; Thursday 16 November 1967: Border 7.30–8.30; Friday 24November 1967: Granada 8.00–9.00

The General
Friday 3 November 1967: ATV Midlands/Grampian 7.30–8.30; Sunday 5 November 1967: ATV London/Southern Television/Westward, Channel/Tyne Tees 7.25–8.25; Thursday 9 November 1967: Scottish 7.30–8.30; Friday 10 November 1967: Anglia 8.00–9.00; Thursday 23 November 1967: Border 7.30–8.30; Friday 1 December 1967: Granada 7.30–8.30

Many Happy Returns
Friday 10 November 1967: ATV Midlands/Grampian 7.30–8.30; Sunday 12 November 1967: ATV London/ Southern Television/Westward, Channel/Tyne Tees 7.25–8.25; Thursday 16 November 1967: Scottish 7.30–8.30; Friday 17 November 1967: Anglia 8.00–9.00; Thursday 30 November 1967: Border 7.30–8.30; Friday 8 December 1967: Granada 7.30–8.30

Dance of the Dead
Friday 24 November 1967: Anglia 8.00–9.00; Sunday 26 November 1967: ATV London/Southern Television/Westward, Channel/Tyne Tees 7.25–8.25; Thursday 30 November 1967: Scottish 7.30–8.30; Thursday 7 December 1967: Border 7.30–8.30; Friday 15 December 1967: Granada 7.30–8.30; Friday 17 November 1967 : ATV Midlands/Grampian 7.30–8.30

Checkmate
Friday 24 November 1967: ATV Midlands/Grampian 7.30–8.30; Friday 1 December 1967: Anglia 8.00–9.00; Sunday 3 December 1967: ATV London/Southern Television/Westward, Channel/Tyne Tees 7.25–8.25; Thursday 7 December 1967: Scottish 7.30–8.30; Thursday 14 December 1967: Border 7.30–8.30; Friday 22 December 1967: Granada 7.30–8.30

Regional TV listings magazines from the time of *The Prisoner's* 1967 broadcast

The card sent out to everyone who had worked on the series, for Christmas 1966

Hammer into Anvil
Friday 1 December 1967: ATV Midlands/Grampian 7.30– 8.30; Friday 8 December 1967: Anglia, 8.00– 9.00; Sunday 10 December 1967: ATV London/Southern Television/Westward/Channel/Tyne Tees 7.25– 8.25; 14 December 1967: Scottish 7.30– 8.30; 21 December 1967: Border 7.30– 8.30; 29 December 1967: Granada 7.30– 8.30

It's Your Funeral
Friday 8 December 1967: ATV Midlands/Grampian 7.30–8.30; Friday 15 December 1967: Anglia 8.00–9.00; Sunday 17 December 1967: ATV London/Southern Television/Westward, Channel/Tyne Tees 7.25–8.25; Thursday 21 December 1967: Scottish 7.30–8.30; Thursday 28 December 1967: Border 7.30–8.30; Friday 5 January 1968: Granada 7.30–8.30

A Change of Mind
Friday 15 December 1967: ATV Midlands/Grampian 7.30–8.30; Friday 22 December 1967: Anglia 8.00–9.00; Thursday 28 December 1967: Scottish 7.30–8.30; Sunday 31s December 1967: ATV London/Southern Television/Westward, Channel/Tyne Tees 7.25–8.25; Friday 5 January 1968: Border 7.30–8.30; Friday 12 January 1968: Granada 7.30–8.30

Do Not Forsake Me Oh My Darling
Friday 22 December 1967: ATV Midlands/Grampian 7.30–8.30; Friday 29 December 1967: Anglia 8.00–9.00; Thursday 4 January 1968: Scottish 7.30–8.30; Sunday 7 January 1968: ATV London/Tyne Tees 7.25–8.25; Southern Television/Westward/Channel 10.05–11.05; Friday 12 January 1968: Border 7.30–8.30; Friday 19 January 1968: Granada 7.30–8.30

Living in Harmony
Friday 29 December 1967: ATV Midlands/Grampian 7.30–8.30; Saturday 6th January 1968: Anglia 7.35–8.35; Thursday 11 January 1968 : Scottish 7.30–8.30; Sunday 14 January 1968: ATV London 7.25–8.30; Sunday 14 January 1968: Southern Television/Westward/Channel 10.05–11.05; Tyne Tees 7.25–8.25 Friday 19 January 1968: Border 7.30–8.30; Friday 26 January 1968: Granada 7.30–8.30

The Girl Who Was Death
Thursday 18 January 1968: Scottish 7.30–8.30; Friday 19 January 1968: ATV Midlands/Grampian 7.35–8.30; Sunday 21 January 1968: ATV London/Tyne Tees 7.25–8.25; Southern Television/Westward, Channel 10.05–11.05; Friday 26 January 1968: Border 8.00–9.00; Saturday 27 January 1968: Anglia 7.35–8.30; Friday 16 February 1968: Granada 7.55–8.55

Once Upon A Time
Friday 25 January 1968: ATV Midlands/Grampian 7.35–8.30; Thursday 25 January 1968: Scottish 7.30–8.30; Sunday 28 January 1968: ATV London/Tyne Tees 7.25–8.25; Southern Television/Westward, Channel 10.05–11.05; Friday 2 February 1968: Border 8.00–9.00; Saturday 3 February 1968: Anglia 7.35– 8.35; Friday 23 February 1968: Granada 7.55–8.50

Fall Out
Thursday 1 February 1968: Scottish 7.30–8.30; Friday 2 February 1968: ATV Midlands/Grampian 7.35–8.30; Sunday 4 February 1968: ATV London/Tyne Tees/Southern Television 7.25–8.25; Westward, Channel 10.05–11.05; Friday 9 February 1968: Border 8.00–9.00; Saturday 10 February 1968: Anglia 7.30 – 8.30; Friday 1 March 1968: Granada 7.55–8.50

Transmission of episodes began on 5 September 1967 in Canada, five days ahead of the UK. The run lasted until 28 November, when after the showing of twelve episodes the series was dropped.

First USA network broadcast: 1 June – 1 September 1968, CBS. *'Living in Harmony' wasn't transmitted during the programme's first US run, but was shown subsequently in syndication.*

Select Bibliography

Books

Alain Carrazé and Hélène Oswald, *The Prisoner -
A Televisionary Masterpiece*
(W. H. Allen & Co. p.l.c., 1990)

Robert Fairclough, *Six of One, Half a Dozen of the Other*
(Maidstone College of Art, 1986)

Chris Gregory, *Be Seeing You... Decoding The Prisoner*
(University of Luton Press, 1997)

S. J. Gillis, *The Gillis Guide to The Prisoner*
(SJG Communications Services Ltd, 1997)

Roger Langley, *The Prisoner in Portmeirion*
(Portmeirion Ltd, 1999)

Ian Rakoff, *Inside The Prisoner*
(B.T. Batsford, 1998)

Matthew White and Jaffer Ali, *The Official Prisoner Companion*
(Sidgwick & Jackson, 1988)

Dave Rogers, *The Prisoner and Danger Man*
(Boxtree, 1989)

David McDaniel, *The Prisoner #2*
(Ace Books, 1969)

Thomas M. Disch, *The Prisoner*
(Ace Books, 1969)

Dean Motter, *The Prisoner a.k.a Shattered Visage*
(DC Comics, 1988-1990)

Hank Stine, *The Prisoner #3*
(Ace Books, 1970)

George Markstein, *The Cooler*
(Souvenir Press Ltd., 1974)

George Markstein, *Traitor for a Cause*
(The Bodley Head Ltd, 1979)

George Markstein, *Ultimate Issue*
(New English Library, 1981)

George Markstein, *Soul Hunters*
(Hodder & Stoughton Ltd., 1986)

Architect Errant: The Autobiography of Clough Williams-Ellis
(Constable & Company Ltd, 1971)

Clough Williams-Ellis, *Around the World in Ninety Years*
(Golden Dragon Books, 1978)

Steven Jenkins and Stephen P. McKay, *Portmeirion Pottery*
(Richard Dennis, 2000)

Alan Barnes and Marcus Hearn, *Kiss Kiss Bang! Bang!
The Unofficial James Bond Film Companion*
(B.T. Batsford, 1997)

Humphrey Carpenter, *Dennis Potter: The Authorized Biography*
(Faber and Faber Ltd., 1998)

Roy Carr, *Beatles at the Movies*
(Harper Collins, 1996)

James Chapman, *Licence to Thrill: A Cultural History
of the James Bond Films*
(I. B. Tauris, 1999)

John Clute, *Science Fiction: The Illustrated Encyclopaedia*
(Dorling Kindersley, 1995)

Paul Cornell, Martin Day and Keith Topping, *The Avengers
Programme Guide*
(Virgin Publishing Ltd., 1994)

Paul Cornell, Martin Day and Keith Topping, *The Guinness Book
of Classic British TV*
(Guinness Publishing Ltd., 1993)

Paul Duncan, *The Pocket Essential Stanley Kubrick*
(Pocket Essentials, 1999)

Christopher Frayling, *Spaghetti Westerns: Cowboys and
Europeans from Karl May to Sergio Leone*
(I.B. Tauris, 1998)

Jonathan Green, *All Dressed Up: The Sixties and the Counterculture*
(Pimlico, 1999)

**Above: The animated
sequence shown before
and after the commercial
breaks. Below: the
slamming bars animation
before the end credits,
used in every episode
except 'Fall Out'**

Kenneth Griffith, *The Fool's Pardon*
(Warner Books, 1995)

Mike Kenwood and George Williams, *Fags, Slags,
Blags and Jags: The Sweeney*
(Uslag Publishing, 1998)

Mark Lewisohn, *Radio Times Guide to TV Comedy*
(BBC Worldwide Ltd., 1998)

Ian Macdonald, *Revolution in the Head: The Beatles'
Records and the Sixties*
(Fourth Estate Limited, 1994)

Arthur Marwick, *The Sixties*
(Oxford University Press, 1998)

Tony Palmer, *The Trials of Oz*
(Blond and Briggs, 1971)

Peter Quennell, *A History of English Literature*
(Ferndale Editions, 1981)

Rock – The Rough Guide
(Rough Guides, 2001)

Dave Rogers, *The ITV Encyclopaedia of Adventure*
(Boxtree, 1998)

Robert Ross, *The Carry On Companion*
(B.T. Batsford, 1996)

Paul Simper, *The Saint: From Big Screen to Small and Back Again*
(Chameleon, 1997)

Time Out Film Guide, 8th ed
(Penguin, 2000)

Magazines

...And Nothing But The Truth (Chapter Arts, 2001)
Dreamwatch (Titan Magazines)
Primetime (Wider TeleVision Access)
SFX (Future Publishing)
TV Zone (Visual Imagination Ltd)
The Morning After (TMA)
Time Screen (Engale Marketing)
Starburst (Visual Imagination Ltd)

Six of One publications

The Making of The Prisoner (1985);
The Prisoner of Portmeirion (1985);
Number 6 (1985-86);
The Prisoner: A Twenty Fifth Anniversary Celebration (1992);
Tally Ho (1993, 1999-2001);
The Long and Winding Road (1996);
In The Village (1999-2001)

Six of One videos

The Prisoner Investigated Volume 1
(TR7 Productions, 1990)
The Prisoner Investigated Volume 2
(TR7 Productions, 1990)
The Prisoner Inspired
(TR7 Productions, 1992)
The Prisoner in Production
(TR7 Productions, 1993)
The Prisoner in Conclusion
(TR7 Productions, 1994)
The Prisoner on Location
(TR7 Productions, 1996)

Documentaries

In Search of The Prisoner
(Sci-Fi Channel, 2001)
The Best of The Prisoner
(MPI, 1990)
The Prisoner Video Companion
(MPI, 1990)
Six into One: The Prisoner File
(Illuminations, 1984)

Index

***Compiled by* Martin Wiggins**

Picture Credits